LAW, DEBT, AND MERCHANT POWER

The Civil Courts of Eighteenth-Century Halifax

In the early history of Halifax (1749–1766), debt litigation was extremely common. People from all classes frequently used litigation, and its use in private matters was higher than almost all places in the British Empire in the eighteenth century.

In *Law, Debt, and Merchant Power*, James Muir offers an extensive analysis of the civil cases of the time as well as the reasons behind their frequency. Muir's lively and detailed account of the individuals involved in litigation reveals a paradoxical society where debtors were also debt-collectors. *Law, Debt, and Merchant Power* demonstrates how important the law was for people in their business affairs and how they shaped it for their own ends.

(Osgoode Society for Canadian Legal History)

JAMES MUIR is an associate professor in the Department of History and Classics as well as the Faculty of Law at the University of Alberta.

PATRONS OF THE SOCIETY

The Osgoode Society is supported by a grant from
The Law Foundation of Ontario.

The Law Foundation of Ontario
Building a better foundation for justice in Ontario

The Society also thanks The Law Society of Upper Canada
for its continuing support.

LAW, DEBT, AND MERCHANT POWER

The Civil Courts of Eighteenth-Century Halifax

JAMES MUIR

Published for The Osgoode Society for Canadian Legal History by
University of Toronto Press
Toronto Buffalo London

Reprinted in paperback 2018

ISBN 978-1-4875-0103-7 (cloth)   ISBN 978-1-4875-2316-9 (paper)

Library and Archives Canada Cataloguing in Publication

Muir, James, 1971–, author
Law, debt, and merchant power : the civil courts of
eighteenth-century Halifax / James Muir.

(Osgoode Society for Canadian Legal History)
Includes bibliographical references and index.
ISBN 978-1-4875-0103-7 (hardback).   ISBN 978-1-4875-2316-9 (softcover)

1. Civil law – Nova Scotia – Halifax – History.   2. Courts – Nova Scotia –
Halifax – History.   I. Osgoode Society for Canadian Legal History,
issuing body   II. Title.   III. Series: Osgoode Society for Canadian Legal
History (Series)

KEN7565.M85 2016   346.716'22509   C2016-903934-X
KF345.M85 2016

University of Toronto Press acknowledges the financial assistance to its
publishing program of the Canada Council for the Arts and the Ontario Arts
Council, an agency of the Government of Ontario.

Canada Council   Conseil des Arts
for the Arts   du Canada

ONTARIO ARTS COUNCIL
CONSEIL DES ARTS DE L'ONTARIO
an Ontario government agency
un organisme du gouvernement de l'Ontario

Funded by the   Financé par le
Government   gouvernement
of Canada   du Canada

Canadä

For Karine De Champlain, with love.

Contents

Foreword

THE OSGOODE SOCIETY
FOR CANADIAN LEGAL HISTORY

In *Law, Debt, and Merchant Power* James Muir analyses a vital issue in our legal history, but one that has not received nearly enough attention to date. This is a path-breaking study of the everyday work of civil law and civil courts, based on the case files themselves and not on reported cases or legal literature or commercial codes. It examines the type of litigation pursued by private economic actors, mostly for debt, how the courts worked, and how the economy operated in a society with very little cash and in which credit was the lifeblood of commerce. Muir employs both quantitative and qualitative analyses of all extant case files and explains how eighteenth-century court procedure worked on the ground. He situates his study against the society and economy of Halifax, analysing who sued whom and why and how the legal system fitted into and shaped patterns of economic relations and activity. Although the author uses statistics to telling effect, the book never neglects the people behind the numbers, so it is infused throughout with individual stories of success, struggle, and failure in a developing and fragile economy in an outpost of empire.

The purpose of the Osgoode Society for Canadian Legal History is to encourage research and writing in the history of Canadian law. The Society, which was incorporated in 1979 and is registered as a charity, was founded at the initiative of the Honourable R. Roy McMurtry and officials of the Law Society of Upper Canada. The Society seeks to stimulate the study of legal history in Canada by supporting researchers, collecting oral histories, and publishing volumes that contribute to legal-historical scholarship in Canada. This year's books bring the total published to 103 since 1981, in all fields of legal history – the courts, the judiciary, and the legal profession, as well as on the history of crime and punishment, women and law, law and economy, the legal treatment of ethnic minorities, and famous cases and significant trials in all areas of the law.

Current directors of the Osgoode Society for Canadian Legal History are Susan Binnie, David Chernos, J. Douglas Ewart, Timothy Hill, Ian Hull, Mahmud Jamal, William Kaplan, C. Ian Kyer, Virginia MacLean, Roy McMurtry, Yasir Naqvi, Dana Peebles, Paul Perell, Paul Reinhardt, William Ross, Linda Rothstein, Paul Schabas, Robert Sharpe, Jon Silver, Alex Smith, Lorne Sossin, Mary Stokes, and Michael Tulloch.

The annual report and information about membership may be obtained by writing to the Osgoode Society for Canadian Legal History, Osgoode Hall, 130 Queen Street West, Toronto, Ontario, M5H 2N6. Telephone: 416-947-3321. E-mail: mmacfarl@lsuc.on.ca. Website: www .osgoodesociety.ca.

Robert J. Sharpe
President

Jim Phillips
Editor-in-Chief

Sadly, there are several people who will not know how much they mattered to this book. During the course of this project my grandmothers, Anna Janzen and Vira Muir, and my good friend in Halifax, Roy Logan, passed away. My friend and law librarian extraordinaire Balfour Halevy cannot share in the joy of the publication of this legal book. I miss them all.

There are several institutions that have supported me: the Social Sciences and Humanities Research Council of Canada, York University, and the University of Alberta all offered me financial assistance at various times to do research or present my findings. The Gorsebrook Institute for Atlantic Canadian Studies provided me office space and more while I did my research in Halifax. Both of my current academic homes, the Department of History and Classics and the Faculty of Law at the University of Alberta offered me some teaching relief to complete my manuscript. The Faculty Evaluation Committee of the University of Alberta provided me the final impetus to complete this book. My unions, CUPE 3903 and the AASUA, managed to secure collective agreements that made it simply possible to be an academic historian.

The research upon which this book is based was carried out primarily at Nova Scotia Archives and Records Management. The archivists and staff there were excellent guides to what was available about the eighteenth century. They made NSARM a great place to work.

I owe thanks to the places where I have presented and published earlier thoughts on Nova Scotian law in the eighteenth century. My first attempts to grapple with the full picture were presented at a number of conferences in Canada and the United States, and were somewhat fleshed out in "The Strange Case of the Schooner *Seaflower*: Law and Business in Colonial Halifax, 1749–1764," presented at the International Seminar on the History of the Atlantic World, 1500–1825 (Harvard University Working Paper #99024). Some of the research I present and conclusions I draw about the Supreme Court first appeared in James Muir and Jim Phillips, "Michaelmas Term 1754: The Supreme Court's First Session," in Philip Girard, Jim Phillips, and Barry Cahill, eds., *From Imperial Bastion to Provincial Oracle: The Supreme Court of Nova Scotia, 1754–2004*. Most recently, I have published a complementary article to this book, "The Fight for Bourgeois Law in Halifax, Nova Scotia, 1749–1753," in *Histoire Sociale/Social History*.

Finally, there are two sets of creditors for whom no offer of repayment will be sufficient. First, as a dissertation, this book was supervised by Paul Craven. Paul was a demanding professor when I first met him in 1994; now he is a very good friend, though often still demanding. When he retired in 2015, a mutual friend and I tried to organize a small party for him; he declined, saying, "The only recognition I look forward to from you is a suitably endorsed presentation copy of your monograph." I am glad I can comply. My supervisory committee also included Doug Hay and Jim Phillips. I doubt I could have put together a better committee of legal historians in one place. The influence of their scholarship and supervision can be seen throughout this book, and I hope all three will accept it as at least a token of my gratitude.

Second, this project began soon after I left my family home in Winnipeg and was finished in my new family home in Edmonton. My parents, Bill and Hilda, and my brother, Dale, have all supported me along the whole of the nineteen years, even as they wondered what was taking so long. They were all much more interested in this project than three scientists could really be expected to be. For the last twelve years I have also had the love and companionship of my wife, Karine De Champlain, and we now have a family of our own. Cameron, Katherine, and Holden have been distracting and exhausting, but a day of writing missed to spend with the three of them and Karine is a day better spent. As I argue in this book, the actions of one can sometimes stand for a whole unnamed family. The book may be mine, but it could not have existed without my family, and no words can thank them enough.

James Muir
Edmonton
May 2016

LAW, DEBT, AND MERCHANT POWER

The Civil Courts of Eighteenth-Century Halifax

1

Introduction

By 1761, Anne Webb, a widow, was operating as a trader in Halifax, Nova Scotia. Exactly when she arrived in Halifax is unknown, but her husband, John, had arrived as early as the founding of Halifax in 1749. By 1752, he was living alone and trading in partnership with Robert Ewer, a militia captain and Justice of the Peace. Sometime later, Anne either married John or joined him in Halifax. In the summer of 1757, he died, and she assumed full responsibility for the business and started trading in her own name. She bought and sold goods from within and outside the colony, working with producers, merchants and traders, and people buying for their own use. Being a widow was not unusual; being an independent woman trader was. In September 1757, only a few weeks after John's death, Anne Webb filed suit for the first time.[1]

In 1761, Roger Hill, a truckman and sometimes carter, had lived in Halifax since at least October 1750, when he married Laetitia Gray there. He first appeared in a Halifax court in December 1750, when he was sued twice and sued someone else. Like Anne Webb, Roger Hill made his living by buying and selling, but he never had John or Anne Webb's status or wealth. As a truckman, he either sold (or trucked) goods out of a shop or from a cart; as a carter, he moved things for people. Unlike the Webbs, who partnered with Robert Ewer, a member of Halifax's governing class, Hill partnered with Robert Cowie, a baker. In 1763, Hill and Cowie secured a land grant for a bay south-east of Dartmouth and named it Cow Bay, after Cowie. Hill died in Halifax on 10 July 1764.[2]

Anne Webb and Roger Hill came from different stations in life, and before now neither has merited mention in any of the many histories of Halifax. Yet both appeared frequently in public records as litigants in civil suits. Anne Webb was the most litigious woman in Halifax in the 1750s and 1760s, suing or being sued in forty-six different actions between December 1757 and 1766. Hill was similarly litigious, being sued thirty-three times, and suing others another twenty times. Hill and Webb, however, were not frivolous, malicious litigants, and while they were involved in a higher-than-average number of legal actions, they were not exceptional within Nova Scotia. In the seventeen years after Halifax's founding in 1749, people there engaged in litigation over private matters at a higher rate than people in most other places in the British Empire in the eighteenth century, or at any other time.

The number of new legal actions initiated in the Inferior Court of Common Pleas, the busiest civil court in Halifax, ranged from 23 per 1,000 to 155 per 1,000 over the first two decades of the city's founding (see table 1.1). It is likely that especially in the years between 1756 and 1766, when the records available do not include clerks' notebooks of all Inferior Court sessions, the number of actions initiated (that is, lawsuits started) is undercounted, and so the litigation rate was even higher. The levels of litigation revealed for the 1750s and 1760s were significantly higher than in England or anywhere else in Anglo or French North America at the time, as far as we now know.[3] They were also significantly higher than in Nova Scotia today, where there were 14 civil suits initiated per 1,000 people per year between 2010–11 and 2014–15.[4] For many people in Halifax in the 1750s and 1760s, litigation was both affordable and easy to initiate, and it played a central role in the day-to-day economy. Suing or being sued was not something that exercised many people; rather litigation was just an ordinary part of doing business.[5] This is a book about those litigious people and the courts in which they sued one another; it is about who sued whom – and why – in such volume.

The abundant records left from the early civil courts in Halifax make it possible to piece together multiple individual actions and the larger social patterns in litigation. The reconstruction of patterns of litigation for individuals allows me to analyse what Haligonians seem to have intended with their litigation strategies. Reconstructing and analysing those patterns of legal actions is only possible with good sets of records. The period discussed in this book begins with the founding of Halifax in 1749 and ends in 1766, a time frame dictated by the sources.

Table 1.1: Population and litigation rates, Inferior Court of Common Pleas,
Halifax, 1750–66

Year	Actions Initiated[a]	Population[b]	Actions per 1,000 people
1750	426		
1751	314	3,200	98
1752	561	4,248	132
1753	321	5,250	61
1754	244		
1755	273		
1756	51	1,755	29
1757	170	3,000	57
1758	138	6,000	23
1759	201		
1760	239	3,000	80
1761	324		
1762	237	2,500	95
1763	387	2,500	155
1764	305		
1765	146		
1766	41		

[a] Nova Scotia Archives and Records Management RG 37 (hx) vol. 1–20 and RG 37 (hx) A1, A2, B.

[b] The sources for the population numbers are: Fingard, Guildford, and Sutherland, *Halifax: The First 250 Years* (1758, p. 6 and 1760, p. 18); Alan Marble, *Surgeons, Smallpox and the Poor* (1751, p. 27, 1753, p. 33, 1757, p. 52, and 1762, p. 70); and Akins, *History of Halifax City* (1752, p. 261, 1756, p. 58, and 1763, p. 69).

Although the records for the Inferior Court of Common Pleas (or any of the other courts) are not complete, they are voluminous for this period; after 1766, the volume of extant records declines precipitously. Much of the analysis about the use of courts relies on my having a significant proportion of all of the litigation represented in some record or other. Otherwise, questions about the ways in which individuals integrated legal activity within their lives become much more difficult to answer.[6]

When people in early Halifax sued one another, it was most often over debt. Plaintiffs and defendants came from a very wide range of occupations and from different classes in the colony and beyond. The centrality of merchants and traders, however, was pronounced. Table 1.2 compares who sued whom on the basis of occupation and status to the extent that the occupation of the litigants on both sides is reported in the records. It is not as full a picture of all plaintiffs or defendants

Table 1.2: Opposing litigant occupations, all civil courts[a]

| | Defendant Occupation | | | | | | | | | | | |
| | Merchant or Trader | | Other Commercial | | Craftsperson | | Sea-based | | Other recorded | | Total | |
Plaintiff Occupation	n	%[b]	n	%	n	%	n	%	n	%	n	%
Merchant or Trader	131	9	91	6	94	7	62	4	118	8	496	34
Other Commercial	29	2	32	2	56	4	25	2	53	4	195	14
Craftsperson	32	2	40	3	74	5	36	2	80	6	262	18
Sea-based	28	2	14	1	26	2	47	3	24	2	139	10
Other recorded	56	4	49	3	81	6	51	4	110	8	347	25
Total	276	19	226	15	331	24	221	16	385	28	1439	

[a] This table includes only actions where the occupation of both plaintiffs and defendants were recorded. For a discussion of occupations, see appendix 2.
[b] Percentage of all of the actions collected on this table (i.e., 1,439).

as will be presented later in this book, but it does provide a nice sense of who sued whom. To show the startling way that litigation clumped around different groups, the table is divided into the four most important occupation categories in litigation in general, with all the other listed occupations placed together in a catch-all category. Merchants and traders alone accounted for more than a third of plaintiffs and were a fifth of defendants in these actions. When the less wealthy, less inter-colonially focused commercial occupations (like retailer, shopkeeper, tavern keeper and truckman) are included, almost half of all plaintiffs and almost a third of defendants were drawn from commercial occupations. Craftspeople (like mason, carpenter, or tailor) made up less than a fifth of plaintiffs but almost a quarter of defendants, often defending themselves against suits from plaintiffs drawn from commercial occupations. The volume of litigation shown in table 1.1 points to how critical civil justice was to the functioning of the economy, while table 1.2 suggests that the legal system was dominated by what I argue was a colonial bourgeoisie.

While Anne Webb and Roger Hill were frequent litigants, the most litigious person in Halifax in the 1750s and 1760s was Malachy Salter, a prosperous merchant, elected member of the House of Assembly, and a Justice of the Peace and Collector of Lighthouse Duties. Not only was Salter the most litigious person in Halifax, he was also appointed as an arbitrator in civil legal proceedings more often than anyone else. What the presence of people like Webb, Hill, and Salter in the courts indicate is that "going to the law" played a critical role in maintaining the economy of Halifax. Merchants and traders constituted a bourgeoisie that was often at odds with Nova Scotia's government officials and its professional and religious elite. The alliance of merchants and traders with government officials and other professionals took time to coalesce as Halifax and Nova Scotia developed into a merchantocracy over the late eighteenth century.[7] In his classic *The Neutral Yankees of Nova Scotia*, J.B. Brebner described the broader political struggle between the bourgeoisie and government for control of the colony in the 1750s and 1760s.[8]

Historians and other scholars from a wide range of theoretical positions have begun again to argue that individuals like the merchant-traders in Halifax should be analysed as bourgeois.[9] For German historian Jürgen Kocka, the bourgeoisie in the eighteenth and nineteenth centuries was composed of "merchants, manufacturers, bankers, capitalists, entrepreneurs, and managers, as well as rentiers, together with their families ... [and] the families of doctors, lawyers, ministers, scientists and other professionals, professors of universities and secondary schools, intellectuals, men and women of letters, and academics, including those who serve as administrators and officials in public and private bureaucracies." Kocka's conception of the bourgeoisie is narrower than the English term "middle class"; it excludes small proprietors, artisans, and other people who were not part of the class that over the eighteenth and nineteenth centuries would challenge and eventually displace Europe's nobility in power. Kocka comes at his use of the term not from Marxist theory but as a historically appropriate term for a newly ascendant class in Europe in the eighteenth century.[10] As capitalism rose to predominate European economies in the seventeenth and eighteenth centuries, so too did the bourgeoisie, displacing at different times and in different constellations the ruling classes of the late middle ages and early modern eras. As Franco Moretti has put it, in the sixteenth and seventeenth centuries the class achieved "bourgeois *legitimacy*: the idea of a ruling class that doesn't just rule, but *deserves* to do so."[11] In Halifax this occurred rapidly and early, displacing no entrenched powers but subordinating, in many ways, the colonial government officials appointed in England or locally. Understanding Halifax's merchants and traders in these terms helps to contextualize the Nova Scotia merchantocracy of the late eighteenth and early nineteenth century within a long tradition of economic analysis, not just Marx but also Weber, Schumpeter, and others.[12]

Canadian historians, whether they have adopted the term "bourgeois" or not and whether they come from left or right, tend to present this class as something akin to Kocka's definition, but with the merchant side given much greater prominence. Thus, Donald Creighton's *Commercial Empire of the Saint Lawrence* is the tale of the rise and fall of a distinct merchant community in the Canadas from the conquest to the eve of Confederation.[13] More recently, Brian Young used the term "bourgeois" as the key to understanding George-Etienne Cartier's place as a member of Montreal's business and religious elite, a "colonial entrepreneurial class," while Don Nerbas has described mid-twentieth-century business-industrial leaders as a "Canadian bourgeoisie."[14]

Bourgeois influence over the practice of civil law was one point of conflict in the early 1750s,[15] and by 1753, if not earlier, the civil law of Halifax was a bourgeois system in terms of its most common users and the results it produced. For most of the 1750s and 1760s, the civil justice system in Halifax at least reflected a broad acceptance of rule in terms of bourgeois interests. This book describes day-to-day legal practices during and after this struggle, what the law's most frequent and wealthiest users wanted, and the result they produced, namely bourgeois law. The law analysed here is a law tailored to meet the needs of the bourgeoisie, however much it proved useful to people from all over Halifax. It is a law imbricated in productive relations and framed in such a way as to regularly secure the interests of creditors over debtors, trade over production, merchants over craftspeople.

The focus on the legal system and day-to-day legal practice helps to make sense of what might otherwise seem to be a lacuna in this book: there is little discussion of Nova Scotia's political history. The 1750s and 1760s were a tumultuous period politically, and at times, as will be seen below, those politics impinged on the civil courts. Perhaps remarkably, however, politics and government regulation or legislation rarely played significant roles in the civil courts. Thus, for example, there is no significant difference in the administration of civil justice before and after the introduction of an elected assembly in 1758. There is almost no reference to local statute law in the Inferior Court. This book is a work of social history; the political story of Nova Scotia in the 1750s and 1760s is not a part of this study.

This is also very much a work of social history as opposed to cultural history, although it is not an argument for the former against the latter. Works on debt in the eighteenth century, especially by historian Craig Muldrew and literary scholar Margot Finn, have discussed the culture of credit relations.[16] While the law plays a significant role in the work of both authors, it is not their primary concern. In this book the law is the primary concern, and debt is important because of its frequency. While I have made use of Muldrew and Finn's discussions of debt, as well as those of others, such as anthropologist David Graeber, their concerns are for the most part distinct from mine. More significant, perhaps, is my decision not to engage in a discussion of legal culture. This is a concept that has positively influenced many of the most recent works on legal history in Nova Scotia, especially that of Philip Girard.[17] In my case, however, the concept offers little in terms of explanatory or analytical power. Following anthropologists Franz von Benda-Beckmann and Keebet von Benda-Beckmann, I share their concern that "there are alternatives to 'legal culture' that are far more precise for descriptive and theoretical purposes." They suggest, for example, that in some cases where legal culture "refers to ideologies or to the values embedded in law, why not call them thus?"[18] In the case of this study, the term offers little to either making sense of what happened in Halifax or to draw connections to other places or times.

I present this law by analysing the way in which legal actions progressed through the system. To do so, I closely follow the legal affairs of a handful of people: Malachy Salter and Anne Webb, both members of Halifax's and the empire's bourgeoisie; Roger Hill, who was most assuredly not bourgeois; and James Monk, a government official in the 1750s and lawyer in the 1760s, who was not much involved in commercial activities but came to have a status in the community close to that of Salter's. Material from many individual litigants, including craftspeople, lawyers and judges, people from within and outside Halifax are used to further illustrate my analysis. I consider *all* of the litigation heard at the five civil (that is non-criminal) courts that met in Halifax in the 1750s and 1760s: the common law Inferior Court of Common Pleas (originally the County Court) and Supreme Court (originally the General Court), and the Courts of Chancery, Vice Admiralty, and Prohibited Marriage and Divorce. The borders between criminal and civil law were ambiguous: the same act could be deemed a criminal assault in one court and a civil assault in another; one person's use of someone else's property might be subject to the civil suit of trover in one and considered theft in another. The differences between criminal and civil law were well understood, even if some disputes could be defined to be put into either system.[19] The courts of first instance, the Inferior Court of Common Pleas and the Quarter Sessions, were distinct even though their bench was the same. There are points below, especially in the discussion of juries in chapter 5, where I will make some direct comparison to studies of the eighteenth-century criminal trial in Nova Scotia and England. But, overall, much as criminal law historians have for the most part ignored civil law in their work, I am setting aside criminal law here. The motivating factors for would-be prosecutors in criminal law are, by and large, different than those for civil plaintiffs, the disputes at the heart of litigation arise from different relationships and events, and the awards made are determined by different principles than criminal punishments (even when imprisonment is the result). The focus of chapters 3 through 6 is the Inferior Court of Common Pleas – the court with by far the most business in the 1750s and 1760s. The majority of actions in that court pertained to debt of some sort, and these actions were almost exclusively civil.

The middle of the book is about the Inferior Court of Common Pleas, preceded and followed by more general chapters. Chapter 2 opens with a discussion of Halifax at its founding, its place in the Atlantic economy, the civil courts and the people who appeared in them (as well as those who did not). Chapters 3 through 7 follow the course of legal actions through the Inferior Court, using suits initiated by Salter, Webb, and Hill and involving Monk as a lawyer in November 1761 and introducing other legal disputes to clarify and illustrate distinctive aspects of the law as practices. Chapter 3 describes the process of beginning a civil action and the variety of litigation that was initiated in the court. Chapter 4 addresses the various ways an action could be resolved and focuses on how litigants could avoid going to trial. Chapter 5 turns to those actions that went to either a jury trial or arbitration, and includes a discussion of the jurors and arbitrators, analysing them in relation to the litigants in the court. Chapter 6 addresses how litigation came to an end: who won and who lost, and how the winners were able to enforce judgments. Chapter 7 starts with appeals from the Inferior Court of Common Pleas to the Supreme Court of Nova Scotia, and then moves on to other civil courts. Exemplary litigation from each of the other four civil courts is described and analysed. The chapter closes with a discussion of two cases in Vice Admiralty as a window into debates about the jurisdiction of the various courts and of the courts in general.

Each chapter contains several elements: first, a description of general court procedures appropriate to the stage being analysed; second, the sources of laws, rules, and practices being invoked; and third, the context of the law, community, and economy in which the litigants found themselves. Although detailed descriptions and analyses of eighteenth-century legal procedure have been done for the criminal law[20] and some parts of the civil law, such as marriage and divorce,[21] this is the first study that recreates the full breadth of civil law procedures in any common law jurisdiction in the eighteenth century. It is distinct from other works on civil justice in the eighteenth-century Atlantic world or Canada because it focuses on the legal structure in practice as a way of illuminating all elements of the non-criminal legal system.[22] Law, legal structure, economy, and culture shaped each other. Understanding how legal process worked and the choices people could and did make within that process illuminate elements of both the legal history of the Atlantic world and the social, cultural, and economic history of Halifax, Nova Scotia, and pre-Confederation Canada.

Through the analysis in these chapters, I make five major arguments. First, although the volume of litigation was unusual and Nova Scotia's courts developed some unique local practices, civil law in Halifax was compatible with other common law jurisdictions, especially England and the other American colonies. Second, Halifax's high litigation rates reflected the circumstances of its founding, its economy, and a population with a high level of transiency. Third, the law developed to meet those circumstances, as the people of Halifax used the law and courts to help resolve their relationship to the city's circumstances. Fourth, the persistence of a high volume of litigation can be explained, in part, by the consistency of the results produced by the courts, which people generally perceived to be effective adjudicators. Finally, the practices of civil law in Halifax adapted to the needs of city's bourgeoisie; where others' interests aligned with the bourgeoisie, the law was useful to them; where others' interests did not, resort to the law was less effective. The law provided a forum to both exercise and balance power in the community. Understanding the importance of bourgeois interests in the practice of the civil law helps to make sense of how and why the law was used to the extent it was. It does not make the law simply a hammer in the hand of an economic elite, but it recognizes how the system of the law came to protect the interests of creditors over those of debtors, regardless of who those creditors and debtors were.

These five arguments mark a tension in this work between the specificity of Halifax and the generality of common law civil court use and practice. All of what is described and analysed here is about Nova Scotia and Halifax in particular. I draw links, often in the notes, to other jurisdictions in the eighteenth century and beyond it, but I present no new research on other spaces and other times and, as I have noted, this study is different in its structure and focus from the other studies of civil law in the eighteenth-century common law world. However, I suspect that in broad strokes, Halifax is not particularly unique: that the civil courts played a role in regulating commerce – especially absent other, informal options – was common, and the buttressing of bourgeois power was part of a process across much of Europe and its colonies in the period of transition to capitalism. This process was uneven over space and time, but Halifax was no outlier.

Legal scholars and lawyers often refer to civil law as private law, the law between private individuals, not between individuals and the public good or the state. Much of the public history of the 1750s and 1760s in Halifax has already been told: the Seven Years War, conflicts and treaties with the Mi'kmaq, the expulsion of the Acadians, or the direct role of the state in the economy. The civil courts were public institutions, and although the disputes brought to them were private, they were resolved in a public setting. This study of litigation in early Halifax brings the histories of private business and private life to public attention.

2

Halifax, a Community of Litigants

They crossed the Atlantic Ocean to get there in the summer of 1749. Fourteen sloops, snows, barques, and other ships carrying 2,576 people: sailors, more than 500 soldiers, and many would-be settlers including "161 farmers, 107 workers in the building trades, 19 shoemakers, 11 butchers, 11 tailors [and] 10 coopers,"[1] all under the direction of Colonel Edward Cornwallis. They stopped in Chebucto Harbour (*k'chibouktouk* to the Mi'kmaq) on the Eastern coast of the Acadian peninsula, and over the remaining months before the snow fell, they built the town of Halifax, new capital of Nova Scotia.

The harbour was large and deep and would turn out to be ice-free all year round. At its mouth were several islands with well-defined headlands on either side. Sailing into the harbour, coming in along the west side of McNab's Island, the people crowding the sides of the ships would see hills rising up from the shore. Passing through a narrows, they would reach a large basin. The islands and headlands provided ideal places for protection from invaders by sea. The high points of land allowed them to watch not only the entrance of the harbour, but other sea and land approaches. The hillsides at the narrows had shallow enough slopes that it would be possible to build a town site.

The ocean they had crossed was also their reason for being there. In 1710, during the War of the Spanish Succession, the British conquered Acadia from the French. With the 1713 Treaty of Utrecht, British control of the mainland of what is now Nova Scotia was confirmed, while the

French continued to control Île Royale (Cape Breton Island), Île Saint-Jean (Prince Edward Island), modern-day New Brunswick, the Gulf of St. Lawrence and St. Lawrence River behind it. On Île Royale they built a massive fortified town, Louisbourg, in its own well-protected ice-free harbour. To the British and their American settlers, the fortress was a constant military threat to British American colonies to the south and a competitor for the important fish stocks of the North-West Atlantic. A force of New Englanders had captured Louisbourg in 1745 during the War of Austrian Succession, but at war's end it was returned to the French over the protests of the New Englanders. A fortress and garrison stationed in Chebucto Harbour would provide protection from Louisbourg for the southern colonies and their fishing fleets. A city to go along with the garrison, and then more settlement of British or Protestant immigrants around the whole of Acadia, would break the ties the Acadians and Mi'kmaq had with Louisbourg, the French, and the Catholic Church, and would hasten the assimilation of these antagonistic or, at best, neutral Nova Scotians. Once established, Nova Scotia could provide fish to Britain and Europe and agricultural produce, wood, and fish to the West Indies in exchange for the manufactured goods it would receive from Britain.[2]

To make Halifax the warden of the North, to use Thomas Raddall's description, would require a massive investment of capital from Britain and labour from the British Isles, the American colonies to the south, and beyond. Louisbourg had taken the French more than twenty years to build. Halifax would have to be built faster – first, simply to house the settlers arriving in Conwallis's convoy, and second, to serve its military purpose. Unlike the earlier British colonies in North America, Nova Scotia would now be not only a Crown colony, but a colony built up by years of significant direct government investment rather than private investment by the settlers themselves or proprietary companies charged with settlement. Jeffers Lennox has shown how much the conceptualization of the space of Halifax was integral to empire, while Julian Gwyn has shown how important imperial fund transfers were to building the colony.[3]

Chebucto had provided protection for a long time before 1749. Throughout the seventeenth and eighteenth centuries, Acadian, American, and European fishers had taken shelter in the bay and dried fish on its shore. The Mi'kmaq had used it for much longer, although by 1749 it was no longer a permanent residence for them either. Preceding the convoy's arrival, Chebucto had been effectively recognized as

Mi'kmaq territory, with no permanent and little temporary presence by British, Americans, or Acadians. Cornwallis was instructed to draw the Mi'kmaq into the British sphere of influence and away from their French and Acadian allies but seemed temperamentally ill-disposed to engaging with them as equals and as the present possessors of the land. In August, two or three violent altercations between Mi'kmaq and British or Americans left several people dead on all sides. Then, in September, several Mi'kmaq men attacked some settlers cutting wood on the eastern side of the harbour in what would become Dartmouth, killing five of them.[4] In reaction, Cornwallis and his council issued a bounty of ten guineas for every Mi'kmaq killed or captured, while the French at Louisbourg offered a bounty on British scalps.[5] Over the next few years, the Mi'kmaq and the people of Halifax alternated between violence, diplomacy, and trade at a distance. On a day-to-day basis, Halifax was effectively shut to the Mi'kmaq – who were, it seems, all too happy to not come to the city in any case.[6]

In 1749, the Mi'kmaq had a much stronger relationship with the Acadians, descendants of French settlers and Mi'kmaq people, than the English who claimed to govern their territory. Although the Acadians had villages or seasonal encampments all through the Maritimes by 1749, most lived in hamlets and villages along the Nova Scotia coast of the Bay of Fundy, at Annapolis Royal, in several Minas Basin communities, and around Chignecto.[7] Soon after the convoy arrived in harbour, several Acadians from Minas arrived at the site overland. They brought with them 100 cows as well as sheep to help stock the new city. In the days that followed, they aided in the initial building of Halifax, and others cut a trail across the peninsula between Halifax and Minas.[8] Nevertheless, the Acadians also remained peripheral to Halifax. The leadership in Halifax was more suspicious than inviting toward the Acadians – much to the contrary of the instructions they received from London. These suspicions grew, rooted in xenophobia and a coveting of the Acadians' farm land on one hand, and a sincere fear of Acadian willingness to take up arms in support of the French on the other. In 1755, spurred on by the fighting in the Ohio River valley that started the Seven Years War, Nova Scotia Governor Charles Lawrence and Massachusetts Governor William Shirley launched a siege of the French Fort Beauséjour on the Bay of Fundy. When it fell, Lawrence found signs of Acadian support for the French and, on that pretext, drove the policy decision that would lead, by the end of the summer, to the forcible expulsion of all of the Acadians who could be rounded up.[9]

Perched on the side of its harbour, Halifax remained primarily focused on the ocean. The Mi'kmaq and Acadians were people to be
feared, envied, and ignored. The town's population ebbed and flowed
with the fortunes of the garrison situated on its shore. Many of those
who arrived in the summer of 1749 left within weeks or months of their
arrival, eventually to be replaced by more who came by boat from the
other Atlantic colonies, the British Isles, or mainland Europe, and who
in turn left again. This exodus was probably encouraged rather than
discouraged by Governor Cornwallis's early decree that any colonist
who left Halifax without his permission would be exiled.[10] The population followed the growing and shrinking garrison in the last years of
peace and war with France in North America and the shifting importance of Halifax vis-à-vis North Atlantic fishery and trade. Although
many of the people in the initial convoy left or died in that first year, the
colony continued to grow to 3,200 by 1751, 4,248 by 1752, and 5,250 by
1753. The population then declined precipitously in the years leading
up to the Seven Years War, with a census in 1755 or 1756 finding only
1,755 people within the town. As the war began in earnest, the population rose again to roughly 3,000 in 1757 and about 6,000 in 1758. At the
conclusion of the war, the population declined again, to around 3,000
in 1760 and 2,500 in 1762–3.[11]

As the population grew and declined, its make-up changed too. The
initial convoys came from England and were made up of people drawn
largely from the British Isles. Halifax and Nova Scotia, however, effectively marked a new northern boundary of New England, and as
many of the original British would-be settlers moved on or died, many
people who arrived later came from the New England colonies and farther south. A third group of people began to arrive in 1750, Protestants
from German-speaking Europe. By 1752, some 339 people in 86 families
lived in the Dutchtown (Deutsch- or German-town) community on the
North West edge of Halifax.[12] In 1753 many of the "foreign Protestants," as they came to be known, moved more than 50 kilometres south
and west along the coast to the new town of Lunenburg, built on the
site of a formerly Acadian and Mi'kmaq village of Mirligueche that had
been destroyed in October 1749 by British troops.[13] Some of the foreign
Protestants, however, remained in Halifax.

Like so many settlements in North America, Halifax had a surplus of
male settlers. It was intended to be a place of permanent settlement for
many who arrived in the first convoy: along with the 1,000 or so adult
men who were not soldiers in the first convoy came 1,030 women and

children. When a census was taken in 1752, there were 1,914 men over sixteen and only 1,122 women (along with 584 boys and 608 girls).[14] However, many of the men listed in the census were likely live-in servants, slaves, or lodgers. The wealthiest men or men most involved in trade often had many more adult men than women in their households. They had the wealth and the business to keep more servants and slaves, who were involved in all aspects of their master's work and were not merely domestics, even as they lived within the master's household.[15]

In the mid-eighteenth century, Nova Scotia's economy relied on grants from the imperial government in London and trade with New England, other British colonies in the Americas and Caribbean, and the British Isles.[16] Its leaders were British governors and British and American merchants and officers who stood looking out toward the ocean and places beyond rather than at the colony itself.

The people who came to Halifax might, like their town, have been oriented toward the ocean, but they built a community with those who joined them around the shore of the harbour. The community was very like other seaside communities in the British Atlantic. They brought the English language, the Church of England and dissenting churches, the common law and their personal expectations of justice. But all of these – the ideas, beliefs, and practices that people brought with them to Halifax – had to fit within the official structures established in and for the colony.

Origins of the Courts

At the third meeting of the governor's council, on 18 July 1749, John Brewer, Robert Ewer, John Collier, and John Duport were appointed as Justices of the Peace for Halifax.[17] An essential element of the English justice system, magistrates were the lowest level of judicial decision-makers. Sitting on their own or in pairs in their own houses, they would be able to hear minor civil and criminal matters (including a wide range of master-and-servant, that is, employment actions), take depositions, and remand accused defendants for trial. For all of this they went unpaid by the state, relying on fees they charged of those who came before them. The limits on what they could hear in terms of the sort of dispute or of the type or value of punishment or award meant, however, that they could not handle the colony's legal matters on their own.

A general court was held at the end of August to deal with a number of criminal matters, with the governor and council acting as the bench.[18] Held to try felonies, the court paralleled the court of King's Bench in England or the higher courts of the colonies. But the fact that it heard only criminal matters meant that the legal needs of the colony were not yet met. In early September, two ships collided in the harbour. When Elijah Davis, captain of one, could not get satisfaction from Ephraim Cook, captain of the other, for the damages caused, Davis went to the governor. Cornwallis had the two captains appoint arbitrators who would be tasked with determining the damages. They found that when the damages to both ships were balanced against each other, Cook owed Davis £14 18s 6d. Cook refused to pay, refusing to recognize the governor's authority absent a court. Although Cornwallis managed to secure Cook's promise to pay Davis, the incident revealed that the colony was in need of a properly constituted civil court.[19]

On 6 December, the governor's council appointed a committee to "examine the Laws of the Plantations & their Regulations with regard to the General Court & County or Inferior Courts." The committee reported seven days later. In preparing his convoy, Cornwallis was instructed by the Board of Trade to set up a legal system based on that established in the older colony of Virginia. Virginia's model was based on the common law and England's legal system, but with some significant differences. Most important was Virginia's hierarchical court structure, which allowed for relatively easy appeals.[20] In these years before the American Revolution, such borrowing between British colonies on the Atlantic coast – either in response to explicit instructions to borrow or through less formal means – was common.[21] The committee used the laws of Virginia as their model for the rules of the courts they presented. Two levels of common law court would be established: a county and a general court. Rules were laid out describing the make-up of the courts, their procedures, and the fee structures for court officers and attorneys.[22] The County and General Courts had both criminal and civil jurisdiction. The County Court would meet four times a year – in March, June, September, and December – following British practice. Its bench would be made up of at least three of the Justices of the Peace sitting together, with the first justice in the commission in charge of the court. Some of the Justices of the Peace would be commissioned as being "of quorum," and their presence would be necessary for the County Court to sit. The General Court described by the committee and established in 1750 would meet twice a year, sitting in late spring and autumn. Its bench would be composed of members of the governor's council, just as it had been in September. Its primary civil-side purpose was to hear appeals from the County Court. A small range of actions could also be heard first at the General Court instead of the County Court, if the litigants so chose. There are no records of this occurring.

In 1751 and 1752, the County Court was remodelled as two courts sitting simultaneously: the Inferior Court of Common Pleas to hear civil disputes and the Quarter Sessions to hear criminal matters.[23] The name Inferior Court of Common Pleas was North American in origin, although it referred to the English central common law court Common Pleas. Common Pleas was originally established to hear disputes in which the king had no interest: essentially private disputes between English subjects. The North American Inferior Courts of Common Pleas followed the same principle, hearing civil disputes rather than criminal ones. The Inferior Courts of Common Pleas differed from their English namesake by being essentially local courts and by having a broader exclusive jurisdiction in practice. The Quarter Sessions kept their English name, but in England they had a limited civil jurisdiction to complement their criminal work. In Halifax, the two courts continued to meet simultaneously four times a year, with some days devoted to Inferior Court business and others to Quarter Sessions. The Justices of the Peace still served as the courts' benches, and the justices who attended often changed from day to day within a session, so long as a minimum of three were always present. This basic structure remained the same throughout the rest of the 1750s and 1760s.

In 1754, with the appointment of Jonathan Belcher as chief justice for Nova Scotia, the General Court was replaced by a Supreme Court. Belcher modelled his procedure for the new court closely on the assizes in Britain.[24] One of the first acts of the colony's assembly, in October, 1758, was to confirm this court structure and its rules. Until 1764, its civil side was confined to hearing appeals, although an appeal meant that a case was tried afresh. I found no actions originating in the Supreme Court before 1766.[25]

In addition to these common law courts, three other courts were established to handle specific other forms of law. After the conquest of Acadia in 1713, a Vice Admiralty Court had been established in Annapolis Royal to handle matters involving shipping and seafaring. In 1749, the court moved with the seat of government to Halifax. The governor in council received petitions from residents in Halifax to resolve disputes that could not be handled by the common law courts or Vice Admiralty. In response, within the first year the council began taking on the roles, as necessary, as a Court of Chancery or a Court of Prohibited

Marriage and Divorce.[26] Cornwallis was initially instructed to establish a Chancery jurisdiction as part of the General Court, with himself as chief chancellor. Even after the criminal and civil jurisdictions of that court were moved to the Supreme Court, the governor remained chancellor and the council acted as the Court of Chancery with the councillors as the court's masters.[27] Similarly, the governor and council adopted the role of a court to hear petitions for divorce and related marriage matters after receiving their first petition to do so in 1750.[28] After an elected assembly was established for the colony in 1758, the assembly passed legislation to establish the court-based process for divorce: legislation approved by the governor and not disallowed by the Board of Trade in London. The legislation affirmed the role of the governor in council to act as a court to hear divorce matters. In subsequent years, the Board of Trade disallowed Nova Scotian legislation aimed at limiting the divorce court's authority on the grounds that divorce was *ultra vires* the colonial assembly. By not noticing the original legislation establishing the court and then disallowing the amending legislation, the Board of Trade effectively allowed Nova Scotia a much broader divorce law than most other places in the British Empire at the time.[29]

The most important of the courts, in terms of use made, was the County Court-cum-Inferior Court of Common Pleas (going forward, all references to the Inferior Court will refer to both the County Court and Inferior Court eras). Between 1749 and 1765, records exist for 4,808 civil actions, of which 4,379 were in the Inferior Court of Common Pleas: 94 per cent of all of the civil actions. The criminal jurisdictions of the Quarter Sessions and Supreme Court, while not insignificant, never came close to matching the volume of civil litigation at the Inferior Court. It was through this court, more than anywhere else, that the people in Halifax came into contact with the law.

Justices of the Peace could also hear certain disputes summarily, on their own or in pairs. These summary hearings, however, did not need to be recorded, and so little direct evidence of the volume of summary work in these years remains. I found records for only sixteen disputes heard summarily, all subsequently appealed to the full Inferior Court The evidence of other times and other places from the end of the eighteenth and through the nineteenth centuries suggests that summary jurisdiction probably was important for certain disputes in the 1750s and 1760s.[30] Simeon Perkins, a Nova Scotia merchant appointed a Justice of the Peace in Liverpool in 1764, left extensive diaries for the period beginning in 1766.[31] From these, we can get a sense of the business he did. Paul Craven, in an important study of Justices of the Peace in New Brunswick from the end of the eighteenth century throughout the nineteenth, relies in large part on justices' notebooks in which they recorded their business.[32] Carolyn Steedman's book-length study of a justice and his weaver neighbour in early nineteenth-century England relies on both the justice's notebook and the neighbour's diary to fully flesh out a justice's work.[33] No such equivalent documents exist for Halifax justices from 1759 to 1766. The number of Inferior Court actions during this period that were clearly appeals from decisions by Justices of the Peace are too few for this book to present a reconstruction of the summary practice in the way the courts were done.[34]

The whereas clauses to a statute of the first elected assembly in 1758 include a note that "the Trial of Causes in a Summary way, before one or two Justices, hath been found very useful and a means of determining many suits with little costs." This statute, like many from the first assembly, codified current practice in Halifax and Nova Scotia. Under it, Inferior Court judges could hear actions for less than £5 summarily. If there were "factual matters in dispute," then the judges could refer it to a jury and, thus, a trial at a scheduled sitting of the court.[35] This was not a ban on lower value disputes coming before the Inferior Court: I found records for sixty-seven actions brought to the court where the plaintiffs could, based on value, have sought a summary hearing. Only seven of these actually went to a jury trial. Thus, regardless of what sort of summary jurisdiction was available, some Halifax litigants were prepared to take small matters directly to the full Inferior Court. If the whereas clause quoted above was truthful, and if Halifax in the 1750s and 1760s conformed to the practice elsewhere in the British Empire, then on top of all of the litigation discussed here involving the Inferior Court of Common Pleas and other courts, there would have been a great deal more litigation over small amounts, employment disputes, and minor assaults. If the surviving records mark the full extent of actual use of summary jurisdiction (an unlikely state of affairs) the conclusion remains that Halifax was a particularly litigious society in the 1750s and 1760s.

The Law in the Inferior Court of Common Pleas

The law the people of Halifax encountered in the Inferior Court was, in essence, the common law, but it was in many ways peculiar to Nova Scotia. Historians have long argued that the courts in Nova Scotia had essentially three ancestors: England, Virginia, and New England.[36]

Moreover, several have asserted that disputes over the sources of law and practice were one front in the struggles between British and New England factions in the community. At the end of 1752, the struggle between these factions came to its first crisis: the "Justices' Affair." Over several months, the colony's merchants and governmental leadership were split over the quality of justice provided by Halifax's Justices of the Peace. A group of merchants (the leaders of the colony's bourgeois) and others claimed to be seeking a more English colony against the actions of the justices who were, it was asserted, New Englanders infecting the law with their colonial views.[37]

At the December session of the Inferior Court, Ephraim Cook, still a ship's master and now merchant and *former* Justice of the Peace, was sued for impersonating a Justice of the Peace and for the wrongful imprisonment that ensued. Cook was a fractious fellow, and in the course of the December trial he managed to get himself imprisoned for contempt of court. His lawyer, David Lloyd, was also clerk of the court, and the bench's handling of Cook's case and Lloyd himself led the lawyer-clerk to publicly withdraw his services as clerk before the end of the court's session.

Two days later, on 29 December 1752, fourteen men petitioned the governor and council, claiming they had "perceived much irregularity and ... partiality in the proceedings of the Inferior Court of Judicature lately held" and demanded a public hearing into the court's conduct "for the discovery of truths which may tend to the publick Good of the province, and to the redress of such Grievances as we labour under."[38] The subscribers to the memorial included Joshua Mauger, one of the two most prominent merchants in the colony; lawyer and governor's clerk William Nesbitt; and John Webb (whose business partner Robert Ewer was one of the justices). The governor and council were irritated by the petition, but also understood that the combination of complainants' identities and the nature of their complaints required a serious response and agreed to hold hearings into the matter. At the beginning of the hearing, the petitioners, styling themselves "the Merchants Traders and Principal Inhabitants of the Town of Halifax," offered a second memorial. This new petition detailed nine complaints against the justices, principally Charles Morris, the chief justice of the court and surveyor general for the colony, and James Monk, a justice and Morris's deputy surveyor. Both Morris and Monk came to Halifax from New England. The new petition had forty-six signatories: thirteen from the first, and several new petitioners from a broader range of people including Roger Hill.

The chief complaint was a general attack on the law that the justices applied:

[G]reat countenance and encouragement hath been frequently given by the said Judges to introduce the Laws and practice of the Massachusetts into the Court of Common pleas in this province which Laws however good and beneficial they may be to the Inhabitants of the Massachusetts yet we conceive are injurous [sic] and detrimental to numbers of people in this Colony ... [these practices] influence the minds of such Jurymen who have been bred under the Massachusetts Law and tend to divide the minds of the people who we Conceive are to be governed by the Laws and practices of England and this Province Only.[39]

In reply, the justices, in their own memorial, replied, "[T]he Laws of the Massachusetts have never been by them at any Time given in Charge to the Jury, or made use of on any decision whatsoever as a Rule to determining the Cause of Proceedings in the said Court." They further argued, "[T]he Libellers are utterly ignorant of the Rules and Practices of the Courts in New England for that in most points they are exactly Conformable to the Practice of his Majesty's Courts at Westminster and the Common Law of England is in Force there as well as in all His Majesty's Plantations in America."[40]

This was probably the most accurate statement made in any of the memorials and petitions. But its application could be more general: it is not clear that anyone was particularly knowledgeable about what the law was in either England or Massachusetts, how the two differed from each other, and how law in Halifax conformed to one, the other, both, or neither. Rather, the appeal to differences between England and New England seems more like a rhetorical device to undermine the authority of Charles Morris and James Monk in particular on behalf of a group of bourgeois merchants and their allies.

Between January 10 and February 1, the council met seventeen times to hear the evidence, none of which was recorded in the council minutes. The council then made its rulings over four sittings in late February and early March. The council found completely for the justices, ruling that the inhabitants did not prove their case in any of the articles of the memorial. The council declared that Halifax legal practice conformed to English law and was free of Massachusetts influences.[41] The council's ruling included many scathing judgments of the Inhabitants' case and a number of pointed criticisms of those involved. This apparent victory for the bench was not as complete as it first appears. On February 28, the council declared that all members of council, men named in the General Commission, and those appointed to be in charge of the settlements at Annapolis Royal, Chignecto, Minas, and Pisiquid were to be deemed to be Justices of the Peace. On March 6, just five days after the final ruling on the affair, the governor recommissioned Charles Morris, James Monk, John Duport, Robert Ewer, and William Bourne as Justices of the Peace and judges of quorum, underlining his faith in them. At the same time, however, Joseph Scott and Sebastian Zouberbuhler were each appointed as both Justice of the Peace and judge of quorum. John Crawley, James Creighton, and Joseph Gerrish were appointed Justices of the Peace.[42] Zouberbuhler was one of the memorialists, while Crawley was likely brother to Edmund Crawley, another of the memorialists.[43] The newly expanded commission of justices ensured that more of the colonial, commercial bourgeoisie were represented on the bench than before, when people like Morris and Monk, reliant on government officers, dominated.

The Justices' Affair was significant in revealing the struggle between much (although not all) of the merchant or commercial community on the one hand and the non-commercial governing elite on the other. Despite the memorialists' characterization of law in Halifax, the day-to-day functioning of the court did not much rely on appeals to English or other precedents. The Inferior Court served a particular function: to resolve disputes between people. In this regard, it was procedure that mattered much more than law. The procedures offered a way to define disputes, to try them if necessary, and to come to a resolution. For residents, the debate about English and New English law was really about what they thought should be the resolutions of disputes, and was not based on any deep or accurate understanding of "the law." As will be clear from the rest of this book, the Inferior Court was important as a forum for dispute resolution, but it was legal process and the opinions of civilians in their roles as jurors and arbitrators that mattered most. The specifics of law were much less important than the structures the courts provided.

The Inferior Court Bench

The chief judge of the Inferior Court for most of the period between 1750 and 1766 was Charles Morris. Morris was from Massachusetts, but had been involved in Nova Scotian affairs since 1746, when he was part of a force of New Englanders who attacked Louisbourg as part of the North American front in the War of the Austrian Succession. In 1748, he returned to lead an expedition to survey the mainland of Nova Scotia. He returned again in 1749 to take part in establishing Halifax by helping survey the town site, which led to his appointment as the chief surveyor of the colony and a member of council. He also began serving as the registrar or clerk of the Court of Vice Admiralty. In December of 1750, he was appointed a Justice of the Peace and began serving as a judge on the Inferior Court. By 1752 and the Justices' Affair, he was in practice the head judge of the court. Each of these positions would secure him a salary from the Board of Trade, allow him to charge fees to those who used his services, or both. In 1764, Morris was appointed an assistant judge of the Supreme Court when its bench was expanded from one judge to three.[44] There is no evidence that Morris was particularly trained for his role as either surveyor or justice, judge or registrar. He was a trusted man of William Shirley of Massachusetts and then Paul Mascarene, lieutenant governor of Nova Scotia in the 1740s. This translated into Morris's being recommended to Cornwallis, which in turn led to his initial appointments. He was either or both an effective civil servant or politically astute; so much so that he remained in the good graces of the governor's office through the terms of several different governors.

James Monk, the other justice to be attacked by name in the Justices' Affair, was also from Massachusetts (although he had been born and educated in Britain) and may have been equally untrained in the law. He arrived in Halifax in the summer of 1749 and was appointed Morris's assistant surveyor that autumn. Like Morris he was given his commission as a Justice of the Peace in December 1750. Monk was never as sure in his position as Morris was, and he was forced to defend himself more than once the year of the Justices' Affair. The council did find him "very unworthy the character a Magistrate ought to support," for his role in a scheme to secure the merchant Thomas Power's property from Power's wife while Power was in prison. Monk and Morris had a falling-out in the late 1750s: Monk accused Morris of favouring Halifax councilmen over others while surveying agricultural land west of Halifax. For his betrayal, he was ostracized by Morris and eventually forced to sell his commission as assistant surveyor to Morris's son. In March of 1760, the governor removed him from his commission as justice for non-attendance of duties, and Monk turned to practising law instead. In the next six years, he became the busiest lawyer in Halifax. He did not remain out of all offices for long: in July of 1760, he was appointed King's Solicitor (solicitor general) for the colony, although without a salary independent of any fees he could earn from the position.[45]

None of the other justices of the peace in the 1750s and 1760s appear to have had legal training either. Appointing amateurs to the office of justice of the peace was commonplace in England and the broader empire.[46] Their role was to deal with simple, statutory matters in summary jurisdiction, not the finer points of law, and a good many books were available to help guide them.[47] When the justices sat at Quarter Sessions and the Inferior Court of Common Pleas, however, they were in essence judges hearing disputes at common law more than statutory law. It was here where the widest variety of disputes could be, and were, heard. The justices' lack of education in the law, and the absence of legally trained lawyers too (see below), served this end. They were, it seems, inclined to accept as within the bounds of law all that was brought before the court, and thus to understand the court's purpose as a forum for resolving disputes in the community, not the place for serious or deep legal argument.

Besides Morris and Monk, the other justices of the early 1750s were drawn from among the elite of the new settlers to the colony. Robert Ewer was a military officer who arrived with Cornwallis and went into trade, forming a partnership with John Webb, Anne Webb's husband. Likewise, Ephraim Cook (whose removal from his commission sparked the Justices' Affair) set himself up as a trader in Halifax after arriving with Cornwallis's convoy as the captain of a private vessel. John Duport also came with Cornwallis and, like Monk and Morris, held paid government offices in the colony, such as secretary to the governor's council, and acted as a lawyer. In 1769, he was made an assistant judge of the Supreme Court before being named the first chief justice of the Island of Saint John (Prince Edward Island) in 1770.[48] The sixth, Joseph Scott, appears to have left little record. After the Justices' Affair, the commission of justices was expanded to include four more: John Crawley, James Creighton, Joseph Gerrish, and Sebastian Zouberbuhler. Of these new justices, Crawley, Gerrish, and Zouberbuhler were all merchants or traders.

The Litigants

Clearly, the residents of Halifax saw the Inferior Court's purpose as resolving disputes in the community as well. As noted in the introduction, the people in Halifax made use of the court at an incredible rate:

from 23 to 155 actions were started for every 1,000 people a year. The heads of more than a quarter of the families named in Halifax's 1752 census appeared as litigants at least once before 1766. Because several "families" in the census often included adults with different surnames (such as live-in servants) who may have engaged in litigation in their own name, and because many of the families listed in the census left the colony within a few years of the census being taken, even this measure likely under-represents how enmeshed households were in the civil justice system. The litigation rates that can be produced are significantly higher than all of the litigation rates I found reported by historians for other North American or common law jurisdictions in the same period. Halifax was a community of litigants.

To fully understand how integral the courts were to Halifax's developing community, it is worth considering some rather large numbers. Between 1749 and 1766, 2,879 individual people were involved in the civil courts as a litigant, juror, arbitrator, judge, justice, lawyer, or surety (guarantor for another person's appearance at a trial or appeal). It is possible to count the separate appearances each individual made in the courts and identify the role they played in the courts each time they appeared. More than anything else, individual people appeared in court as litigants: a plaintiff suing or a defendant being sued. Most appeared in only one legal action: of the 2,512 individual people who sued or were sued, more than half (1,293) were involved in only one action, and three-quarters (1,886) appeared in three or fewer actions (going forward, when I use the term "infrequent litigant," I will be referring to this group of 1,886 people). But, these infrequent litigants account for only one-quarter (2,672) of all of the appearances made by litigants. Four hundred twenty-two people were litigants in four to nine actions; combined, the infrequent litigants and these 422 accounted for half of all litigation appearances. The other half of all litigation appearances (5,069) were made by 204 individuals (8 per cent of all individual litigants) who sued or were sued ten or more times. The most frequent litigants were 56 individuals (only 2 per cent of litigants) who sued or were sued in 27 or more distinct actions. They represents one-quarter (2,644) of all of the appearances made by litigants (the term "frequent litigant" refers to this group of 56). In much of the analysis below, I will contrast the 1,293 infrequent litigants with the 56 frequent litigants as groups who took part in the same proportion of litigation but for whom litigation was a very different part of their lives. Many of the people of Halifax experienced suing someone or being sued, but most of the time the courts served a small proportion of the population.

More can be said about the people who appeared in the courts as a way of understanding who used the courts and why. In particular, it is possible to evaluate litigants based on their gender (and, to a degree, their family status), their occupations and class, and where they came from. The differences between frequent and infrequent litigants will make it possible to begin to explain the place of civil courts in Halifax's society.

Gender and Family

The litigants were overwhelmingly male: 2,256 individuals involved in the courts were (likely) men, compared to 154 who were (likely) women. The men made 9,780 appearances as litigants, roughly four appearances per person, while the women made 320 appearances, or two appearances per person. Not only were women less likely to sue or be sued, they were less likely than men to sue frequently: 137 (89 per cent) of the female litigants appeared in three or fewer actions, compared to 1,649 (73 per cent) of male litigants. On average, women accounted for only 3 per cent of plaintiffs or litigants. The greatest proportion of women litigants was in 1761, when 6 per cent of all litigants were women.[49]

Women's relatively low participation rates as litigants and men's disproportionately high participation rates can be explained in two complementary ways. On the one hand, the greater the extent to which women were integrated within family economies, the lower their participation rates would appear to be. There was a general expectation in the common law that husbands had legal responsibility for their wives, for their debts and credits, and for torts involving them.[50] Thus, Edward Lush's wife purchased a wide variety of goods from the merchant Charles King in the first few months after Halifax was first established. She did this for the household, which by 1752 was composed of five adult men, one boy, and herself. When King decided he, or perhaps his wife or servants, had extended enough credit to the Lushes, it was Charles King who sued Edward Lush for the debt.[51] In the 1759 action *Rock v. Maguire*, John Rock sued, even though the debt in question was for credit extended by Mary Rock, his wife.[52] It is not clear how free married women in Halifax were to sue or be sued in their own name, but in practice they seem to have sued or been sued in their husband's names. Married women were regularly (although not always) identified as litigants when they sued or were sued for defamation and assault, but even in these cases, wives who were identified as victims or perpetrators were not always identified as plaintiffs or defendants.[53] In only twenty-two appearances by women as litigants are they identified as a "wife."

On the other hand, Deborah Rosen and Cornelia Hughes Dayton, historians of other colonial jurisdictions, have argued that women's participation rates are a reflection of their "level of independent participation in market activities."[54] In other words, the greater the extent to which women, single or married, produced or traded goods or provided services *separate* from the other adults (particularly adult males) in their family, the higher their participation in the courts as litigants. In comparison to the women in Rosen's study of New York in the eighteenth century, women in Halifax made up a greater proportion of litigants than in rural areas of the colony but a smaller proportion of litigants than in New York City.[55]

Mary Whitehand appeared as a litigant eight times. In one action she appeared as a co-defendant with her husband, and in one action she was identified as a "widow." In most actions, however, she was described as a "sole dealer." Whitehand appears to have been acting as a femme sole trader: a married woman who operated in trade and law as if she were single and independent of other male supervision of her trade (as by a father or trustee). She apparently had the power to contract independent of her husband and sued or was sued to enforce those contracts without him.[56] Femme sole traders existed in London in the eighteenth century, but their legal status was more ambiguous outside of the city. Marylynn Salmon has found statutes covering femme sole traders in only Pennsylvania and South Carolina of the British North American colonies, although she found women claiming to be femme soles operating elsewhere in the colonies.[57] There were no ordinances or statutes defining femme sole traders for Nova Scotia before 1766. There were, however, women who appeared in court as innkeepers, milliners, and practitioners of other occupations. Some may have been single or widows, but it is likely that some, like Mary Whitehand, were married but traded and litigated independently.[58]

Femme soles were not the only women to sue and be sued in their own right. Widows who attempted to wrap up their deceased husband's affairs or who continued to run the family business predominated among female litigants. Widows appeared as litigants 172 times, 54 per cent of all appearances by women as litigants. The existence of femme sole traders and the comparatively liberal divorce law (discussed in chapter 7) suggests that women in Halifax in its early years had greater legal, and probably personal, freedom than in contemporary England or than they would have had even in Nova Scotia later into the colonial period.

Nevertheless, women were excluded by law or practice from other legal roles, such as those of juror or arbitrator. The formal spaces of law were essentially male spaces, and women's involvement as individuals arose in exceptional circumstances.

The absence of women from the written records of law should not be understood as their real and complete absence. In the documents of law, women were often not seen – but they were there. As the Lush and Rock litigation hints at, litigation between two individual men was often actually litigation between families. Women (and children, for that matter) were active in the life of Halifax, constantly engaged in exchanges of goods and services and, with that, the accruing of debt and extension of credit. They also engaged in personal exchanges, the sharing of local news, and thus the building of community knowledge that helped to determine whether someone or some family should continue to receive credit or if some clearing of accounts and even litigation was necessary. At extremes, that knowledge, be it about creditworthiness or sexual behaviour, could spill into accusations of slander or even physical confrontation and assault.

Families were at times nuclear, made up of husbands and wives and children, but could also be extended, including three or more generations within a single household or adult siblings who operated individually or as a single unit, depending on the circumstances.[59] The servants and slaves in a household also often had the power to enter into all sorts of exchanges themselves, sometimes as individuals and sometimes as representatives of the family. In the latter case, they too could be sued, not as themselves but through the family head.[60] Just as husbands stood in for their wives in litigation, fathers could stand in for children, masters for servants and slaves, and brothers for sisters and minor brothers. The documents and language of legal activity hide this wider family and community dynamic. So, while the numbers of male and female litigants do point to the levels of both female independence and male domination, they are not simply or directly representative of this. In much of what is to follow, it is necessary to remember that the men suing each other (and also the women suing and being sued) are often merely representatives, signifiers if you will, of their families, their households.

Occupations: Status and Class

The documents created for actions often contained several pieces of information about the litigants: their name, where they lived, and a description of what they did or of their status. Thus, a litigant could be described by occupation as "merchant," "mantua maker," or "black-smith," but also by their position in the community as "gentleman," "esquire," "wife," or "widow" (although the masculine equivalents of the latter two, "husband" and "widower,"[61] never appeared). Some terms could do double duty; "yeoman," for instance, meant both an independent farmer and someone with a status below that of gentle-man.[62] The occupational and status labels were applied by oneself as a marker of self-perception and by opponents as a marker of how the person was understood by the opponent and the broader community. The terms served a necessary purpose of identification, and so what-ever descriptor was used, it had to be reasonably close to the actual oc-cupation or standing of the person in question or risk a challenge to the writ. As a whole, the terms used allow us to get a picture of what the litigants did, their class, and their standing in the community.

Although the court was used by a broad swath of the community, the Inferior Court served primarily as a commercial court or a court for people engaged in trade and commerce. Table 2.1 summarizes the appearances as litigants for those occupations with the most individ-ual litigants. The table is divided between craftspeople, commercial people, and labourers. As can be seen, more than half of the fifty-six frequent litigants were drawn from merchants and traders, and almost two-thirds of the frequent litigants had commercial occupations. By way of contrast, craftspeople, like bakers or carpenters, made up only one-seventh of the frequent litigant appearances. Craftspeople made up the largest group of infrequent litigants. The nine most common crafts occupations for litigants were bakers, blacksmiths, butchers, car-penters, coopers, housewrights, masons, shoemakers, and tailors. As the last column of table 2.1 shows, half or more of the individual liti-gants who were described with each of these occupations, except ma-sons, appeared in court three or fewer times. By contrast, half or more of the individuals who were identified in most commercial occupations appeared as litigants in seven or more actions. In practice, truckmen like Roger Hill were engaged in commerce, but their median number of litigation appearances was more similar to that of craftspeople. A handful, including Hill, however, sued much more often, drawing their mean number of appearances closer to other commercial occupa-tions than most crafts. Labourers' litigation patterns more closely re-sembled craftspeople's. Overall, while individual craftworkers would be involved in only a small number of legal actions, most commercial

Table 2.1: Select occupations and litigation appearances

Occupation	Number of individuals[a]	Number of people making 3 or fewer litigation appearances[b]	Number of people making 27 or more appearances	Mean number of appearances	Median number of appearances
Craftspeople					
Baker	25	15	2	8	2
Blacksmith	17	11	1	7	3
Butcher	16	7	0	7	2
Carpenter	75	39	1	5	3
Cooper	20	12	0	4	2
Housewright	28	14	0	5	3
Mason	18	8	1	11	4
Shoemaker	19	13	0	3	2
Tailor	23	12	2	7	3
Commercial					
Merchant	140	53	28	16	7
Retailer	73	23	11	12	7
Shopkeeper	25	8	6	18	8
Tavern keeper	35	7	7	15	9
Trader	112	36	20	15	8
Truckman	18	11	2	11	3
Other					
Labourer	84	58	1	3	2

[a] This includes all individuals ever described with one of these terms or a compound occupation term including one of the terms (e.g., a merchant-brewer would be included in the merchant category). Because occupation terms were, to some degree, fluid, it is possible that an individual could be counted in more than one of the rows.

[b] The numbers in this column and those in the columns to the right of it are based on the total number of appearances made by an individual who was ever described by any of the terms in the occupation column, including those appearances where the individual was described with a different occupation or did not have an occupation included.

litigants would be involved in several actions. The Halifax civil courts were courts that involved a large proportion of the Halifax population from all levels, but the courts were still primarily used by people engaged in commercial activity, that is to say, following on Kocka's and Moretti's definitions, the bourgeois.

One group remarkably under-represented in civil litigation was the military. Halifax was a garrison town, with a sizeable naval and army presence for much of the 1750s and 1760s. Soldiers and naval sailors rarely made appearances in civil litigation as soldiers or sailors. Of course, they could rack up debts along with others, especially toward retailers, tavern keepers, and the like. But they are simply not identified by military terms in the records in any great number. They were involved in Halifax life, and with the law. Jim Phillips and Allyson May found that in the same period as the one covered in this book, thirty-six of the fifty-nine male accused murderers were soldiers or naval sailors.[63] I have two possible explanations for the relative absence of military men in the civil courts records. First, their potential creditors may have been unwilling to extend them much credit, as their status as sailors and soldiers made them even more transient than the civilian population. Second, to the extent they appear, they may not appear as soldiers or sailors. For instance, they may appear as plaintiffs while moonlighting as labourers, carpenters, or housewrights. I have no positive evidence to either suggestion; the former seems rational on the part of creditors and the latter seems reasonable to the extent that the soldiers and sailors were given any freedom to work away from their garrison or ship. Army officers appear intermittently in the records as defendants sued for victualling contracts, but these, too, are rare instances.

The Halifax Courts and the Wider World

Halifax was the centre of the colony of Nova Scotia, at least for the British, American, and European Protestant settlers, and was itself part of a wider imperial trading network in which the colony was a new and small part. The court use reflected this. Litigants in the court came from all over the Atlantic world and beyond.[64] Until 1759, the Halifax court was the only inferior court for the entire colony. When four additional counties were created west and south of Halifax (Cumberland, Kings, Annapolis, and Lunenburg) people in those colonies could bring local suits to their own inferior courts. Halifax's Inferior Court remained the court for north-eastern Nova Scotia and, when Nova Scotia was greatly expanded by British success in the Seven Years War, became briefly the court for Cape Breton and Prince Edward Island.

Unsurprisingly, the court was first and foremost a court for the people of greater Halifax. Beside the town of Halifax and its immediate suburbs, by 1766 several other communities of various sizes had sprouted up around Chebucto Harbour or the north-west arm on the other side of Halifax's peninsula: larger places like Dartmouth and Sackville, and smaller places like Point Pleasant, Gottingen, and Dutchtown. Four-fifths of the people who litigated in the courts were from greater Halifax; making up nine-tenths of all litigation appearances.[65]

A very small number of new settlers had moved into Annapolis Royal when it was capital of British Nova Scotia after 1713. With the founding of Halifax, more new settlements of English-speaking and German-speaking settlers were established: Lunenburg for the foreign Protestants, Canso for fishing operations, and after the expulsion of the Acadians, throughout the Annapolis Valley. After the second siege of Louisbourg and then the end of the Seven Years War, some people moved to Cape Breton Island. A little less than a tenth of the individuals who appeared in the courts were from other parts of Nova Scotia, accounting for about a twentieth of all litigant appearances in Halifax. Almost as many litigants came from the rest of British North America, primarily the New England colonies but also from places farther south along the Atlantic coast of North America, Newfoundland, or after 1760, from Quebec. These people made many fewer appearances as litigants than did the Nova Scotians, however. A much smaller number of individual litigants came from the British Isles, the West Indies, or other parts of the world.[66]

One's role in court was, for people from away, determined by where they lived. Nova Scotians were more than twice as likely to be defendants in the Halifax courts than they were to be plaintiffs, while people from farther away were roughly three times as likely to be plaintiffs over defendants.[67] This pattern is reflective of the flows of credit and capital into and out of Halifax: Halifax was the seat of government, the law, and business in Nova Scotia; credit flowed out from Halifax to the other English and Protestant settlements in the colony, and people from those settlements owed more to Halifax than Haligonians owed them. According to local ordinances and then acts by the assembly, foreign creditors could not collect on debts accrued before someone settled in Nova Scotia, unless the debts arose to pay for passage or for goods shipped to Halifax. Debts accumulated after a person settled, however, could be collected in Halifax's courts.[68] The people in Halifax – especially the merchants, traders, mariners, and fishers engaged in international trade – turned to more prosperous people elsewhere for their credit. Those creditors (or their local agents) came to Halifax's courts for remedies when debts went unpaid.[69]

The Acadians before 1755, and the Mi'kmaq for the entire period under study here, were not only not residents of Halifax by and large, they were not a presence in the civil courts. I found no positive evidence of any Acadian or Mi'kmaq person appearing in the Halifax civil courts. They were, in the 1750s and 1760s, communities apart, both geographically and in terms of the civil law. While the civil courts were part of the colonial state, their role in colonization was one of exclusion. The absence of Mi'kmaq and Acadian people in the civil courts was a result of their exclusion from the regular commercial activities of the new colonizers. The echoes of colonization were also essentially absent from the civil courts. Thus, the agents responsible for treating and trading with the Mi'kmaq do not appear in the civil courts in that capacity; the movement of the planters onto Acadian lands likewise did not create immediate civil legal disputes, though the planters did eventually appear in the courts.

A Selection of Litigants

The conjunction of these patterns of gender, occupation, and place can be better understood by comparing Anne Webb, Roger Hill, and two other frequent litigants, Malachy Salter and James Monk. Webb was the only woman among the fifty-six frequent litigants (those who sued or were sued twenty-seven times or more). Roger Hill was the only truckman in that group. Nevertheless, both were in many ways typical of certain types of frequent litigants, and their litigation patterns reflected their status in several ways. Webb, as she came into business on her own, called herself and was termed a trader. Traders appear to have engaged in providing some things to their final users, but most of the time moved goods within Halifax and Nova Scotia: taking up consigned and unconsigned trade goods brought into the colony and then passing them on to retailers, shopkeepers, and craftspeople in the town and beyond. They also bought up the produce of people from the town and the rest of the colony, selling it on to local and visiting merchants and mariners involved in international trade. Webb extended credit to many people and found herself indebted to only a few. Thus, she was a plaintiff in almost three times as many actions as she was a defendant. Most of the people she sued were from Halifax, but about a tenth of the time she sued people from other parts of Nova Scotia (see table 2.2).

Roger Hill, by contrast, although he made his livelihood largely from buying and selling goods, was, as a truckman, engaged in very local trade. He bought from many people and sold to many. In the process, he was constantly needing credit and extending it. His business was rather marginal, and he was sued half again as many times as he sued others. All of the people who sued him, and all the people he sued, were from within Halifax, as table 2.2 shows.

Webb's and Hill's litigation patterns become even more defined when compared to the patterns of other frequent litigants. The merchant Malachy Salter, the single most litigious person in Halifax in the period, as Susan Buggey has noted, was described by some contemporaries as a "'Litigious troublesome Man' 'who has treated us in a Barberous cruel manner.'"[70] He was a plaintiff in 110 actions and a defendant in 30. Born in Boston in 1716, Salter had already established himself in coastal shipping, distilling, and financing fishing expeditions before he arrived in Halifax in 1749. Salter arrived in Halifax sometime in 1749 or 1750 and quickly established himself as a merchant, first in partnership with John Kneeland and then on his own. In his mid-thirties when he arrived, Salter had already been involved in running his uncles' Boston distillery and in taking part in trade up and down the coast of North America and into the West Indies. In Halifax, he quickly established himself as a merchant of some repute and with a comparably extensive fleet of ships for merchants in the town. In September of 1762, he lost both his commission as a Justice of the Peace and his appointment as Collector of Lighthouse Duties. Although he had government appointments, sinecures, and contracts from time to time, he did not keep them for long and was much more reliant on private trade for his wealth than some of the other prosperous merchants of Halifax, like Joshua Mauger or Thomas Saul.[71] One of the leaders of the New England faction in Halifax, he held several government positions or protected monopolies, although often for only brief periods. Although he did not side with Joshua Mauger and the other merchants in the Justices' Affair, he was never close to government, and in 1777 he would be indicted for sedition in support of the American rebels. His business in Halifax turned on shipping – bringing in goods and shipping out fish and other produce – as well as some local manufacture and privateering in times

Table 2.2: Residence and litigation patterns

| | | Home of Opponent | | | | | | | Total | |
| | | Halifax | | Nova Scotia | | BNA | | Unknown | Opponents | Actions[a] |
Litigant	Role	N	%[b]	N	%	N	%	N	N	N
Anne Webb	Plt	29	88	4	12	0	–	1	34	34
	Def	6	67	2	22	1	11	3	12	12
Roger Hill	Plt	17	100	0	–	0	–	5	22	20
	Def	35	100	0	–	0	–	4	39	33
Malachy Salter	Plt	89	88	9	9	3	3	18	119	110
	Def	25	68	2	5	10	26	5	43	30
James Monk	Plt	27	93	1	3	1	3	3	32	27
	Def	33	87	4	11	1	3	1	39	38

[a] Some actions featured several opponents.
[b] Percentage of actions where opponent's place of residence is known.

of war.[72] In 1761, Salter was a prosperous merchant, a member of the elected House of Assembly, and a newly appointed Justice of the Peace and Collector of Lighthouse Duties. Almost all of Salter's litigation was against people in Halifax or the rest of Nova Scotia, but more than a quarter of the people who sued him came from other parts of British North America. Salter was engaged in the courts in other ways too: Salter was the most frequent arbitrator in the period, acting in that role sixty-six times over sixteen years.

The justice and then lawyer James Monk was not, unlike Webb, Hill, or Salter, involved in trade. His income until the late 1750s depended on his government contracts and after that primarily on his work as a lawyer. He had a higher status than Hill; he appears to have been wealthier, and socially was certainly placed higher in the community (at least before his falling-out with Morris). Like Hill, he was a defendant more often than he was a plaintiff, but the differences were not great. Almost everyone he sued was from Halifax, while only twice did he sue someone from either the rest of Nova Scotia or British North America. Most of the suits against him were also initiated by Haligonians, although about a tenth came from people resident in other parts of Nova Scotia, and once he was sued by people from away.

The tailor Peter Mackey also went to court many times: he served as a juror in fifty-one different actions. Little is known about Mackey. He was not listed as the head of a household in the 1752 census, although it is possible he resided in someone else's house as a servant or lodger. He first served as a juror in the September 1753 session of the Inferior Court, and last served in the September 1763 session. By the end of the 1750s, Mackey owned a house that he let out for eight shillings a week, although in litigation over the house his tenant described it as "not fitt for any Gentleman to Lodge in."[73] In total, he was involved in only three actions as a litigant: he sued his tenant for a debt, and was himself sued once for a debt and once for his involvement in a fight between two others.[74] Like many other craftspeople and others of middling income or less, Mackey attended the courts regularly, but not so often as a litigant.

Conclusion

The civil courts established in Halifax in 1749 were the forum for conflict resolution among the settlers in Halifax. The civil courts were used to deal with the specific, often small, conflicts that arose between private individuals in their economic and, to a much lesser degree, social relationships. These were conflicts that, taken together, spoke to the place of Halifax within Nova Scotia and the broader British Atlantic world. They were also conflicts that reflected the roles of men and women in the colony. They were conflicts that reflected the relationship between commerce and craft, between, in the end, merchant capital and productive capital and labour. The litigants in the civil courts, and especially in the Inferior Court of Common Pleas, were drawn from all segments of Halifax's population, from among the new settlers to the rest of Nova Scotia and from the broader empire. But the courts were dominated by a small group of frequent litigants, all but one of them male and the largest portion of whom came from the wealthiest of commercial occupations. It was a court that was simultaneously a court of the entire city and of the elite. The ways in which these masses of litigants, and the small number of frequent litigants, moved their disputes through the courts are the subjects of the remaining chapters of this book.

3

Initiating Actions

On 16 November 1761, Daniel Wood, clerk of the Inferior Court of Common Pleas, issued sixteen writs to call defendants to trial in December. Each of these represented a new trial or action that could begin at the session. By the time the court would begin sitting, fifty-six new actions were to start and another two were to be taken up again, continuing on from the September session of the court. Of these actions, we know the issue in sixteen: eleven were for debts, two for assaults, and one each for breach of contract, trespass, and recovering on an earlier judgment of the court (*scire facias*). This was a smaller load than average for the Inferior Court in the early 1760s but the sorts of cases were typical of the court's business.

Of the sixteen writs issued that day, three of the actions involved Anne Webb, Roger Hill, and Malachy Salter as plaintiffs or defendants. Their three actions can be used to demonstrate and explain several aspects about initiating litigation in the 1750s and 1760s. First, they can be used to show the writs, other legal documents, and forms of action employed in Halifax and inherited from English law. Second, they can demonstrate the role of lawyers in shaping litigation. Third, they can be used to develop an analysis of why people would sue when they did. Through describing what happened in Hill's, Salter's, and Webb's cases, this and the subsequent chapters will show how actions were initiated, progressed through courts, and came to an end. Studying processes and practices can show how the Inferior Court operated, why and how litigants used the court, and how court actions played into broader relations within the colony. At points in each chapter there will be digressions to show and explain elements of the Inferior Court legal process not captured in these cases.[1]

Issues behind Initiating Debt Litigation

When Haligonians sued, they most often sued over debt. Debt was common, and almost all transactions in early Halifax were on credit.[2] The community had very little circulating money,[3] and its economy developed not with the exchange of coins and bills but with the extension of a great deal of credit and the accumulation of significant debts. It was not a barter economy.[4] Rather, the value of most things was priced monetarily, in pounds, shillings, and pence. Exchanges were completed either for similarly valued goods or services or on credit. A day's work by a carpenter, for example, might be paid for with an agreed upon amount of food and drink. More often, however, exchanges were handled on ledger transactions, with credits and debits often lasting months, if not years.

Such reliance on debt and credit was common throughout the Atlantic world in the eighteenth century, and was essential for sustaining the networks that linked the economies of the United Kingdom, Africa, the Caribbean, North America, and mainland Europe.[5] Within communities around the Atlantic, credit networks – local, intercolonial, and international – formed the basis of most economic transactions.[6] Halifax in the 1750s and 1760s was a new city on the Atlantic coast, but from the very moment of its founding as a base for the Royal Navy and the new capital of Nova Scotia it was very much part of the Atlantic world. The legal practices developed in Halifax were drawn from laws, practices, and experiences in other parts of the British Atlantic,[7] while the local debts often involved goods or capital drawn from or prepared for places all over the Atlantic world. A study of litigation in early Halifax becomes a broader history of the British Atlantic world, colonialism and merchant capitalism of the long eighteenth century,[8] and how the common law spread through the Atlantic and came to what would become Canada.[9]

Table 3.1 shows that in the Inferior Court more than three-quarters of all actions were directly related to debts. As already suggested, actions like trover and ejectment may have also resulted from debts for goods, land, or rent, so that an even greater proportion of the actions were

Table 3.1: Varieties of debt in Halifax courts

Debt Type	Inferior Court		Supreme Court		Vice Admiralty		Total	
	N	%	N	%	N	%	N	%
Total Actions[a]	2284		113		105		2502	
Debt Actions[b]	1750	77	52	46	27	26	1829	73
	N	%[c]	N	%	N	%	N	%
account	879	50	25	48	1	4	905	49
bond	22	1	0	0	0	0	22	1
note	476	27	13	25	0	0	489	27
note & account	31	2	1	2	0	0	32	2
work or wages[d]	94	5	3	6	25	93	122	7
miscellaneous / undefined	248	14	10	19	1	4	259	14

[a] Includes only those actions for which the matter in dispute is known. Thus, I have excluded actions for which no cause of action is known or it is too vague (e.g., it is a trespass on the case with no details).

[b] This includes only those actions for which the records clearly show them to originate in debts. Thus, cases of ejectment or trover are excluded because, while they may originate in a debt between the parties, this may not be the case. I have also excluded *scire facias*, which arose when someone failed to pay court ordered damages. While these are akin to debts, the actions do not arise from one person extending another credit.

[c] Per cent of the debt actions in the particular court or, under "Total," for all three courts.

[d] Includes actions described as "debt for wages on account."

likely debt cases. The table provides comparisons with the Supreme Court and Vice Admiralty to show that the two next busiest civil courts in Halifax also heard a large number of debt actions.

The litigation Anne Webb, Malachy Salter, and William Fury each initiated on 16 November 1761 were based on debts; in each case the defendant owed the plaintiff money or value for credit extended earlier. Where it is possible to determine what led to an action of trespass on the case, more than half were for "debts on account" (or some variation of this phrase), that is, for debts accrued through the trading of goods, services, or labour. Another quarter were for debts by note. These are debts that might originally have been accrued for any number of reasons, but were written down as promissory notes in which the debtor/defendant promised to pay the creditor or assignee/plaintiff a certain amount of money by a certain day.[10] At the Inferior Court of Common Pleas, more than three-quarters of the actions for which reasons for initiating the action are recorded were clearly for debts of one type or another (see table 3.1).

The types of debts suggest something about the economy and society of colonial Halifax and the place of the courts. Half of the debt actions in the Inferior Court were for accounts. The large number of account debts speaks first to how economic transactions occurred within Halifax: people extended credit routinely and payments were made in kind or when hard currency was actually available in the colony. Most of the time, most people did not have enough hard currency to buy all they needed. This was not particularly exceptional of colonial (or even metropolitan) local or even international economies. Moreover, despite the fact that the population was constantly in flux, people were willing to extend credit rather readily. Working on credit for weeks, months, and even years was a necessity in a colony where currency was rare and where much of the local production was aimed at foreign markets at some distance from the colony. Even the trade that occurred far from the colony was frequently on account.

The persistence of account seems to show that Nova Scotia differed from other North American colonies. Bruce Mann has traced a shift from account debts to debts by notes in Connecticut's courts between the 1710s and 1730s. He argued that the shift reflected and promoted wider changes in the economy. The expansion of both volume and distance of trade required a credit system that was rational and predictable. It is not that trade was not handled by accounts, but that debtors were regularly required to acknowledge their debts through a written note promising payment. The legal certainty of debts on notes allowed creditors greater assurance of their trading relationships when they could no longer rely on the sanctions of a relatively small and insular community. This in turn was a sign of a commercializing economy. Accounts were often of a commercial nature, but Mann asserts that notes "[t]ogether with paper currency, which was a public variant of private credit instruments, [were] written instruments [that] forced people not only to calculate in monetary terms, as they had always done, but to deal in monetary terms as well."[11] Thus, for Mann, even debtors and creditors "who customarily traded on book accounts ... made their accounts over into formal credit instruments as the price of further dealing."[12] Where suing on account persisted into the 1750s and later, it reflected local or temporal peculiarities. Thus, account debts persisted in larger towns because, Mann reasons, "the trust that underlay book debt in the earlier [small] towns could also arise in relations that were frequent and repeated [as might exist for retailers in large towns]."[13] Or, in the 1760s, Mann found a return of suing on account in rural areas and reasoned that due to the needs of the wartime economy, creditors were more convinced of the solvency of farmers and thus felt the need to convert accounts to notes less strongly.[14]

Account debts dominated in Halifax and their persistence does *not* show less of a concern for secure, predictable transactions than that shown by people in Connecticut at the same time. Rather, while the largest account debt was for £926 19s 7d (three times larger than the largest debt on a note), the median claim for an account debt was £12 14s 2d, more than £2 less than the median for debts on notes (£14 17s). This suggests that many creditors would seek a promissory note to secure debts that grew to a certain size without being cleared.

The occupations of creditors who favoured either accounts or notes are suggestive of the way accounts could persist, be changed into notes, or exist as notes from the start. Tavern keepers, who would typically extend small amounts of credit over several visits, sued twenty-one times on accounts, but only two times on notes. For example, Thomas Power, a tavern keeper, sued mariner Francis Picket for £3 4s 7d at the June 1757 Inferior Court. The account grew over many months. In total, there were twenty-two entries, the largest for more than three gallons of red wine (13 shillings) and for a loan of 12 shillings in cash. The rest was made up of individual nights at the tavern, such as when Picket had "liquor in company 2 bowles punch and 2 mugs" for 2s 8d; "2 mugs flip" for 8d (flip was a cocktail served warm or cold and made of rum, or other liquor, sugar, sometimes eggs and sometimes beer); and "wife mug beer and gill of rum" for 6d (the gill was a quarter pint).[15]

Tailors, who would produce a specific product or set of products for a client and rarely had regular interactions with the same clients, sued on notes nine times compared to five times on accounts. What debt led to a note of hand is usually unrecorded. Tailor David Belcher sued James Shepard in March 1758 for a debt on account from September 1757 for £9 19s 9d, including cloth, buttons, garters, waistcoats, and £1 10s labour in making a suit. At the same session, tailor Thomas Butler sued writing clerk William Firth for a note of hand worth £5 10s. The note was signed on 18 June that year, and the writ of attachment filed on 9 August. On 3 November 1757 Thomas Butler sued Frances Piggot on a £4 note of hand dated 28 October 1757, six days earlier.[16] There is even evidence of tailors taking other people's notes as payment. On 30 June 1760 Thomas Bleigh sued Kenneth Sutherland for a £3 3s 6d note from May 7. The note was originally made out by Joseph Torrey, who signed it over to George Louttit, who in turn signed it over to Bleigh. The note circulated quickly; it took less than two months for the note to change hands twice and for an action to ensue.[17]

Merchants, traders, and retailers all sued more frequently on accounts than on notes, but as the volume and value of their intercolonial trade decreased, they sued more frequently on notes: merchants sued on accounts almost two and a half times more often than on notes (148:64), traders a little less than two times more often (48:26), and retailers almost at equal volumes (15:13). This pattern of greater reliance on notes as the size of the commercial enterprise shrunk requires some explanation. It may be that for small and more locally oriented the trading enterprise, turning accounts into notes became more necessary to ensure payment before the trader or retailer had to pay off their own debts.

Merchant's accounts were both similar to and radically different from accounts like Francis Picket's with Thomas Power. When the merchant Jonathan Binney, from Halifax, sued Boston merchant Ebenezer Lowell in 1754, he presented an account dating from the late 1740s. The first part of the account listed an October 1748 order whereby the Boston firm Burch & Badger would pay Lowell £231½ on Binney's behalf. In April and June 1749 Binney appears to have paid Lowell another £112½ in cash. In exchange Binney received £120 worth of lemons (roughly 7500 fruit), a £5 cheese, fourteen pounds of sugar for £3, and another £12½ of "sundries for [my] family." In total, Binney claimed that he had received only £149 15s 5d worth of goods and was still owed £194 3s 8d (or goods equal to that value).[18] Several elements of this account need parsing. First, the account here was for a much longer period than those discussed above. Merchants, especially transacting over long distances and with great volumes, could let credit (or debt) sit for a long time before circumstances would provoke them to clear the books. Binney, for example, could have used his credit with Lowell to purchase more or sign it over to someone else to pay other accumulated debts. Second, credit could be purchased in advance. Moreover, credit was both the result of cash paid and orders made on others. The use of orders allowed people to transact business at great distances without sending cash (which could be stolen, lost, or otherwise misappropriated). They also served to knit merchants from disparate communities together.[19] In Binney's case, his first payment was made by a third party based near Lowell with whom Binney already had credit or enough of a reputation that they were prepared to advance money to Lowell. Third, the account unexceptionally mixes goods traded as part of the merchants' enterprise (the lemons) and goods for personal and family use, one more reminder that family needs and business needs were imbricated, regardless of class.

A suit between London-based merchant John Blackburn and Halifax tailor Charles Terlaven reveals other elements of the trading credit-debt relationship. Terlaven signed a note to Blackburn on 28 July 1761 for £51 7d to be paid back three months later. The debt was for cloth and hose, and Terlaven had listed the conditions:

Provided I dispose off the Above Goods to the Officers of the Provencials or so much thereof as I shall dispose off, after which time I will Allow him Interest for the Same till it is paid, which is to be at the Same time as the Provincials under Col. Twing now Commanded by Col[e] Arbuthnot are Paid by the Province of Massachusetts and also Promise to Pay Said John Blackburn the Amount of what goods Shall be sold to any other Person in Six Months from this Date[.]

Terlaven tried to limit his liability for the goods based on his capacity to contract with the army. The contract was missing, however, any description of how the goods could be returned to Blackburn in the event that Terlaven did not sell anything. Blackburn finally had Terlaven sued at the December court in 1763. He claimed to have received nothing from Terlaven in the meantime, and expected £3 6s 10d in interest added to the initial debt (the jury did not award the interest).[20]

There were other suits that were common. For instance, while artisans, labourers, and other workers sued for account or note debts, they also sued for wages or for work done. Wages were usually for a certain amount of labour measured in time; work done was for the production of a particular thing or the completion of a certain task. Half of all the actions entered into by carpenters and labourers were for work or wages (nineteen by carpenters, ten by labourers); fishers sued for work or wages in 30 per cent of their actions, and housewrights and mariners each sued for work or wages in 20 per cent of their actions.[21] Craftsmen sued for payment for work done more often than even the numbers in table 3.2 show. At times the product of their labour could be defined with a clarity that allowed them to sue on account and, like all creditors, workers of one sort or another could demand a note of hand for their labour. But as workers, these artisans and others would also enter into arrangements where they simply provided their labour in a contract of service or for services. These would lead to wages and work done suits. In *Freedom Bound*, Christopher Tomlins reports that in Massachusetts in the seventeenth century most wage suits were modelled as debt suits based on the failure of the employer to pay the agreed sum on completion of the contracted work or task. In the eighteenth century, Tomlins finds a rise in *quantum meruit* suits where workers sued for the value of the work finished at the point of litigation.[22] Wage suits in Halifax relied on both traditions though the phrase *quantum meruit* was not used. As will be seen in chapters 4 and 5, such suits were the most contested of debt suits in Halifax.

Debt actions came about because creditors needed the money or value of the debt or feared that repayment would become impossible. Some of the other actions were initiated for similar reasons. For example, the *scire facias* arose when a successful plaintiff had not been able to collect on the judgment they had received. An ejectment or a suit of trover could arise because a tenant or debtor had failed to pay what they owed the plaintiff. The launching and timing of all of these suits was at least in part determined by the same considerations as debt cases. Other actions, however, were initiated for different reasons. Assaults and defamations, for instance, were launched soon after the assaults had occurred or defamatory comments had been made. Such actions were directly reactive: plaintiffs felt they had been wronged and wanted retribution, punishment, to clear their reputations or achieve similar results. The actions on debts initiated on 16 November 1761, however, are illustrative of much more than the importance of debt in Halifax, and to those actions this chapter now turns.

Meany v. Hill: Summons and Attachments

Between 21 January and 10 February 1761, Roger Hill bought 30 bushels of "Indian Corn" (that is, corn or maize) from William Meany for £6. Hill gave Meany £2 in cash and 2 cords of fire wood valued at £1 4s (there were 20 shillings to the pound and 12 pence to the shilling). Sometime later, Hill gave Meany another shilling. In November, Meany hired James Monk as his lawyer and had him prepare the documents needed to sue Hill for the remaining £2 15s. Monk took out a writ of summons from Wood while filing with the court a copy of the account between Meany and Hill and a declaration by Meany describing how Hill's debt was incurred. The writ of summons was essentially the same whether the action was heard summarily (by a single Justice of the Peace at any time) or by the Inferior or Supreme Court.

Each writ was prepared by the clerk of court with the plaintiff or the plaintiff's lawyer. The summons instructed the provost marshal or his deputy to find the defendant and demand the value stated on the writ or summon him, her, or them to trial on the date specified. In addition, the writ informed the provost marshal, and thus the defendant, of the form of action (debt, trespass, etc.). The provost marshal then returned the writ to the court, noting if the defendant had been found and, if so, when and where. A formulaic document, much of the writ's wording corresponded to model writs brought from England. At first, the entire writ was hand written, although eventually some forms were produced to cover the boilerplate text at the beginning and end of each writ.

Here is an example of one writ from 1753, with the original spelling:

Halifax Ss
George the Second by the Grace of God of Great Brittain France & Ireland King Defender of the Faith &c.
To the Provost Marshall of Nova Scotia or his Deputy Greeting
We Command you that you Summon William Hunstable of Halifax within the Province aforesaid Mason (if he may be found in your Precinct) to Appear before Our Justices of our Inferior Court of Common Pleas next to be Holden at Halifax within and for the County of Halifax aforesaid on the first Tuesday of March next then and there to Anser the suit of Benjamin Gerrish of Halifax in the County aforesaid Merchant. In a plea of Trespass upon the Case For that the Deft[t] at Halifax afores[d] upon the 21 Day of February Current was indebted to the pltf. in the Sum of Fifty one pounds Eleven Shillings and Seven pence half penny Sterling to Ballance the Acc[t] hereto Annexed and then and there

promised to pay the same on Demand but fails thereof tho' Demanded, To the Damage of the Said Benjamin Gerrish, as he saith, the sum of Sixty pounds; hereof fail not and have you then there this Writ and your Doings thereon according to Law upon the said first Tuesday of March Next
Witness Charles Morris
Esq[r] This Twenty third Day of February in the twenty Sixth year of our Reign
Annoque Domini 1753
[Signed] John Ker, Clerk
Endorsed [by] [Otis] Little Att.o[23]

The writ opens with a greeting on behalf of the King to the provost marshal, who will execute the writ. It then instructs the provost marshal to summon William Hunstable to appear at the next sitting of the Inferior Court of Common Pleas to respond to the legal action against him initiated by Benjamin Gerrish. Both men are identified by where they live (Halifax) and by their occupations, so as to ensure the writ is served on the correct person (although the plaintiff's occupation could be left off). If either party was a widow, widower, executor, or agent then the original creditor, debtor, or party would also be named. What followed identified first the form of action, which identified how the plaintiff's complaint could come before a court (discussed below), and then a description of the specific complaint, in this case a debt for goods purchased on credit. Because it is a debt, Gerrish, the plaintiff, asserts that he asked Hunstable to pay the debt, that Hunstable promised to do so, and that it was still not paid. Gerrish then demands £60 in damages. Finally, the date and location of the session at which the defendant is summoned to appear are identified. The writ closes with the date it was issued and a signature by the clerk of the court who prepared the writ, along with an endorsement by the plaintiff's attorney, who requested the summons.

By the late 1750s, the structure of the writs had changed. In general they looked like the writ above, but the specifics about the plaintiff's actual complaint were removed or abbreviated. These, instead, appeared in a declaration the plaintiff would prepare to accompany the writ. In the declaration, the plaintiff would again identify the form of action, but would also provide a more detailed account of the events that led to the action than would appear in a writ. For some debt cases, like on promissory notes, this meant that the declaration was not significantly different than the writ. In other cases, where there was an extensive history of credit extended and partially repaid, or where the dispute was an assault or defamation, the declaration could be quite long and descriptive and differ from the writ. Of course the descriptions in the declarations could have been shaped by the plaintiffs to suit their positions to a degree. The declarations, however, were made under oath by the plaintiff and had to conform to the evidence, written or oral, that would be presented to the court prior to or at trial.

In his action against Hill, Meany's goal was to recover the £2 15s still owed to him. Nevertheless, the summons demanded, as per general practice, that Hill turn over to Meany £6. In this case, the demand was clearly related to the original debt, but it was also for more money than Meany claimed in his declaration to be owed. Even in attachments there would often be a difference between the demand in the writ and the damages claimed in the plaintiff's oath and declaration. Frequently in debt cases, as here, the plaintiff would demand the full value of the original debt and then elsewhere in the summons or in the declaration only claim the outstanding balance. In cases where none of the original debt was paid, or where the original debt was for an odd sum, the demand would often be equal to the next highest pound, five pound, or ten pound value. Claims made in declarations were usually for the value owed that could be demonstrated by written evidence of the debt the plaintiff could produce before trial. For the 1,800 Inferior Court actions between 1750 and 1766 where both the demand and the claim are recorded, demands were on average 126 per cent of the value claimed by the plaintiff.

To serve the writ the deputy provost marshal (the provost marshal himself appears to have never served a writ) would take the writ and a copy to the defendant's home and present them to the defendant. One was left with the defendant (usually the original, with a wax seal of the court affixed to it) and the other was returned to the clerk. On the bottom or back of the returned copy, the deputy provost marshal would state when, where, and to whom he served the writ and would then sign it.

The writs had to be served on the defendant personally. For a summons, if the deputy provost marshal did not find the defendant or a family member to whom the writ could be taken, he would leave it at the defendant's home and note that this is what he had done. This, however, only worked if he could be assured that the defendant was still in Halifax. If the defendant had left town or otherwise disappeared, the provost marshal returned the writ unserved, with the notation "*non est inventus*" or "not found." Considering the size of Halifax, the deputy often knew if the defendant was out for the moment, away for a short while, or gone. It was usually only in the last case that a defendant would be reported not found, as this ended the legal action. Defendants who were away were often represented in court by a lawyer or someone else who would ask for a continuance until the individual's return. One example is John Webb's action against fish merchant Edward Lukey in 1756. The deputy returned the writ with the note, "I Cou'd not find the Def^t or any thing to Attach but I left him a Copy hereof at his Usual place of abode." When the action came to court in September it was continued to the next session because Lukey was still out of the colony.

Webb's writ to summon Lukey was a type of the writ of summons called an attachment, which further ordered the provost marshal to "attach" some portion of the defendant's property and to the value demanded, to take bail to that amount, or to imprison the defendant. Plaintiffs seeking attachments were required to prove the damages and swear out oaths to the value they claimed they were owed (for summons, no swearing of an oath was required). The proof had to be in writing and show the specific value owed, and so attachments were available to plaintiffs who sued for debts based on accounts (as in *Webb v. Lukey*) or promissory notes. In actions with more subjective demands, like slander or assault, damages could not be so easily proven, and so attachments were not available to plaintiffs. In *Meany v. Hill*, Meany could have sought an attachment, but because Monk filed his papers without him, Meany could not swear an oath to the debt.

Attachments had to be served slightly differently because of what they entailed. On the reverse of the writ copy he returned to the clerk, the deputy provost marshal would record specifically what he attached. Most often the defendant's house and lot were attached, but at times the deputy provost marshal would attach specific household items or trade goods, like the defendant's tools or the family's plates. Instead of attaching property, however, he could take bail in cash. When he attached goods or property, it appears that the deputy left them in the possession of the defendants, but if the defendant presented cash to the deputy, the cash appears to have been taken into court. The defendant could continue to use the goods pending the outcome of the action without using them up, but the cash could be spent and disappear.[24]

When there was no property or cash to attach, the deputy could attach the defendant's body, that is, he could imprison the defendant. Asserting that a body was attached on the writ did not necessarily mean the individual was actually imprisoned until trial. Rather, the defendants were left free but would be threatened with imprisonment. At times leaving the defendants free could pose a problem. In 1762, for example, John Butler sued brewer William Amies and Deputy John Callbeck attached Amies. On the reverse of the writ, Callbeck recorded "By Virtue of this Writt I have Attach'd the body of the within Nam'd Defend & at the Request of the Pltf he was not put in goal & he made his Escape." In other cases it is clear the defendant was imprisoned. In 1761, for example, soldier John Wright was imprisoned while awaiting trial on an action launched by the merchant Joshua Mauger.[25]

Determining who should be imprisoned and who should simply be attached with the threat of imprisonment was left, it appears, to the plaintiff. In other jurisdictions, the plaintiff would be required to cover the cost of imprisonment for debtors. If this was the case in Halifax, which is likely, some plaintiffs were probably deterred from imprisoning defendants prior to trial to save costs. The plaintiffs had to consider the likelihood that the defendant would decamp. Although Amies did leave the colony, Butler may have thought that as a brewer with a functioning business Amies was likely to stay in Halifax. In contrast, Mauger might not have been convinced that a soldier like Wright was likely to remain in the colony. It is not always clear on the document's face or on allied documents from the action, if "imprisonment" actually led to time in gaol. The attachment also did not make imprisonment after the conclusion of a trial much easier. As will be seen in chapter 6, imprisonment at the end of an action occurred following a set procedure.

The requirement of presenting written proof of the debt in the form of a note or account to get an attachment meant that imprisoning putative debtors prior to trial was more difficult in Halifax than in eighteenth century England.[26] Attachments were used less frequently than simple summons, and when they were used, the majority of attachments led to attaching land, goods, or cash rather than imprisonment (see table 3.2). In about 40 per cent of cases goods or land were attached, and so the deputy provost marshal took nothing away. In a quarter of the cases he did take bail and something of value actually exchanged hands. In a tenth of cases the defendants simply satisfied the claim on the spot, referred to at the time as "compromising," and the action was brought to an end immediately. In a little more than a tenth of cases the only record is that the defendant was summoned: no attachments are recorded. Imprisonment was the option in few cases, and in even

Table 3.2: Returns of attachments, Inferior Court of Common Pleas

	Land	Goods	Bail	Gaol	Not found[a]	Summoned[b]	Satisfied[c]	Total
N	199	53	161	50	35	81	63	642
%	31	8	25	8	5	13	10	100

[a] The defendant was not found and the writ was returned to the court unserved.
[b] The writ records that the defendant was summoned and there is no record of any attachment.
[c] The writ records that the defendant "compromised" or "satisfied" the plaintiff's claim, which means that the plaintiff and the defendant came to some out-of-court settlement and the action was concluded when the writ was returned to the court.

fewer was the defendant not found. In practice in Halifax, attachments offered only limited additional security to plaintiffs that they would receive satisfaction for any decision made in their favour.

The declarations and the writs were formulaic documents, and much of what was written in them may only have loosely corresponded with the events that gave rise to the legal dispute in the first place. Common law tradition allowed for a narrow range of possible forms of action: assumpsit, account, covenant, debt, detinue, ejectment, replevin, trespass, trespass on the case, and trover. The writs were often constructed around legal fictions that would describe the real events in the stylized form of the specific writ, even if that language had little correspondence to the facts asserted. The declarations, although including the language of the fiction, would usually describe what had actually happened.[27] In the case of trover, for example, the plaintiffs would declare they had "casually lost" the property in question, even if they would next acknowledge that they had lent or rented the property in question to the defendant. Typically in actions such as for assault or defamation the "real" actions would be interwoven with or follow the fictional formal language expected for the writs. In debt cases, such as *Meany v. Hill* the formalities of the writ and declaration included when the debt was contracted and for what purpose. The written evidence of the debt, such as the account in this case, which was appended to the declaration, detailed the history of the transactions between the parties and recounted who exchanged what and how and when exchanges took place.

When Roger Hill was served with the writ, he would have understood what it meant, in general if not in the intricate specifics of its language. This was not only because he already had significant experience with the courts, but also because enough of the writ and declaration presented to him were in clear, common language that he could read it or have another read it to him. Because of this, Meany's intentions and his own obligations to the court would be clear. Additionally, the deputies in Halifax all appear to have been literate, and so they may have actually served this function for illiterate defendants when they served the writs. He might, however, have wondered why he was being sued at all. Meany only demanded £6 from Hill – significantly less than the £16 median value of demands at the Inferior Court, where three-quarters of all actions were for £10 or more. Such a small demand and claim, however, were not unheard of, as the smallest demand at the Inferior Court was for £3 and the smallest claim for only 15 shillings.

Salter v. Pratt: Causes of Action and Use of Lawyers

Daniel Wood also issued a writ on behalf of Malachy Salter against the shipwright Joseph Pratt on 16 November 1761. This was the second of at least three legal run-ins between Salter and Pratt. A little over a year before, in September 1760, Pratt sued Salter for £10. In 1761, Salter sued Pratt for £6, and in April 1762 Salter sued Pratt for £8 on a note of hand (a promissory note) worth £5 and accrued interest. In all three cases the plaintiff pled the defendant had committed a "trespass upon the case." This was the most common of all writs issued for the Inferior Court of Common Pleas: 85 per cent of all actions were on the case, while the next most common, ejectment, accounted for only 4 per cent.[28]

For over 500 years by the 1750s, civil suits at the English courts of Common Pleas and King's Bench had to be in the form of a specific writ, such as trespass. Each of these writs applied to a very precisely defined and narrow range of injuries.[29] For example, the original writ of trespass applied to, in the words of historian Cecil Fifoot, "direct and unauthorised interference with land, goods or person." Thus, if a tenant burned down his house through careless use of the fireplace, then the landlord could not sue under trespass because the tenant's use of the fireplace was authorized. If a widow's house was burned down because her neighbour's fire got out of control, she could not sue the neighbour under trespass because her fire was indirectly caused by the neighbour (that is, he had no intention of burning down her house). Nor could a person sue if his injury was caused by the failure of another party to act.[30] The original writs created bizarre circumstances in which justice in the common law courts seemed impossible. Say, for example, that a family bought fish from a fishmonger on credit, then, reasonably, ate the fish, and finally, failed to pay for the fish. The fishmonger could not sue on trespass, because he willingly gave them the fish. He could not sue under trover, which returned to the plaintiff goods improperly in the defendant's possession, because they no longer had the fish to return it. He could not sue under debt or assumpsit because, reasonably, there was no written agreement or other proof of the promise to repay or to act as required by these writs.[31] Nevertheless, it is clear that the family owed the fishmonger for the fish they got from him and ate. To deal with this, and related problems, beginning in the mid-fourteenth century, writs of trespass *sur le case* or "on all the manner according to the case" began to be issued and used. "Case" might be thought of as "in this case," referring to the specific facts that gave rise to the issue at hand. The plaintiff was given the space in the writ to identify the specific facts that gave rise to a legal wrong.[32] By the time Halifax was founded in the mid-eighteenth century, the writ of trespass on the case was understood in fairly broad terms. In the 1755 popular book *Every Man His Own Lawyer*, the writ was described as applying for "Redress of Wrongs and Injuries, done without Force, and by Law not provided against," that is, covering everything that was not otherwise covered by a more specific writ.[33] Historians of both old and New England have found that case remained common in the 1600s and 1700s. In the 1600s, actions on the case made up four-fifths of the actions in one court in England, and case was used frequently in New England.[34]

In Halifax, following North American custom at least,[35] trespass on the case was used in a wide variety of disputes, even where another writ might have been sufficient. The power of case, and its potential problem, lay in the pleading showing that some wrong had been done that deserved compensation. With the courts willing to accept this very broad use of the writ, there was little reason to try to make the facts conform to the more specific requirements of the other writs. Thus, even when the evidence necessary to prove other causes of action was available, trespass on the case was used. Salter's writ against Pratt describes the action as "trespass on the case debt by note." Between 1749 and 1766, Halifax plaintiffs used more than fifty different terms like this to describe the specific complaint in an action on the case. Debts on accounts, that is, for credit usually issued over time in exchange for goods, or by (promissory) notes were the most common, but trespass on the case was also used for assaults, theft, and wrongful imprisonment. The last four, at least, could have been sued with one of the other writs. At times it was even compounded with the names of other writs, like debt,[36] trover, *scire facias* or replevin. This suggests that in the mid-1700s, the application of case was wider than that contemplated in the treatises of the day or perhaps even in the practice in England and New England.

The practice that developed in Halifax diverged even further from that in other jurisdictions. As described in the previous section, descriptions of the wrongs migrated from the writs to declarations over Halifax's early years. Yet the author of *Every Man His Own Lawyer*, following the custom of the writ going back to its origins, called for a description of the wrong to be included in the writ proper. The judges, clerks, and lawyers of Halifax seem to have come to a general agreement on this practice, as is demonstrated both by what was recorded in the writs and declarations and what was not done about them – defendants did not plead to abate an action (that is, have it thrown out) because the plaintiff failed to explain the case in the writ itself.

The use of case so broadly can be explained on four grounds. First, it appeared to be much more fluid than the other writs. Plaintiffs did not have to present their injury in a way that, on its face, was legally compensable if it was defined as "on the case": essentially any wrong could be described on the case of its own facts and at trial the plaintiff could argue over why the injury deserved court enforced compensation. Second, the Inferior Court judges were not themselves lawyers educated in England. They had not been trained in the fine precision of the common law writs. Nor did their authority rely on their unique or special knowledge of the writs. The justices did not actively claim or seek to display "their learning with an eloquence that often rivalled that of leading statesmen," as Douglas Hay has described the assize judges of England at the same time.[37] Halifax's justices could rely on their resolving people's problems as being central to their authority. Local lawyers were likely a third important reason for the use of case. Lawyers were used a great deal in Halifax. In at least 75 per cent of actions, plaintiffs hired lawyers. Thus, it was lawyers who prepared most of the writs, and it was often lawyers who acted as the clerk as well. For example, Daniel Wood, clerk of the court in 1761 was also, at various points over the period, a practising lawyer. Lawyers got into the practice of pleading on the case for all manner of wrongs; defence lawyers accepted this and did not attempt to have the action tossed out due to a failure in its form. In situations where plaintiffs represented themselves, it was the clerk, in drawing up the writ, who could help them define their action, and case provided an easy way to do this. The rather open method of pleading actions in the case persisted in Halifax because the bench accepted the broad use of case as well, either following the practice set out by their clerks in preparing writs or on their own accord.

While plaintiffs relied on lawyers in most actions, defendants hired lawyers in at least 17 per cent of cases as well. The disparity is partly explained by the number of actions that never went to trial (discussed in chapter 4), and partly because the records that remain are predominantly plaintiff-side and so use of lawyers by defendants may be unreported. Many defendants probably saw little value in going to a lawyer if they knew the claim against them was accurate and if they had no intention of challenging it. Some defendants who defaulted, that is, failed to make any defence, or confessed to the claim against them may have sought legal advice or had a lawyer appear for them, but most appear to have not.[38] While plaintiffs had good reason to hire lawyers to ensure their cases were properly prepared and presented to the court, defendants who had no intention of defending may have had no need to hire lawyers. Moreover, the successful party could count on the court charging at least some portion of their lawyer's fees to the losing party. Defendants who expected to lose would have to face paying for two lawyers, their own and the plaintiff's. Defendants would, however, want to turn to a lawyer when they believed they could win, the delaying tactics a lawyer could employ would help them, or the lawyer could help reduce the damages awarded against them. Overall, it was more likely that plaintiffs would hire lawyers than defendants, and what remains remarkable about Halifax is how many of them did so. We do not know who Salter's lawyer was in November 1761. When Pratt sued Salter in 1760, Pratt hired James Monk to be his lawyer. Two years later, when Salter sued Pratt a second time, Monk was Salter's lawyer. In the early twenty-first century such routine switching of sides by lawyers is almost unheard of in Canada where it would be considered a conflict of interest and potentially prejudicial to the original client. In Halifax in the 1750s and 1760s this was not an unusual experience.

Most of the lawyers in Halifax represented people only once or twice. Although Monk, for instance, represented seventeen clients ten or more times, three-quarters of his clients for whom there are records only hired him for one or two actions. From the client's perspective, some clearly did favour particular lawyers. Anne Webb only used three lawyers, favouring William Nesbitt up to 1761 and then exclusively hiring James Brenton; Roger Hill likewise favoured Nesbitt and his partner George Suckling in the 1750s, and turned to David Lloyd in the 1760s. Malachy Salter, by contrast, used attorneys in at least seventy-two different actions, hired eight of the ten men he could have hired, and used as many as four different lawyers in a single year. By spreading the work about, Salter maintained a business relationship with all of the lawyers. This may not have meant that he received special treatment when he was sued. Rather, by maintaining a business relationship with the entire bar, Salter and those like him could ensure that they always had a lawyer they could turn to when necessary.

This sharing of lawyers may have something to do with the small size of the bar in the 1750s and 1760s. Between 1749 and 1766, ten men acted regularly as lawyers. Three had started practising in 1750: John Ker, Otis Little, and Daniel Wood. By 1752 four more men had joined the profession: Joseph Kent, David Lloyd, William Nesbitt, and George Suckling. Until 1759, these seven men were the only men to practise law in the colony and two of them, Little and Ker, dropped out of the profession in 1754 and 1755 respectively. In 1760 two more men started to practise, James Monk and James Brenton, and shortly after, Richard Gibbons Junior began to practise regularly.

The men who practised law moved in and out of legal practice or supplemented their lawyerly activities with other work, including legal work. Several of them, including Otis Little and Joseph Kent, were appointed as or acted as clerks for one or another of the courts, or had other sinecures instead of or in addition to their private practice. Others were connected to Nova Scotia's government elites in other ways: Monk, for instance, had been Charles Morris's assistant and a Justice of the Peace before he began practising law. William Nesbit was the clerk to the governor and council in the early 1750s, and Richard Gibbons Junior's father was deputy provost marshal for the colony while he himself served as clerk for the Court of Vice Admiralty.

A lawyer could help plaintiffs in trespass on the case matters; an experienced lawyer was almost a necessity in the other causes of action that were often more complex or reliant on extensive legal fictions. For example, the actions of trover and ejectment were used by owners to reclaim their property. Ejectment applied to land, trover to all else. In a trover writ the plaintiff asserted that he or she "casually lost" the thing in question and that the defendant found it and "converted" it to her or his own use. In practice, however, the goods sought in trover may have been sold but not paid for, stolen, loaned, or held by the defendant as security for a debt subsequently paid. At trial all that the plaintiff needed to prove was that the goods were once his or hers and they were now unlawfully in the defendant's possession. The defence needed to show that the defendant's possession was *and remained* legal. Neither side worried much about whether or not the goods were actually "lost" and found. The specific requirements of the writ (the "casually lost" in this instance) could often be legal fictions: facts asserted for the purpose of conforming to the requirements of the form of action even if they did not actually match the real events in question.

Ejectment made the most elaborate use of fictions. Originally, ejectment allowed a householder to challenge the title of another person re-
siding on the land in question. The action arose in the middle ages and
granted leaseholders similar rights to freeholders in removing squatters
by allowing a tenant to remove the previous tenant or other illegal oc-
cupant from a piece of land without involving the land's owner. When
compared to the cost of having to prove title through the chain of title,
ejectment developed into a relatively inexpensive way to determine or
assert title to a piece of land regardless of the plaintiff's tenure. However inexpensive, though, ejectment was truly complex. The plaintiff
would initiate an action by a fictional Mr. Thrustout against a fictional
defendant, Mr. Holdfast. Thrustout claimed to have signed a lease with
the real plaintiff for the land in question. When he attempted to take
possession, however, Thrustout found Holdfast living on the land and
sued him to have him leave the property. The plaintiff or their lawyer
would impersonate Holdfast and write a letter to the real defendant
announcing both the lawsuit and Holdfast's intention to default the action and leave the land, resulting in a confirmation of the real plaintiff's
tenure by confirming the plaintiff's right to lease the land to Thrustout.
Holdfast would suggest that if the real defendant had some interest in
or claim to the land, however, then he or she could contest the action in
Holdfast's place. At trial, the real defendant would replace Holdfast, the
real plaintiff would replace Thrustout and the competing claims to the
property would be tested. Ejectment was a relatively common action
in Halifax, contrary to the experience in New England and the middle
colonies, where it was first shorn of its fictions and then replaced by an
expanded use of trover to include real property as well as goods.[39]

Webb v. Fury: Timing

On 16 November 1761, Anne Webb took out a summons against William Fury. Webb initiated many legal actions, but this one was unusual
for her. At both the September 1758 and the immediately preceding
September 1761 sittings of the court she initiated eight actions. In
March 1763, she initiated four actions at once. The action against Fury
was the only one she initiated at the Inferior Court for the December
1761 sitting.

Initiating several lawsuits at once was common practice in Halifax.
Many circumstances could lead to such practices. Plans to leave the

colony, dissolving a partnership, clearing an estate, or being sued one-self, could all lead a litigant to try to clear up all or several outstand-ing accounts or debts. Webb's eight lawsuits in September 1758 were a direct result of her husband's death and her need to either wind up or take over his firm. The suits of 1761 and 1763 may likewise have related to long-standing debts first extended by John before his death, or from Anne's continuation of the Webb business on her own.

The suit Webb launched against Fury stood on its own, but it fol-lowed eight actions she launched just three months earlier. The nine actions all grew out of credit extended by the Webb business. The deci-sion Anne Webb made both to pursue all of these actions and to pur-sue Fury after the rest are not precisely recorded. To understand her choices, it is possible to infer from what was in the actions themselves, and how they were similar to others' choices to litigate. It is likely that these nine actions are best understood as marking a single impulse to turn to the courts. The specific reason Webb sued Fury in November might be understood best as there being some reason why she did not, in the end, sue him at the September court: perhaps she approached him before she initiated the action and he suggested he would repay her without going to court, but he failed to do so in the agreed upon time. Perhaps he was out of the colony and so she postponed suing him until he returned. Perhaps Webb had not figured out what exactly Fury owed her by the time she sued the other eight people in the summer, although this is less likely than the other options because she could use the process to determine what he actually owed her. In any case the specific time she chose to sue Fury was related to the eight suits she launched in summer for the September 1761 court.

Plaintiffs chose to sue several people at once or defendants were sued by several people at one time almost exclusively over debt. All business in Halifax in the mid-eighteenth century involved extending credit and going into debt. People would often bargain with each other over the exchange values of what they offered and what they received, for ex-ample, how much a coat would cost and how much chopped wood would be worth the same. If it became necessary to go to court, then the accounts of credit extended and payments made would track all of the exchanges in monetary terms, which was necessary because the courts could offer no damages except in monetary value.[40] The exchanges could be immediate: people could trade one thing for another on the spot. In many cases, however, trade happened over time: goods would be given on credit on one or several occasions with an expectation of repayment in goods, cash, or labour at a later date. The creditor could continue to extend more credit or refrain from seeking repayment for as long and to such value as she or he trusted that the debtor would be able to repay or until the creditor needed something to pay her or his own creditors.

The choice to threaten to use or actually initiate actions in the courts could arise in a variety of ways. Dealings between individuals might, for a variety of reasons, end in litigation for reasons strictly internal to those relationships. For instance, William Meany appears to have decided by late autumn 1761 that Roger Hill was unlikely to continue to make payments of one form or another on his debt without being prodded. Malachy Salter may have decided to use the courts as part of a larger struggle with Joseph Pratt, initiating the action in November 1761 because the possibility to sue arose. Anne Webb made a business decision by mid-summer 1761 to clear as many of the long-standing debts owed the family business as possible. For Webb, litigation came about not because of one recalcitrant debtor, but because her records showed a great number of people to be indebted to her or her company and she needed to clear the debts and balance her accounts.

Clumps of litigation like these by Webb were not generally a surprise to defendants. Creditors often tried to encourage the paying off of debts before having to sue. Many creditors announced their intention to sue anyone with outstanding debts in the *Halifax Gazette*, a local broadsheet that specialized in publishing news from away and local advertisements. These seemed to spike in the days and weeks leading up to a session of the court. A typical advertisement from 1752 read:

Whereas Messi. Joshua Mauger, William Nesbitt, Benjamin Gerrish and Samuel Shipton, are appointed Trustees by the Creditors of Israel Abrahams and Israel Abrahams and Company to receive all the Money, Goods, and Effects of the said Abrahams, and the said Abrahams and Company, and to distribute as they receive to said Creditors. This to give Notice (as the Trustees are in possession of the Books) to all persons having Accompts[41] open with Abrahams or the Company, that they immediately come and settle and pay their Ballances to the Trustees at the House of Joshua Mauger, as they would avoid being prosecuted at the next June court.[42]

This advertisement explicitly threatened legal proceedings against those who did not pay off their debts. It was also rather wordy, even given the general form of such advertisements. A shorter advertisement appeared in a September issue of the *Gazette* the same year:

All Persons indebted to the Estate of Richard Rance, late of Halifax Baker deceas'd, or to his Widow Mary Rance since his Decease, are desired to make Speedy Payment to said Mary Rance to prevent further Trouble. And those to whom said Estate are indebted are also desired to bring their Accompts in order for a speedy settlement, as she intends to leave this Colony.[43]

Here the advertisement not only seeks debtors but creditors as well. When almost all of the transactions between people involved extending credit and acquiring or paying off debts, these sorts of advertisements were essential. Not only did these ads potentially catch off-book debts, they also eased the need to track everyone down. Once, hopefully, most of the debts had been cleared, the creditors could go after only the recalcitrant and large debtors who remained.

The advertisement for Mary Rance and Anne Webb's clumps of litigation in 1758, 1761, and 1763 also point to the way in which business, litigation, and family were integrated. Both women were widows faced with several decisions on the death of their husbands including whether or not to carry on the business and to stay in Halifax. Regardless, they would have to either close off the debts owed to or by their husbands or renegotiate them in their own names. These moments reflected a shift from one person in the family who was carrying on the business to another. But in many cases what they also reflected was a shift not in who was doing the business but in whose name the business was being done. Families were integrated economic units, and there may have been a tightly prescribed division of labour between husbands, wives, and children. Men who worked on fishing vessels and other ships worked in primarily masculine environments, at least while at sea and some skilled craftsmen, like masons and housewrights, do not seem to have worked alongside their wives when on job sites. For most others in Halifax, except perhaps those in the civil service or some professions, a man's job was in fact the family's job. On John Webb's death, Anne Webb was not left with a business she did not understand. On the contrary: although Webb on his own or in partnership appeared in legal documents as an individual, Anne appears to have been involved to varying degrees in the day-to-day trade in which the Webbs engaged.

When Anne sued in 1758 to finalize accounts entered into with her husband and in 1761 and 1763 in an effort to close accounts long in arrears, she was making decisions about more than the continued viability of the business. She was ensuring that her family could be sustained. In doing this she was not doing something radically different from when her husband John Webb engaged in similar suits on his own or in partnership with Robert Ewer.[44] The money they hoped to receive through the process of legal action would in turn go to paying off their own debts or buying new trade goods. All of this, in turn, allowed the family to sustain itself. Although litigation appears in the records to generally be the province of men, the family's actions and needs were often behind the transactions that created debts and the decision to litigate.

All this goes to explaining the timing of litigation: it was timed not necessarily for purposes that today would be understood as strictly business and was often timed for the purposes of family as well. The creditors a debtor faced were not always, or, at least in Halifax's courts, even very often strictly, business creditors. Rather, the credit to be repaid was often for personal expenses, the things the family needed to live day-to-day or month-to-month. Clumped litigation, in which Anne Webb most frequently engaged, could often be necessitated by needing to meet larger business creditors or otherwise reflect a business imperative, but such decisions almost always involved a family imperative simultaneously. Individual actions, like Meany suing Hill, might be prompted by specific concerns about an individual debtor's capacity to pay. Having let the debt stand for some time, litigation might have been understood as a necessity because intermittent payments had slowed or ceased without repaying all that was owed. Litigation in these cases could serve to encourage repayment, either before trial or by securing a verdict and then court order that would allow the creditor to collect more vigorously (see chapter 6). In cases where there had been several transactions over time or where the value of what was exchanged was particularly open to debate, conflicts could arise about how much was, in fact, owed. In these cases the court, especially juries or court appointed arbitrators, could evaluate the value of things or labour and clarify what was still owed. Litigation could thus be chosen because the parties could not otherwise come to an agreement. In other cases, like Salter's suit against Pratt, litigation could occur because the option to sue arose, and it could have the effect of extending the conflict by other means or be an irritant to the other side. In still other cases, like those on promissory notes, the timing of litigation could, at least in part, be based on when it was legally possible to seek repayment. In these cases, however, the date a note came due only marked the point at which litigation could begin, not when it had to occur. Finally, for actions that were not over debts, the timing of litigation was often more clear: assault and defamation actions usually occurred soon after the incidents in question.

Conclusion

The actions that Anne Webb and Malachy Salter initiated, that Roger Hill had initiated against him, and on which James Monk worked on 16 November 1761 were routine. Webb and Salter had sued before, Hill had been sued before, and Monk had not only sued and been sued, but he had also worked as a lawyer helping initiate suits many times before that day. For these four, and for the many more who initiated actions for the December 1761 session of the Inferior Court, starting litigation, suing, and being sued were routine, or at least not uncommon. Law suits were initiated when they were and for the reasons they were because of the needs of the plaintiff or the potential deficiencies of the defendant. The actions that were initiated followed the basic forms set out in the English common law and practised, with some changes, for centuries.

The prevalence of trespass on the case and of suing on account, however, distinguishes Halifax and Anglo-Nova Scotia from both the other English colonies in North America and from England. Some of these distinguishing traits may have to do with the state of the colony at the moment. With a small bar of mainly untrained lawyers, simple procedures that effectively and efficiently did what clients needed may have made the most sense. In a colony relatively new and sparsely populated, at least by those who made regular use of the courts, practices like suing on account debts may have made sense in a way they would not later as the economy and society developed. The forms of action were determined by common law traditions and not by the actually existing economic and social relations in the community. The frequent use of trespass on the case shows that the people of Halifax were not operating their economy or thinking about the law in the narrowly defined ways demanded by most writs. Haligonians felt wrongs, injuries, and a need for security. In each case, they defined those things that they believed could or should be resolved in the courts.

In the centuries since, some elements of these practices have changed, and some have not. In the nineteenth century the courts in Nova Scotia, as in England and other parts of the common law world, disposed of the forms of action and writs that were used to define suits and initiate actions in the 1750s and 1760s. While the system of writs was replaced with a much simpler system, a variation of which persists to this day in Nova Scotia and in the rest of Canada, we should not mistake the appearance of change for real change. In practice the traditional forms of actions had been disposed of by the 1750s in Halifax. The reliance on trespass upon the case spoke to a simple method of initiating litigation despite the apparent formality of the forms of action.

4

Avoiding Trial

When plaintiffs began law suits it was usually because they wanted something that they believed was rightfully theirs: the repayment of a debt, the return of their property, a restored reputation, or something else. Choosing a lawsuit as the method of getting this always meant that they could end up in court, but when William Meany, Malachy Salter, and Anne Webb started their actions on 16 November 1761, they likely did not expect to end up making their claim at a trial. When the court met in late November, each of the actions was on the order for the court. In each case, the litigants were called, and in each case the defendants, Roger Hill, Joseph Pratt, and William Fury, chose not to defend themselves: *Webb v. Fury, Salter v. Pratt,* and *Meany v. Hill* all ended in default, as did many of the actions at the Inferior Court of Common Pleas. Trials of one sort or another were possible, but the majority of all actions initiated in the Inferior Court ended without a trial. Trials were costly affairs: in most cases each side would have to pay for a lawyer and usually the loser would be required to pay court costs for both sides. At the Inferior Court a number of procedures or options could bring an action to an end, either with a hearing of some sort or without. How a plaintiff came to secure a verdict, a judgment, and payment of what the court ordered (satisfaction), or came to a realization that victory or satisfaction was impossible depended on many things. The legal action arose out of some particular problem between the plaintiffs and defendants. The process taken to resolve the action spoke to how the parties understood the problem and their relationship to one another. Initiating a legal action was not necessarily a particularly aggressive tactic on the plaintiff's part, and the way defendants in particular decided to respond through the legal process illuminated how legal processes were integrated with general commercial and even social interactions within Halifax and between the people of Halifax and places beyond the communities around Chebucto Harbour. This chapter begins with a review of the various ways an action could be concluded. It then turns to a discussion of the default and other ways in which litigants ended an action and avoided trials, providing a description of the process and presenting explanations for why an action was resolved in one way or another. The next chapter describes the two most common forms of trial.

Resolving Actions

To a modern reader not particularly familiar with the law in practice today, it is likely surprising that more than two-thirds of all actions in the Inferior Court of Common Pleas ended without a trial of some sort. After all, going to court appears to be central to the law. Nevertheless, today, every stage of the legal process can be so expensive that many potential litigants try to limit their reliance on or even avoid lawyers and the legal system to resolve their disputes.[1] As will be seen in chapter 6, the costs of trials in Halifax in the 1750s and 1760s were not insignificant. In situations where there was little or no way for a litigant to win it made sense to avoid a trial. A trial could delay the inevitable loss, but would also increase the costs to both parties. The best option for many defendants after the initiation of an action was forgo the trial and cut the whole process short.

Actions were initiated by plaintiffs. Once they had done so, however, control over the process passed to the defendants. Defendants chose whether or not to contest a claim against them and how to go about doing so.[2] Although, as will be seen, plaintiffs usually received judgments in their favour, defendants could use the selection of process to various ends, from outright victory, to limiting the amount they would, in the end, owe a victorious plaintiff, to delaying their repayment. Because, in most cases, the defendants and not the plaintiffs chose the way an action would be resolved, one element of this and the next chapter will be in part to explain why a defendant would choose a particular process and what a defendant would do to lead to a certain process. There will be some reference back and forth to compare the ways actions could be resolved with or without a trial.

The variety of ways an action could be resolved was quite broad. Defendants who knew they would lose outright, or believed they could not significantly reduce the damages awarded against them, could default, confess to an action, or try to make some agreement with the plaintiff before the court's session. Plaintiffs who decided they would not win or who came to an agreement with the defendant outside of court could nonsuit or withdraw their actions. If defendants believed the action against them was legally unsound, as opposed to factually unsound, they could ask the court for an abatement. Judges could also dismiss actions on their own accord when faced with a plaintiff's failure to mount a legally sound action. If some sort of hearing was required, the litigants could have a jury trial by a regular, or in some cases, special jury, or opt for arbitration. By the mid-1760s, even some defaults would result in hearings by juries of inquiry.

As table 4.1 shows, at the Inferior Court defaults predominated: of the 3,172 actions for which some resolution is known, 1,317 or 42 per cent ended in default. The next most significant ways a trial could be avoided were by the plaintiff withdrawing the action (13 per cent) and by the defendant confessing to the plaintiff's claim (9 per cent). The remaining methods of avoiding trial were much less common in total: dismissals occurred in 3 per cent, abatements in 2 per cent and nonsuits in 1 per cent of actions. Trials by jury were, next to defaults, the most common way of resolving disputes, but only 565 actions ended this way (18 per cent), while 348 ended with arbitrations (11 per cent). The remaining methods of hearings (special juries, juries of inquiry, and trials by judges alone) each occurred in less than 1 per cent of actions. While more than two-thirds of actions ended without a hearing, the proportion may have been even greater. Hearings of one sort or another resulted in the creation of more documents. Defaults, withdrawals, and confessions did not: rather these results may have been recorded by the clerk on the writ or mentioned in the bill of costs. It is reasonable to conclude that when fewer documents remain from an action it is because fewer were created in the first place and that the action ended in some way other than a hearing or trial.

As will be discussed in chapter 7, the processes available and used in the other civil courts were more constrained. Although the Supreme Court was a common law court too, almost 90 per cent of the actions that reached that court ended by trial, mostly by jury, or arbitration.

Table 4.1: Processes by court

Process	Inferior Court		Supreme Court		Admiralty		Chancery		Divorce	
	N[a]	%	N	%	N	%	N	%	N	%
default	1317	42	1	2	4	4				
nonsuit	43	1								
confession	277	9	1	2	2	2				
withdrawn[b]	407	13	6	9	1	1				
abatement	50	2								
dismissed	98	3			2	2				
jury trial	565	18	36	55						
special jury	24	1	6	9						
inquiry	17	1								
judge trial	26	1	3	5	94	91	9	75	3	100
arbitration	348	11	13	20			3	25		
	(n = 3172)		(n = 66)		(n = 103)		(n = 12)		(n = 3)	

[a] In some instances an action may end up going through more than one of the above process (for instance, a defendant defaults but then moves for a trial). The total number for each column refers to distinct processes, not actions.
[b] Withdrawn includes actions returned "agreed," "compromised," or "satisfied."

Almost the same proportion of Vice Admiralty actions ended in trial by judge, which was the only option once an action reached a hearing. Although the number of actions for Chancery or the Court of Prohibited Marriage and Divorce was much smaller, in both cases all actions ended in trial by the court. The volume of actions started, the wide range of disputes that could be brought, the relatively low cost of any action in the court, the fact that the vast majority of actions in the court were receiving their first hearing and the procedures available in the Inferior Court all account for its much larger proportion of actions that ended before trial.

Default and Nonsuit

Defendants defaulted when they did not appear in court to answer their summons to trial. At first, defaults were recorded on the day the action was to be heard, but this soon changed so that defendants were required to give notice of their intention to go to trial a week before the opening of the courts' sessions. Failure to do so would result in the court finding the defendant in default and issuing a judgment for the plaintiff. Defendants who failed to announce their intention to challenge the plaintiff's claim could get these default judgments set aside with some ease, but almost all defendants who defaulted appear to have intended to do just that. Thus, the default was essentially a failure by the defendant to act, and it exists in the historical record as a silence. This poses significant challenges to the historian trying to interpret and explain what was occurring. Understanding the motivation behind any particular default is now impossible, but by looking at the patterns of defaults for individuals and the community as a whole, some plausible explanations can be offered.

When Joseph Pratt, William Fury, and Roger Hill all defaulted in 1761 they were doing what a great many defendants did every session. Default was the most common method of bringing a common law action to an end at the Inferior Court of Common Pleas in Halifax. Nor were the three men strangers to the process. Fury was a defendant in 22 actions and defaulted in at least 16. Pratt defaulted both times the resolution of an action against him is known. Hill was sued more times than either Pratt or Fury, and the resolution of 47 of these is known. He defaulted 15 times (32 per cent) – less frequently than the other two, but it was still one of his two most favoured options, along with arbitration, which he also entered into 15 times.[3]

When defendants defaulted they would be responsible for the plaintiffs' damages and costs in pursuing a legal action. Before 1765 defendants would have no opportunity to challenge the plaintiffs' claimed damages (the introduction of the jury of inquiry changed this, as will be seen in the next chapter). Defaulting would result in low costs, however, especially as opposed to a trial or arbitration. This meant that defendants could engage in rational decisions about whether or not to default even when they knew they owed the plaintiff something. This is certainly what Roger Hill appears to have done. Of 15 actions where he was sued for £8 or less, he defaulted 8 times; of 12 actions where he was sued for £10 or more he defaulted only twice. The greater the claim against him, the less likely he was to default instead of taking another course. Even if Hill disagreed with the demand or claim the plaintiff made in a small value suit, if the difference between his accounting and the plaintiff's was less than it would cost him to go through a trial or some other process, then it would make sense to default. The more demanded of him, the greater the chance that any discounting he could achieve through some other process would be greater than the court costs he would incur. Thus, the greater the value of the suit against him, the more sensible it was to not default.

There were other reasons to default too. As will be seen in chapter 6, some judgments were never successfully executed. Defendants who had no intention of paying back what was demanded of them regardless of whether or not they accepted that a debt was owed had no reason to do anything but default. Some defendants may have left Halifax between the time they were served and the time of judgment. Still others might have defaulted because they did not understand the process of the courts or because of other mistakes or misunderstandings.

It is unlikely that many defaults occurred because defendants did not understand what was happening and let time run out to challenge. Defendants could appear before the court at the actual session and petition to have a default against them reversed so they could enter a plea and adopt another process. On 25 November 1760 the Inferior Court issued a default judgment against Joseph Jones for a defamation suit by Benjamin Leigh that was to be tried in December. When the court session officially started several days later Jones's lawyer James Brenton presented the court with the following affidavit:

Joseph Jones the Deft in sd Cause maketh Oath that being Ignorant of the rules & practice of Law, he did not make timely Application to an Attorney for to make an Appearance for him in said Cause by which means he was defaulted therein.[4]

The clerk, Richard Gibbons, recorded the "Default struck off" and Jones was able to enter a plea and proceed to trial. Defaults were struck off in thirty-seven cases. There is no record of a petition to reverse a default being denied by the court. The small number of rescinded defaults (3 per cent of all defaults) suggests that most defaults were the intentional strategy of defendants.

Brenton's pleading that Jones was ignorant of the rules and practices of the Inferior Court was an acceptable way of explaining Jones's behaviour in a petition, but this may not have accurately explained his or others' actions in being in default and seeking it reversed. When defaults were struck off, most went either to trial (13) like *Leigh v. Jones* or arbitration (10) and 4 were dismissed by the court. But another 6 were withdrawn by the plaintiff and in 5 the defendant confessed judgment instead. Replacing a default with a confession essentially replaced one judgment for the plaintiff without a hearing to another judgment for the plaintiff without a hearing but with defendant acknowledgment. The withdrawal meant there would be no judgment at all. This suggests that the plaintiff and defendant were negotiating some out-of-court resolution when the default was issued. If they came to some other agreement than the original demand or claim, the reversal of the default would ensure that the newly agreed upon damages were the value the defendant paid.

Defendants were not the only ones who could default. When a plaintiff failed to do something required to properly bring an action, such as failing to file a declaration when those were required or failing to attend court, then the plaintiff was nonsuited and the action died.[5] For example, the merchant Jonathan Binney attempted to sue Ebenezer Lowell, a Boston merchant at the September 1754 session of the Inferior Court. Binney sued for a debt on account of £21 13s 2½d. Lowell entered a plea stating his intention to defend the action. Neither Binney nor his lawyer George Suckling, however, presented to the court a copy of the account or a replication (the necessary written reply to a defendant's plea), nor did they formally withdraw the action. Binney was nonsuited and the court awarded Lowell 14 shillings costs. Binney launched another suit against Lowell for the December session, provided all of the appropriate papers this time, and won all that he demanded at a jury trial.[6] Only seven of the forty-three nonsuits appear to have been re-tried like

Binney v. Lowell, however, suggesting that plaintiffs nonsuited for reasons other than error too. Although unrecorded, the two most likely reasons for nonsuits are that the defendant compromised in some way with the plaintiff, making the action unnecessary at least for the moment, or that the plaintiff decided a loss was inevitable.

The Inferior Court of Common Pleas heard a wide variety of actions, ranging from the various debt actions, which were the most common, to assaults and defamation. Table 4.2 shows the number and percentage of suits going through the various processes for the seven most common forms of action. It seems that defendants chose how to respond to an action based on the sort of action it was. For example, 90 per cent of the *scire facias* actions were defaulted. *Scire facias* was a special writ used to get execution on a judgment that was more than a year old (see table 4.2). The writ asked the defendant to come to court and show why the court should not issue a writ of execution. In these cases, the issue of indebtedness had already been tried, and the only question would be if some satisfaction of the original judgment had been made but was not recorded by the court nor acknowledged by the plaintiff. Faced with a *scire facias*, most defendants would see no reason to defend themselves.

As discussed in chapter 3, the majority of Inferior Court cases were debts on accounts and debts on notes. In both cases, the majority of suits were defaulted: 69 per cent of note cases, 55 per cent of account cases. In total, only 17 per cent of note cases went to trial or arbitration and 34 per cent of account cases went to trial or arbitration. Note debts were based on written promises to pay the specified amount. In a normal note case there would be little the defendant could do to challenge the debt. In account cases, there was potentially more room to challenge the plaintiff. One could call into question the value of the goods, labour, or money exchanged with the plaintiff to lower damages. The potential to argue over the value of the debt is most clearly seen in debts for wages or work done. Although 32 per cent of these cases ended in default, 24 per cent went to trial and 35 per cent went to arbitration. Especially when the work done could be examined, defendants could try to have someone else evaluate the work and set a different price. Juries could evaluate work done, but arbitrators, appointed from within the trade or among the trades customers, could do this even better.

The more space for disagreement between plaintiff and defendant over the amount owed, the less likely the action was to be defaulted. This was even clearer where the actions were not debt related and

Table 4.2: Process and sorts of actions, ICCP

Action[a]	Process	N	%
scire facias	Default	28	90
(n = 31)	Confession	0	0
	Nonsuit	0	0
	Withdrawal[b]	1	3
	Abate / Dismiss	0	0
	Trial by Jury[c]	1	3
	Arbitration	1	3
debt by note	Default	211	69
(n = 304)	Confession	19	6
	Nonsuit	1	0
	Withdrawal	18	6
	Abate / Dismiss	2	1
	Trial by Jury	40	13
	Arbitration	13	4
debt on account	Default	330	55
(n = 600)	Confession	31	5
	Nonsuit	6	1
	Withdrawal	25	4
	Abate / Dismiss	2	0
	Trial by Jury	115	19
	Arbitration	91	15
debt for work	Default	22	32
(n = 68)	Confession	1	1
	Nonsuit	0	0
	Withdrawal	5	7
	Abate / Dismiss	0	0
	Trial by Jury	16	24
ejectment	Default	19	31
(n = 61)	Confession	0	0
	Nonsuit	0	0
	Arbitration	24	35
	Withdrawal	6	10
	Abate / Dismiss	0	0
	Trial by Jury	36	59
	Arbitration	0	0
assault	Default	4	11
(n = 38)	Confession	1	3
	Nonsuit	0	0

Table 4.2: (*Concluded*)

Action[a]	Process	N	%
	Withdrawal	1	3
	Abate / Dismiss	1	3
	Trial by Jury	17	45
	Arbitration	14	37
defamation	Default	6	21
(n = 29)	Confession	0	0
	Nonsuit	2	7
	Withdrawal	0	0
	Abate / Dismiss	1	3
	Trial by Jury	14	48
	Arbitration	6	21

[a] The action types were chosen because each occurred at least 25 times. The 18 actions described as "debt by note and account" are counted in both "Debt by Note" and "Debt on Account." The 27 actions described as a variation of debt on account for work or wages are counted in both "Debt on Account" and "Debt for Work."

[b] "Withdrawal" includes actions returned agreed, compromised, or satisfied.

[c] "Trial by Jury" includes trial by special jury, but does not include actions that went before a jury of inquiry.

there was even more space for disagreement. Although 31 per cent of ejectments were defaulted, all of the rest were taken to a jury trial. Ejectments turned on disputes over who had claim to a piece of land and, more importantly, the home upon it. If the defendant-resident lost, he, she, or they would have to move out. Even if the disagreement between the parties was rooted in a debt, this was a dispute with a very specific remedy, and the implications for the defendant demanded a defence in most cases. In cases like defamation and assault the implications of a damage award were more remote from the action, but the cases were most often about real altercations and conflicts between the parties. Defendants were unlikely in most cases to simply acquiesce to the plaintiffs' version of events or claims for the damage caused: 69 per cent of defamation cases ended in a trial by jury or arbitration, 82 per cent of assault cases ended in trials or arbitrations. Nevertheless even in these disputes default was possible. As table 4.2 shows, six defamation cases and four assault cases (21 per cent and 11 per cent, respectively) were defaulted. Over all, as the issues in dispute became more contestable,

Table 4.3: Process in common law actions by size of claim

Claim in £	Actions n	No trial[a] %	Abate[b] %	Jury[c] %	Arbitration %
$x \leq 5$	493	83	5	6	5
$5 < x \leq 10$	525	77	4	13	5
$10 < x \leq 20$	458	69	2	17	12
$20 < x \leq 30$	183	64	1	20	14
$30 < x \leq 40$	96	54	4	26	16
$40 < x \leq 50$	71	56	3	21	20
$50 < x \leq 100$	145	55	3	25	17
$100 < x \leq 200$	80	45	4	28	24
$200 <$	45	44	2	38	16

[a] No trial includes defaults, confessions, nonsuits, and withdrawals.
[b] Includes abatements and dismissals.
[c] Includes jury and special jury trials.

the proportion of actions that went to trial or arbitration increased; despite this some defendants defaulted in every kind of action. In total, defendants at the Inferior Court of Common Pleas defaulted in 42 per cent of actions, dong this more than going through any other process to get to a judgment.

While the type of action helps explain why defendants would not default, more needs to be said to account for all of the debt actions that did not end in default and the other sorts of actions that did end that way. Roger Hill seemed to treat the value of a suit against him as one determining factor. Similarly, for other defendants at the Inferior Court, the value of the suit against them seems to have helped determine their chosen course of action. As table 4.3 shows, when sued for £5 or less, more than 80 per cent of actions ended without a trial of any sort by the defendant defaulting, confessing, coming to some agreement with the plaintiff, or the plaintiff nonsuiting or otherwise withdrawing. As the value of suit rose, however, the number of suits ending without a trial declined, so that by the time a suit was worth more than £30 only about 55 per cent of actions ended without a trial, and when suits were worth more than £100, less than half of suits ended without a trial. Matching this decline was a rise in the percentage of suits ending in trial or arbitration. The number of suits dismissed or *successfully* abated wavered between 1 and 5 per cent without following a particular pattern.

There was some correlation between the pattern of choosing whether or not to default and occupation. As table 4.4 shows, craftspeople and labourers were overall more likely to default or otherwise avoid trial than to go through with a jury trial or arbitration, especially when they were defendants. People with commercial occupations were also generally inclined to avoid trial, although merchants and traders, when defendants, opted for jury trials or arbitration more than half the time. By contrast, when merchants and traders were plaintiffs, most of their actions ended without trial or arbitration. This can be explained to a degree by the fact that merchants and traders sued craftspeople, people with smaller commercial operations and many others would often be suing for relatively small sums. When merchants and traders were sued, however, especially by other merchants and traders, it was often for a large sum.

These patterns are interesting in several ways. First, although there is a significant decline in the number of actions that ended without a trial as the value of the suit rose, default remained an acceptable response. However important the law was in guaranteeing economic transactions, the trial as a process by which a claim was proven was not essential in most cases. Second, the proportion of successful abatements and dismissals does not change following a clear pattern: while 5 per cent of actions under £5 were abated or dismissed, 4 per cent of actions of £100 to £200 were also dismissed or abated. There are dips and rises in between, but the numbers suggest that abatements and dismissals were determined independently from their value. This makes sense: errors can be made regardless of the value, and while defendants who faced larger potential losses may have been more inclined to look for errors, the court was unlikely to find them where they did not exist. Where they did exist, it was in a defendant's interest, no matter how small the value of the suit, to see it abated as paying no damages was always better than paying even a small damage award. In debts on account, the form of debt easiest to contest next to debts for wages and the single most common type of action, it was the value of the claim more than any other factor, including the plaintiff's occupation or the litigation experience of either party, that appears to have convinced a defendant to default or to resolve the dispute by some other process.

To test this thesis, I employed a statistical analytical technique called logistic regression analysis. Regression analysis tests the statistical strength of relationships between dependent and independent variables to predict certain results. I theorized that the decision whether

Table 4.4: Processes in common law actions by occupation and role

Occupation	Actions		No trial[a]		Abate[b]		Jury[c]		Arbitration	
	Plt	Def	Plt	Def	Plt	Def	Plt	Def	Plt	Def
Craftspeople										
Baker	13	16	10	11			3	4		1
Blacksmith	7	29	6	14			1	5		5
Butcher	6	15	4	10			1	4	1	1
Carpenter	40	45	23	41			8	3	9	1
Cooper	10	12	1	12			4		5	
Housewright	9	11	4	10					5	1
Mason	12	12	7	6			2	4	3	2
Shoemaker	7	11	2	9			3		2	2
Tailor	13	10	9	6		1	3	2	1	1
Commercial										
Merchant	238	52	149	18	2	1	71	26	16	7
Retailer	26	44	18	24	1		4	13	3	7
Shopkeeper	8	15	6	7			2	4		4
Tavern keeper	24	30	12	17		1	9	8	3	4
Trader	77	91	54	51			13	29	10	11
Truckman	13	13	10	6			1		2	7
Other										
Labourer	19	29	10	28			4	1	5	

[a] No trial includes defaults, confessions, nonsuits, and withdrawals.
[b] Includes abatements and dismissals.
[c] Includes jury and special jury trials.

or not to go to trial was likely determined by the value of the claim, as in Hill's case, plaintiff and defendant occupation, and plaintiff and defendant experience with litigation. In general there was a 31 per cent chance that any action initiated would not end in default. Roger Hill's threshold appears to have been £10, but he was both involved in an exceptional amount of litigation and not particularly wealthy. After some analysis of the data, I tested to see if a threshold of £20 would be better. I found that in those cases worth £20 or more there was a 75 per cent chance that the defendant would choose not to default.[7] The combination of variables most likely to lead a defendant to not default were if the claim was equal to or over £20, the defendant had experience as a litigant, the plaintiff had no experience as a litigant, and the plaintiff was not a merchant or trader. With this combination of variables, there was an 84 per cent chance the defendant would choose not to default.[8] Other possible variables on their own or in combination, like litigation experience on its own, were far much less predictive of defendant choices.[9] Although defendant experience was important, the size of the claim is the most important factor in these models.

Default remains an option in contemporary Canadian law. In the Nova Scotia Civil Procedure Rules, for instance, plaintiffs can ask for a default judgment against a defendant when the defendant has failed to file a statement of defence with the court within the time prescribed by the rules and the plaintiff has notified the defendant of their intention to seek a default judgment.[10] Other Canadian common law jurisdictions have similar rules.[11] In all jurisdictions, plaintiffs must seek to find defendants in default, rather than it being automatic.

Confession

Defendants could also confess to the pleas against them. Akin to criminal confessions, defendants would appear in court and make a formal statement confessing that the plaintiffs' pleas were correct and that they were indebted or otherwise owed the plaintiffs a specified amount. At first glance it may seem odd that defendants confessed considering the availability of default. Confessing, however, allowed defendants to exercise limited control over the proceedings against them. As a method of resolving actions, confession's utility rose and fell with changes to the procedures of the Inferior Court. As will be shown in chapter 6, when defendants defaulted, the judgments against them would generally be equal to what was proven by the documents the plaintiffs could provide to the court. If the defendant agreed with the value claimed or demanded by the plaintiff, then defaulting would be a sensible option for defendants. Plaintiffs and defendants, however, did not always agree. When they disagreed but the difference was not large the defendant may not have seen any point in contesting the plaintiff. In many cases, however, defendants sought to correct the plaintiffs' claims.

One example arises in an intercolonial suit from 1761. Halifax merchant or trader Nathan Nathans was sued by two New York merchants, Mathias Van Aelslyn and Judah Hayes, for a bond he signed. Bonds were agreements to complete some trade transaction by a certain date or be liable for a larger sum in penalty. The bonds were enforceable by a court in the jurisdiction of either party. Bonds were an essential component of cross-Atlantic trading,[12] although they appear to have been less common in Halifax in the 1750s and 1760s than in other parts of the empire or in intercolonial trade especially. Nathans made his bond with Van Aelslyn and Hayes in May 1757 when he promised to pay them £127 7s 7d sterling (£141 10s 7½d Halifax currency)[13] in three payments between 1757 and 1758. If he failed to do so, Nathans committed to paying the penal sum of £254 15s 2d sterling, or twice the base amount. On the back of the bond provided to the court were records of two payments from 1759 totalling £30 13s 4d sterling. The balance outstanding at the time he was sued was £96 14s 3d sterling. When David Lloyd, Van Aelslyn and Hayes's lawyer, filed the writ on their behalf, he claimed £254 15s 2d and demanded £270 sterling in total.

Despite his bond, Nathans took exception to being asked to pay so much. He wrote to Lloyd, "Sir, Please to Confess Judgement for Me in Action Brought Aginst Me on Bond by Jadaha [sic] Hayes & Mathias Van Aelslyn of New York to March inferior court of common pleas for the sum of one hundred & Six pounds fourteen shillings & three pence[.]" Apparently this was sufficient for Hayes and Van Aelslyn, and so Lloyd took the letter, as Nathans requested, to court and judgment was made against for £106 14s 3d sterling. Nathans confessed for the equivalent of what was outstanding on the original debt on the bond, converted to Halifax currency. He might have achieved the same result going to trial on the bond, but by this route he made an offer to pay his creditors what they were owed on the original debt without facing the possibility that the bond would be enforced as it was written and for its full value.[14]

Confession was also useful when defendants attempted or threatened to go to trial but decided against it in the end. William Fury may have defaulted when Anne Webb sued him in November 1761, but in a different action nine months later he confessed judgment instead. Fury, a distiller, gave the carpenter William Ingolls the following note: "I promise to pay Wm Ingolls or Ord^r on the First day of June next ensuing the date hereof the Sum of Sixteen ... this 15th day of Feby 1762." But Fury did not repay Ingolls on the first of June, nor did he do so during the rest of June and July. On July 26, Ingolls swore out a writ of attachment against Fury demanding £20, but claiming only the £16 promised in the note.[15]

Fury hired James Brenton as his lawyer and Brenton entered a plea on his behalf stating "The Deft by James Brenton, his Att^o comes and Defends the force & Injury . . . & saith that he owes the plaintiff nothing & of this puts himself upon the country." This was the standard form for a defendant's plea: an assertion that they did not do what they were accused of, and then a statement that they were willing to go to trial (that is, putting themselves upon the country). In the most common plea in a debt case the defendants would say they were "not indebted in the manner and form said," rather than Brenton's plea that Fury "owes the plaintiff nothing." The most important part to Fury's, and any other defendant's, plea was a denial of the plaintiffs' assertions and claims and a statement of the willingness to defend against them at trial.

Ingolls's lawyer Daniel Wood made a written reply to Fury's plea by asserting that Fury was "liable and did promise" to pay Ingolls the £16, which Fury "hath not denied wherefore for want of a sufficient please in that behalf the plaintiff prays Judgement with costs." The difference between Fury's plea that he "owes the plaintiff nothing" and the normal debt plea to be "not indebted in the manner and form said" was the key here. Wood was asking the court to rule that Fury's plea was insufficient to go to trial and to thus find for Ingolls without a trial or even oral argument by Fury's lawyer. The wording of Fury's plea was unusual, but the judges of the Inferior Court accepted it and rejected Wood's request for judgment in favour of Ingolls. This was not the only time when there was an oddity in the pleading, but the judges of the Inferior Court never accepted a plaintiff's argument that a difference in the structure of a pleading was sufficient to find for the plaintiff.[16] Having his motion rejected, Wood submitted a new reply on Ingolls's behalf saying he was prepared to go to trial too. The written reply or "replication" to the defendant's plea was a required step to move the action to trial. Usually all they did was, as with Wood's second plea, assert the plaintiff's willingness to go to trial as well. Fury at the last moment changed his position. Instead, Brenton submitted to the court a letter from Fury stating "I confess judgement for sixteen pounds and Costs." No trial was had and judgment was for Ingolls for the full £16 and his costs.

There is no record of why Fury changed his mind. He may have wanted to challenge Ingolls's claim only to be convinced out of doing so by his lawyer or someone else. A debt on a note when the note existed, as it did here, was difficult to defend against unless the defendant had some evidence to show that the note had been repaid or that the plaintiff had no right to sue the defendant for the note, which could happen if the note had been signed over to someone else. If Fury confessed because Ingolls had the better case, then his initial plea may have been a bluff, intended to try to scare Ingolls away from the suit, or an attempt to delay while he tried to negotiate a different repayment schedule outside of court. If the bluff or renegotiation failed, the defendant could still go to court and confess judgment, as Fury did here. As will be shown in chapter 6, the cost of a confession was not usually very different from a default, so there was little disincentive to trying to scare an opponent off or negotiate a better deal.

A third reason defendants confessed was to control, to some degree, when they paid the plaintiffs. For example, John Shippey used confession, among other means, to delay paying Giles Harris, Jonathan Hill, and Richard White. At the December 1750 sitting of the court, Shippey had Hill's and White's cases dismissed, while Harris's was continued until the next session in March. By March 1751, Shippey came to an agreement with Harris, Hill, and White to turn the matter over to arbitrators. The arbitrators never reported to the court, but in the June 1751 sessions Shippey confessed to all three debts with the provision that payment be delayed one month.[17]

Two other examples from 1750 show how confession could be used to control the structure of repayment. At the September 1750 session, John Shaw was sued by three different creditors. He confessed judgment on the condition that one of his creditors, Samuel Shipton, act as trustee for all three in distributing Shaw's house and other assets.[18] In another 1750 action, Ben Allen agreed and confessed to a debt owed John Jones with the condition that James Monk supervise a repayment plan of one shilling per week.[19] In another action, the confession was used to balance competing claims. James Chapman sued Robert Erskine for unpaid wage. Erskine agreed to confess to the debt, but only once Chapman agreed to work for half a day in exchange.[20]

Shippey, Shaw, Allen, and Erskine all used confessions as a way to wrest some control over the process of paying debts they seem to have acknowledged as their own. For Shippey, it was part of a longer strategy to delay judgments, and thus delay a court order to pay. When he finally confessed, the confession set out a time table for repayment, not just an acknowledgment of the debt. Ben Allen's confession likewise set up a schedule for repayment. John Shaw exercised some control in appointing who would be responsible for selling his assets, and thus, perhaps, in limiting what would have to be sold. Finally, Robert Erskine was able to secure more work out of Chapman before having to pay him for any.

There were a wide variety of uses made of confession in Halifax, but overall confession seemed to be a process used by defendants to control litigation against them. Historians of England and Virginia have found similar practices to those in Halifax, but have interpreted confession as a device used by creditors to secure payment of a debt sometime after the court session.[21] This interpretation is not convincing in the Halifax case. For instance, it would be unlikely that James Chapman would demand that he work an extra half day when he was suing for unpaid wages from earlier work. More generally, the litigation itself was the threat the plaintiffs held over the defendants. Given the other options defendants had, confession is better understood as a process by which they could exercise greater control over judgment against them than through defaulting or even trials or arbitrations, which *might* change the value of the damages, but would not change the payment methods.

The records of confessions are concentrated in two periods: 244 of a total of 277 are from the period between 1749 and 1754. Changes in procedure in the early 1750s may have accounted for the decline in confessions after this period. When defendants were required to announce in advance of the session that they intended to defend themselves or be found in default, then confessing became more involved: defendants would have to make a plea of defence and then later confess. This is clearly what William Fury did, but for many the additional steps may have made the process less appealing than simply defaulting or, where significant differences existed between plaintiff and defendant, actually mounting a defence at trial or arbitration.[22] The second moment occurred after the introduction of juries of inquiry in 1764. To be discussed more in chapter 5, the juries of inquiry significantly raised the court costs involved in defaulting. Confessing debt would avoid the jury and thus limit costs. It appears that confessions were useful when they suited defendants' needs, when they were less expensive than other options, and when they did not disproportionately require more work or cost more money.

Withdrawals

Actions could be withdrawn by the plaintiff before a judgment was rendered because of a default, confession, trial, or some other process. The withdrawal stands between the processes of default and confession, which usually stood for the defendants' acquiescence to the claims against them, and the other processes available that all involved contesting the plaintiffs' claims in some more direct way. Withdrawals occurred when an action was satisfied or compromised prior to the court's session or when the plaintiff otherwise decided to end the action without it being contested.

Satisfaction and compromise were recorded 92 times. In 15 of these cases, the deputy provost marshal returned a writ of summons or attachment with the note "satisfied" and no further action was taken. In these cases, it appears that the defendant either gave the deputy provost marshal the claimed amount to turn over to the plaintiff or the defendant paid the plaintiff prior to or at the time the writ was served. In the other 77 actions, either the marshal or clerk recorded on the writ that it had been compromised, which is to say, the plaintiff and defendant came to some compromise and the action was concluded. For example, on 16 February 1764 the merchant Thomas Hardwell swore out a writ of attachment against Josiah Adams, a block maker, for £7. Five days later, Hardwell wrote a note on the back of the clerk's copy of the writ: "Received a note of Hand from the Defendant for the within Debt and Cost which when paid is in full [satisfaction] of this Writ." Below this he signed his name. The deputy provost marshal then wrote on the writ, "The within is Compromised between the parties" and signed his name. This ended the action and it was dropped from the Inferior Court's March session.

In another 315 cases, actions were recorded as being withdrawn, often without any record explaining why. Certainly some of these were also satisfied or compromised, but not all. Plaintiffs could also withdraw actions when they believed they had limited or no chance of success. One example of this, at the Supreme Court, involved an appeal by James Quin after he was sued by and lost to John Fillis at the Inferior Court (appeals will be discussed in detail in chapter 6). Quin, as executor of Thomas Ahern's estate, was sued by Fillis at the March 1763 session of the Inferior Court. When Quin lost both an attempted abatement, described below, and then trial by jury, he appealed to the Supreme Court. On 15 May 1763, a jury was empanelled to hear the new trial. At that moment, Quin withdrew his appeal. Having lost at the lower court, Quin appears to have decided at the last moment that he would have no chance at winning at the Supreme Court either.[23] It was better to withdraw, even that late in the appeal, than to continue to accumulate costs in a losing battle.

Withdrawals were made by plaintiffs, but in many cases they withdrew their actions at the initiative of the defendant. This is most clear in those withdrawals following satisfaction or compromise in which the defendant either paid the plaintiff or made acceptable arrangements to do so. Thus, in *Hardwell v. Adams*, the defendant still controlled the process: it was Josiah Adams's initiative to give Thomas Hardwell the promissory note that led to the compromise and thus the end of the action. Quin's withdrawal was more clearly a decision made by the plaintiff, or in this case, the appellant. People could initiate legal actions only to decide at some later point that success was so unlikely that withdrawing was the best option to prevent having to pay accumulating costs to both the court and the other party.

Abatement and Dismissal

Abatement and dismissal, the last two processes to be discussed in this chapter, differ substantially from the others and mark out a middle ground between avoiding trial and a full trial. Both required the judges of the court to make a decision about the viability of the action, and so some element of the plaintiff's claim was "tried" even if no actual trial occurred. They belong in this chapter rather than the next, however, because they both occurred prior to any examination of the evidence; they both were evaluations of the legality of the plaintiff's claim, irrespective of the accuracy of the evidence.

Having been served, defendants could enter a plea of abatement, asserting there was some defect or error in the plaintiff's writ or declaration. Giles Jacob's *A New Law-Dictionary*, first published in England in 1729, included, by 1743, a list of reasons for abatement:

Insufficiency of the matter, or the Uncertainty of the Allegation, by Misnaming the Plaintiff, or Defendant, or the Place; or to the Variance between the Writ and Speciality or Record; of the Incertainty of the writ , count or declaration; on account of the Death of either of the parties before Judgement; or where a Woman Plaintiff is married before or depending the suit; and for several other causes[.][24]

Not all of these were pled in Halifax. For example, there was no plea of abatement made because a female plaintiff got married in the meantime. Nevertheless the wide range of options for seeking an abatement made it an attractive option to defendants who wished to debate the reach and application of the law and legal processes to particular civil disputes. In Halifax, a defendant could plead abatement or demurrer, common in Connecticut in the 1700s, but the judges treated them as meaning the same thing.[25]

Upon receiving a writ of summons or attachment, the defendant would enter a plea in writing seeking an abatement. The plea would explain the reasons for seeking the abatement and conclude with the statement that should the plea fail, the defendant wished to go to trial on the matter. A copy of the plea would be delivered to the plaintiff who would reply in writing. These replies, referred to as "replications," would attempt to show the error identified by the defendant did not exist or was minor, or, in the later 1750s and the 1760s, or they would include a motion to amend the impugned documents so that the action could continue. The judges would evaluate the written reports and rule to abate the action, which would end it, allow the plaintiff to amend the writ or declaration to correct an error, or reject the plea and send the action to trial.

James Quin's attempt to abate an action by John Fillis was introduced in the last section. Appointed executor for Thomas Hearn's estate, Quin was served with a writ demanding £25 owed to Fillis. Quin's attorney Daniel Wood moved for an abatement because Fillis's writ and declaration identified the debtor as Thomas Ahern, while Quin was executor for a Thomas *Hearn*. James Monk, Fillis's lawyer, replied saying that "Thomas in his lifetime was called Thomas Ahern as well as Thomas Hern" and offered to pay the cost of amending the plea and declaration should the court see fit to demand it. In this case they did not, the abatement was rejected entirely, and the case proceeded.[26]

Quin had been successful in an earlier attempt at abatement. In August of 1762 the merchant Henry Ferguson and the auctioneer Philip Hammon sued Quin and Daniel Heffernan, called a yeoman, as executors on a bond of John Porter's. Ferguson and Hammon asserted that

Quin and Heffernan had entered into a penal bond worth £200 on 20 February 1760, to be paid to the plaintiffs whenever they required it if the conditions of the bond were breached. Quin and Heffernan were the executors of Porter's estate, and thus were expected to cover Porter's outstanding debts, including his bond to Ferguson and Hammon, out of the estate's assets. Quin and Heffernan challenged the claim against them and sought abatement on two grounds. First, they asserted that they should be sued to render an account to show what assets they held, to whom they had made payments, and from whom they had received payments. Second, they claimed that no evidence had been appended to the declaration or writ that showed that they were the proper defendants in this case. In their replication, Hammon and Ferguson claimed

the stile of An Action upon an Obligation is an Action of Debt upon Specialty agreeable to the form & precedents of Law as the plt have Declared. And the plts further say that they are ready in Court to produce Evidence of their Executorship & that the Obligation is Annexed to the plts Declaration & therefore ready to be produced.

In other words, the bond was evidence of a debt and so that was how they should have, and did, sue. Further, they could produce evidence at trial that the defendants were Porter's executors and thus the proper defendants. The court rejected this replication and abated the action.[27]

In an earlier case the error seems, in retrospect, less important. In launching a 1757 suit, mariner Thomas Bryant contended in his writ that the tailor Michael Sexton,

on the first day of March last was indebted to the Plt in the sum of Four pounds three Shillings & four pence for the like sum of Money by the Deft of George Greensword before that time had and received to the Use of the Plt & there promis'd to pay the Same on demand but fails thereof tho' demanded.

Essentially, Bryant claimed that Sexton received from George Greensword £4 3s 4d before 1 March 1757 and promised to pay that amount to Bryant when it was demanded. The explanation in the declaration Bryant filed was more confusing. Sexton's defence, as laid out in his plea of abatement, was that Bryant's writ was insufficient because,

the Plaintiff has not any where in his said Declaration alleged that the said

Michael made the Promise, in said Declaration mentioned or alleged, to any person whatever which he ought to have done.

Bryant was required in his writ *and declaration* to establish the legal basis for a debt to show that the defendant was indebted and had promised to repay the same to the plaintiff. Whether or not the promise had happened was a question of fact to be debated at trial, but the assertion of the promise was necessary to make the writ and declaration complete. Although he made the assertion in the writ, quoted above, he did not state so in the declaration, and thus Bryant's declaration was insufficient to demonstrate that a cause of action actually stood against Sexton. The judges accepted Sexton's plea and Bryant's action was abated.[28] In both of these cases the plaintiffs were expected to provide basic legal elements in their pleadings, including a proper defendant, proper cause of action, and proper claim of a breach of law. Failure to so include these elements resulted in abatements.

Other failures or gaps in the forms did not lead to successful abatements. When London merchant John Blackburn sued Halifax tailor Charles Terlaven in 1763, Daniel Wood sought an abatement. Wood argued that neither the original writ nor the copy served on Terlaven were endorsed by Blackburn's attorney or had a warrant from Blackburn authorizing legal action on his behalf. James Brenton, Blackburn's local lawyer, asserted they were good, noting the rules and practice of the court in Halifax did not require that the attorney endorse the writs. Nor did practices require that he, as Blackburn's attorney, file a writ of attorney proving just that. The court sided with Brenton and the plea of abatement was rejected.[29]

At times the pleas of abatement could be very complex, but they had to have a clear basis in law and the actual documents filed or pleadings made. Jonathan Hoare was sued for defamation by Charles Morris, the chief judge of the then County Court in March 1751. Morris claimed Hoare had called him "a damned lyar and a Cursed Rogue." In response, Hoare's lawyer John Ker tried to secure an abatement twice, on three grounds.

In his first plea, Ker offered two grounds. First, he asserted that Hoare was improperly held on bail. An attachment could only be issued and bail only be taken when the plaintiff had sworn out an affidavit specifying the value of the damages sustained. No such affidavit or declaration existed in this case. Second, Ker asserted that the form of the writ was wrong because it did not follow "the Same form and manner as in England," as ordered by the governor and council.[30] In particular, he asserted that writs should be directed to the defendant, but that the writ presented to Hoare was directed to the provost marshal or his deputies (Ker called them sheriffs) instead. To support this, Ker cites examples from Jacob's *Law Dictionary* where writs directed to the sheriff were proper, but states that there was no precedent for a writ to be directed to the sheriff in a personal action for damages, as this was.

Both grounds were dispatched, but the reasons were not recorded. On the first, the writ served on Hoare was a summons, not an attachment, and so no bail appears to have actually been taken. This being the case, it was odd for Ker to claim that bail was inappropriately demanded. He did suggest that his argument on this may not be accepted, however, when he introduced his second argument with the phrase, "If it Shall be Alleged by the plaintf that the Defft is not in Court on Baill But on Summons …" Although such passages are common in modern legal pleadings, one can hear the undercurrent of recognition by Ker that his pleading was weak. The second argument is intriguing: if Ker was found correct then all of the writs of summons and attachment to the court would be invalid because all were directed to the provost marshal, instructing him to summon or attach the defendant for the reasons described in the writ. In early editions of Jacob's *Law Dictionary* (the first edition was in 1729) a writ was described simply as "the *King's Precept*, in Writing under Seal, commanding some Thing to be done touching a Suit or Action." In one entry, a writ of inquiry of damages is described as "a judicial *Writ*, that issues out to the Sheriff upon a Judgment by Default …"[31] It is perhaps possible that Ker relied on these definitions, and assumed that writs were to be directed to the defendants unless otherwise specified, as in the writ of inquiry. By the 1743 edition, however, Jacob's *Law Dictionary* provides the following definition: "Writ, signifies in general the *King's Precept* in Writing under Seal, issuing out of some Court, directed to the Sheriff or other Officer, and commanding something to be done in relation to a Suit or Action, or giving Commission to have the same done."[32] Ker's claim about the writ is not contradicted by the *Law Dictionary* in its earliest editions, but his argument is, in fact, wrong.

When his first attempt at securing an abatement failed, Ker offered a second reply to the writ with a third ground for seeking abatement: that defamation can only be claimed against the real, economic damage caused by the effect of the words, and not against the utterance of the words alone. For this proposition, Ker relied on the third edition of William Style's *Practical Register* from 1694, a guide to the rules and practices of England's common law courts first prepared in the 1650s. Ker asserted that for Morris's suit to go forward he should have made a statement under oath recounting the damages actually sustained by Hoare's words. Ker went on to cite Jacob's *Law Dictionary* again on the proposition that when words can have multiple meanings, the court should follow the mildest meaning.[33] Ker's third ground was an argument about law, but it turned to some degree on the evidence: on what real damages, if any, Morris claimed to have sustained from Hoare's calling him a liar and rogue; and what possible understandings of rogue were available to the court to determine the effect of Hoare's words. Both could be tested at trial by a jury. Again Ker's plea was rejected and the matter went to trial.[34] It is not particularly surprising that Ker's attempts at abatement would be refused by the court regardless of plaintiff. The fact that the plaintiff was the chief judge of the court, however, may certainly have coloured the proceedings to some degree too. The rest of this case will be picked up in chapter 6.

Ker's attempts at securing an abatement were poorly constructed; they relied on legal arguments that appear to have been unsupported either in fact or in law. Coupled with the fact that he was asking a bench led by Charles Morris to abate an action initiated by Charles Morris,[35] it seems highly unlikely that he could have been successful. It was an interesting strategy to adopt. In different circumstances it might have been aimed at getting the judges to make an error so as to allow for an appeal or writ of *certiorari*, but such things were not necessary in Halifax, as chapter 7 will show.[36]

There were no successful abatements in 1751, despite Ker's efforts, but 31 actions were successfully abated in 1752, almost two-thirds of all of the abatements recorded up to 1766 (see table 4.5). Abatements became a political issue in 1752 in the months leading up to the Justices' Affair. In March 1752, the Inferior Court judges petitioned the governor and council to make a rule for Halifax that "no circumstantial error in the copy of the process shall abate the writ unless the ... mistake ... may operate to the disadvantage of ye Defendant." Where an abatement might be granted, they recommended that "the plaintiff may amend such Error upon the agreement of the parties and application to the court and paying costs arisen so far provided they be no such material errors as may annul the process in law." These two rules would limit the grounds for abatement and give plaintiffs the opportunity to keep actions moving forward with the agreement of the defendant and the

Table 4.5: Abatements and dismissals over time

Year	Number of abatements	Per cent of total actions[a]	Number of dismissals	Per cent of total actions
1750	3	1	34	10
1751	0	0	22	7
1752	31	6	20	4
1753	7	2	13	4
1754	3	1	6	3
1755	2	1	1	0
1756	0	0	0	0
1757	1	1	0	0
1758–60	0	0	0	0
1761	1	1	0	0
1762	2	2	1	1
1763	0	0	2	1

[a] Abatements as a percentage of actions concluded in the Inferior Court that year.

court. The council rejected the first, citing it as being "very prejudicial to the defendant," but it did accept the second, allowing writs abated for some error to be amended with the agreement of the parties.[37]

At the March session, the Inferior Court justices abated eight actions. In June, the first session after their appeal to the governor and council was rejected, thirteen actions were abated. In the September session another seven were abated. In both the March and June sessions they abated more actions than had previously been abated by the court in total. The sudden increase seems to speak to some crisis in the law, and considering the timing in conjunction with their appeal for a change in rules, it seems to some degree manufactured by the judges to pressure council for a change in the rules.

The process for abating counted on the bench coming to an agreement of some sort, apparently by a vote among the sitting justices. With the Inferior Court often having five or more judges sitting at a time, this could be difficult. At the December 1753 court, Richard Tritton sought an abatement against an action by David Rogers. The basis for the plea is lost, but what happened next is recorded: after both parties' lawyers were "fully heard the Clerk was Ordered to put the Question to [the] Court Whither the Writt Should Abate or not." At this session, six justices were sitting at the Inferior Court bench. The clerk recorded, "The Court being Equally Divided they Continued the Consideration hereof to a fuller Court."[38] The action was heard again at the next session, in March 1754. Once again the lawyers made their cases, and "it was Carried that the said Writ do abate by a Majority of Three to two upon which the Court Ordered that the Said Writ do Abate and they Allowed the Defendants Plea And Passed Judgment Against the Said Plaintiff for the Defendants Costs which is taxed at Nine Shillings."[39] At both sessions the same six justices were reported as sitting and the clerk did not record who was actually present at each of the two hearings.

In December 1752 the judges petitioned the governor and council again, asserting that the failure to fully adopt their March recommendations had created a "great inconvenience" and seen "Justice ... delayed." The governor and council were now convinced to change the rules more completely. The original writ was still required to "contain thereon the Plts and the Defts true Christian name, place of abode, occupation, trade, mistery, or degree and bear true tests with the time of issuing the said summons, process or writt." Nevertheless, broad restrictions on abatements were now introduced:

No Summons, process, writt, Judgment or other proceeding in any of the Courts of Justice within this province shall be abated [or] arrested ... for any kind of circumstantial or clerical Error or mistakes nor thro the defect and want of form only, Provided all the Essential and Substantiall matters thereof be plainly sett forth therin necessary to proceed upon the merits of the case or be contained in such Judgment made thereon, and where the person and Case may be rightly understood and intended by the Court, and the Court on Motion made in such case may order the amendment therof.

If there was a failure in the form, the problem writ could be amended on the spot; if there was a problem in law, the writ could be abated. In addition, errors in the *copies* of writs produced by or for the court could not be used as the basis for a successful abatement.[40] The effect of this change was immediate: from thirty-one abatements in 1752 to six in 1753 and to four between 1754 and 1766.

The short-term implications of this change in rules are unclear. As the new rules were promulgated just days before the beginning of the Justices' Affair, it may be that this correspondence between judges and governor played some precipitating role. The demands for changes made by the judges may have prompted some to see them as moving away from a formalistic and strict interpretation of the law imagined to be "English" and towards the more forgiving, intent-based practice of New England. The evidence for this is weak, however: no specific mention of the abatement changes is made in any of the petitions. Moreover, the effect of the changes seems to be of differing value to the petitioners in the crisis. The problem with abatements is that they allowed otherwise justly indebted or accused defendants to escape or delay judgment for a session or more through errors made by the plaintiffs, lawyers, and clerks. Successfully abating an action might lead to it being reintroduced three months later, or it could be dropped entirely. When a writ was served against the wrong person then abatement was appropriate, but when, as in *Morris v. Hoare*, it was used to try to avoid judgment when a legally sound complaint was laid against the rightful defendant, abatement was an obstruction. Changing the rules for abatement meant that the judges could ignore many such petitions without having to appear as if they were being capricious in their decision-making. For frequent plaintiffs like Joshua Mauger, then, abatement was a potential nuisance; for frequent defendants like Roger Hill, however, abatement could be very useful.[41]

The same justices who petitioned for restrictions on abatements dismissed 20 actions in 1752, having already dismissed 22 in 1751 and 34 in 1750. Dismissals, like abatements, ended litigation, usually prior to trial, because of some failure on the plaintiff's part. They differed from abatements because dismissals were made by the bench on their own initiative, or at least without written argument from the defence. Dismissals operated as a way for the bench to independently shape how Halifax's plaintiffs sought legal remedy.

Dismissals were present from the very beginning of the county court. At the very first session *Dugan v. Poor* was dismissed because the debt at its core was contracted outside of the colony, and the governor had proclaimed that Nova Scotian residents would be protected from creditors on debts accrued prior to coming to Nova Scotia. Other early dismissals from the earliest period were effectively nonsuits: *Turner v. Fielding* from the first session was dismissed because the plaintiff Samuel Turner failed to appear, while *Grant v. Smith* at the same session was dismissed, "the parties not appearing."[42] In later months, several actions were dismissed for "want of service" of the writ, while others were dismissed because the plaintiff failed to produce all the necessary paperwork, such as declarations or for a failure to swear by the plaintiff to the plea.[43]

In the face of an inexperienced and untutored bar and general public, the bench seems to have used dismissals as a way of ensuring that the rules were followed. At times this could be significant, as in one 1751 action dismissed because "The Defendant not being Charged with anything in the Writt."[44] Most dismissals were for failures in making a proper legal case or following the rules: the plaintiff's failure to make a declaration explaining the action,[45] the plaintiff forgetting to swear to the claim for an attachment,[46] and the defendant not being served with a true copy of the writ.[47] Others were the result of the defendant's condition, such as being in the Navy,[48] in prison,[49] or dead.[50]

Most of the records of dismissals come from the Inferior Court minute books. Once it is clear that plaintiffs' lawyers were recorded, there were 27 dismissals where the plaintiffs appear to have been unrepresented and 34 where they clearly had a lawyer. Of those 34, 23 plaintiffs had the same lawyer: William Nesbitt, one of the people who signed the complaints in the Justices' Affair.[51]

The number of dismissals a year and their proportion of all actions declined after the justices petitioned for the changes in abatement rules as well. In 1753 there were thirteen dismissals, seven less than the previous year, but six more than the abatements the same year. In 1754 there were only six dismissals, still twice the number of abatements that year. In the years the followed, the numbers of dismissals were even lower: four in total between 1755 and 1766. The parallel decline of both abatements and dismissals suggests they need to be understood together.

There are several possible explanations. First, it may be that the number of dismissals and abatements was dependent on the accuracy of plaintiff legal actions: if plaintiffs, their attorneys, and the clerks became progressively more skilled at initiating actions then the opportunity for abatements and dismissals would decline. The problem with this explanation is that it suggests that defendants, their lawyers, and the judges were better at picking out problems with plaintiff documents than the plaintiffs were at preparing them, but the lawyers and the litigants were often the same people, while the bench was no more legally trained in the early years than the bar. Second, the declines might not be related: abatements might have declined because of the bench's hostility to them and the change in rules, while dismissals might decline somewhat later because of a change on the bench: the increase in the number of justices following the Justices' Affair or the arrival of the English-trained Jonathan Belcher in 1754 as chief justice for the colony. Third, the change might be the result of a desire on behalf of the bench to better facilitate the use of the courts for debt collection: abatements and dismissals allowed defendants to win, and by limiting both, plaintiffs became more likely to win.

Choosing to Avoid Trial

When a plaintiff nonsuited, the decision might have been theirs alone; likewise in some cases of withdrawals. When a case was dismissed it was possible that the defendant had no intention of contesting the action or could not do so and the dismissal was simply based on the court's own evaluation of the plaintiff's materials. In most cases, however, the processes by which an action came to an end were determined by the defendants. They could choose to try to make some agreement with the plaintiffs in advance, to confess to the claim, to default, or to contest the action through pleas of abatement or by seeking a trial or arbitration.

As will be seen in chapter 6, the loser of any legal action was almost always compelled to pay not only their own legal fees but those of the winner as well. This included lawyers' fees as well as the costs associated with each stage a legal action went through. Trials by jury and arbitrations cost a great deal more than anything else, so defendants who thought they would lose had a great incentive to avoid trial or arbitration.

The selection of process to end actions may have rested with defendants, but the volume of actions that ended without trial or arbitration says something more about the place of civil law and the Inferior Court within Halifax society. Legal action was not, it appears, necessarily a sign of broken relationships between people. On the contrary, it appears to have been one part of normal commercial, and even just inter-personal, relations. Launching an action did not end discussion; on the contrary discussion continued well after litigation was initiated. Plaintiffs could use litigation to prompt defendants to act on outstanding differences by making agreements in advance of trial or, when defendants went into default, to secure their claim with a court order to compel payment if necessary.

This does not, however, mean that litigants did not contest the claims made against each other. Even while avoiding trial, defendants could contest claims against them, explicitly through pleas of abatement, effectively by coming to an agreement with the plaintiff for a sum less than claimed, or implicitly by defaulting when they had no intention of ever paying. Or, they could contest the plaintiffs' claims by going to trial or seeking arbitration, the themes of the next chapter.

5

Going to Trial

On 17 November, 1761, Roger Hill initiated an action for debt against Anne Webb. As discussed in chapter 4, Hill defaulted when William Meany sued him, and William Fury defaulted a suit by Webb at the same session. Webb, however, was not prepared to default to Hill. Rather, their dispute was tried before a jury in December.

Every action initiated at the Inferior Court could end in a trial, and even with the various ways to avoid trial, almost one-fifth of actions ended in a trial before a jury. While historians of other North American common law colonies have found that, by the 1750s, very few actions ended in trials before juries, in Nova Scotia this remained an important procedure, the next most common to defaulting.[1] Both Deborah Rosen and Bruce Mann identify the needs of a commercializing market economy as the reason for the change away from jury trials by mid-century. Rosen, for example, argues that the decline in the number of jury trials in New York by mid-century reflected a change in the law towards greater certainty by "supplying clear standards for interpreting contracts and ... enforcing them predictably." Merchants would thus avoid challenges in court by employing notes of hand and other written instruments, while "craftsmen, farmers, and women valued the more traditional juridical function" of jury trials. In addition, she suggests that "craftsmen's and farmers' dominance on juries" led to a "greater likelihood of a favourable verdict" for the defendant.[2] Halifax, although a new city, was enmeshed in markets both within the colony and beyond, yet jury trials remained an important aspect of all civil litigation, including debt litigation.

Litigants could also opt to have the court refer their matter to arbitration. The option used by the governor and council to resolve civil disputes in 1749 lived on in a local process built upon arbitration procedures from England and New England. Just as with jury verdicts, arbitration awards were enforced through a rule of the court. As will be seen, however, there were significant differences between the processes of choosing jurors and choosing arbitrators.

In either case, the litigants' disputes were turned over to community members rather than officers of the courts. Defendants regularly chose to take actions to trial or to court-ordered arbitration rather than default or make a deal with the plaintiff. Jury trials and arbitration did not result in substantially different outcomes from other processes in many cases. They did not impede, and may rather have furthered, commercial development. Through the jury, a large number of people who were infrequent litigants were integrated into the court system and inculcated with the values it supported, especially the payment of debts, even by enforcement if necessary. They learned through experience to come to verdicts in similar ways and on similar terms, and thus ensure consistency. Experienced arbitrators did much the same thing. An understanding of how jury trials and arbitrations occurred and who made the decisions reveals the conservative and commercial nature of both. At the same time, a study of jury trials and arbitrations shows how the courts operated when serious conflicts between litigants arose. The first part of this chapter will explain how jury trials and court-ordered arbitrations operated in their multiple forms. The chapter then turns to a comparative analysis of jurors and arbitrators to show how the selection of both helped ensure that the process of trial was less uncertain than other historians have presumed.

Trial by Jury

The records that remain of *Hill v. Webb* are typical of trials: the initial documents that set out the action remain, so we know that Roger Hill sued Anne Webb on a debt on account. Hill claimed that in April and May 1757 he sold Webb a variety of small goods, including bread and wood, to a total value of £22 7s. For this debt, still unpaid some four years later, Hill demanded £27 in damages. Both Hill and Webb hired lawyers to represent them. Hill was represented by David Lloyd while

Webb was represented by James Brenton.[3] Although a smaller percentage of debt actions went before judge and jury than defamation, assault, or ejectment actions, trials for debt accounted for 192 (55 per cent) of the 349 jury trials where the cause of action is known.

For most trials, little documentation of what happened remains. The plaintiffs or their lawyers would present their case, including both written evidence and witnesses. Defendants would then present any written evidence they had along with their witnesses. It appears that the plaintiff could speak directly to the meaning of the written evidence. A sheet of paper prepared by the clerk recorded the names of the jurors who heard the trial. Evidence and arguments were presented by both parties at the trial. At times, witnesses had written depositions that were taken in advance of trial and presented as part of the hearing. At other times, witnesses would appear and give only oral testimony. Testimony was not recorded by the clerks, but both sides could examine the witnesses. For *Hill v. Webb*, no evidence from the trial itself remains other than the copy from Hill's account book that was attached to his writ and declaration. No witnesses are listed as appearing.

After the parties concluded, the judges charged the jury. A simple charge was recorded on the same sheet of paper as the jurors' names: "Your issue is to try whither or Not the Defendant is indebted to the plaintiff in way and manner as Laid in the Writt and Return your Verdict according to Evidence."[4] The charge would ask the jury to decide if the defendant had acted as the plaintiff alleged and thus owed the plaintiff some sum. There are no records of longer or more complex charges than this. It is possible that the judges took some time in explaining the law and evidence to the juries before allowing them to retire to consider. However, as will be seen later in this chapter, most juries were composed of several experienced jurors. This experience, combined with the relatively narrow range of disputes juries regularly heard, and even the bench and bar's limited legal education might have meant that more involved discussions of the law were felt to be unnecessary to deliver or too difficult to articulate to be a common practice.

The jury then deliberated and came to a verdict. There is no evidence to suggest that the jury retired from the courtroom to come to their verdict; at English criminal trials at the same time, jurors often did not leave the courtroom to deliberate.[5] Once arrived at, the verdict was inscribed on a sheet of paper, usually in the form "We find for the plaintiff the sum of ..." and signed by the jury foreman (if he was literate). In

Hill v. Webb, the jury returned its verdict for Hill, awarding him the £22 7s he claimed he was owed.

The trial jury was made up of twelve men selected from a panel of jurors summoned for every session. Jurors would be summoned through a venire, a special writ from the court requesting the provost marshal (or his deputy, who again did the work in this case) to summon a group of men to serve as jurors at the upcoming session of the court. The venire for the December session was issued on 30 November 1761, calling thirty-nine men. Nine of the men were unable to serve: two were fishing, three were out of the province, one was away from Halifax, one was a constable, one was not found and so not served, and one was currently in jail (and also claimed to be a constable). A jury of twelve men was then selected from the remaining pool to act as jurors in the trial. Of these, seven had occupations listed at least once in other actions (the jury summons did not usually include this information). Alexander McCulloch, in thirteen appearances as a litigant, was variously identified as a merchant, trader yeoman, gentleman, and truckman, although most often as either a merchant (five times) or a trader (four times). Nathan Levy, also a frequent litigant, was usually identified as a trader (twenty-two times), although once he was identified as a yeoman. McCulloch straddled the ground between merchant and trader, while Levy as clearly the latter; both were probably of a status or activity closer to Anne Webb than Malachy Salter. The other five jurors who had at least once been identified by an occupation seem to have been artisans or labourers. Ezekiel Averall, the jury foreman, had been identified as a housewright or carpenter; Cornelius Ulman was a carpenter. John Cobright was a shoemaker and James Ray a baker. Michael Bourk had four different terms applied to him over six litigant appearances: twice called cooper and twice yeoman, he was also identified once as a "yeoman and labourer" and once as a truckman. Thus, two of the men worked primarily in commerce and trade, four as artisans, and one as both artisan and in low-level commerce. As will be seen below, this sort of jury was typical at the Inferior Court.

Some trials left many documents, which provide a fuller picture of the trial process. Benjamin Leigh sued Joseph Jones for defamation in December 1760, after a series of incidents in late August of that year. On September 11, Leigh and Jones met before two justices of the Inferior Court, Scott and Duport, and a clerk, so Leigh could have several men make depositions. Edmund Keating, a Virginian and mate of the ship *Sally* made the first. He claimed that on August 26, Jones had come on board the *Sally* and enquired about her cargo. Told it was consigned to Leigh, Keating reported that Jones said, "[I]f Mr Leigh had the cargo the captain would go away without the Money, for Mr Leigh could not pay for it without he borrowed the Money, and [Jones] did not know any Merchant that would lend it him, and signified that Mr Leigh's Credit was very bad, and that for [Jones's] on part he would be damned if he would Trust [Leigh] with five shillings." Later, Keating visited Jones in his shop. There, Jones repeated the accusations against Leigh and suggested the he and his partner Robert Campbell were willing to purchase the *Sally*'s cargo for a fair price.

Next, Leigh deposed Hezekiah Brewer, master of the *Sally*. Brewer was newly arrived in Halifax, and thus presumably did not have a good sense of the Halifax merchant community. Brewer told the justices that Keating had reported to him Jones's claim that "[I]f he let Mr Leigh have the Cargo he might wait some time for his money" as well as other aspersions against Leigh's character. Brewer claimed he was thus "fearfull of putting the Cargo in Mr Leigh's Hands." When Brewer finished, Jones then questioned him further. Brewer conceded that, in fact, he had allowed Leigh to handle the cargo anyway, because, as he put it, "[O]n Enquiry, I found that Mr Leigh was a Person of Credit."[6]

Leigh arranged for two more depositions by James Brodie and James Middlesex Walker, who reported on conversations with John Cann, the co-owner of the *Sally*. Cann himself was unavailable to be deposed or to appear at trial because he was still in Virginia. Both Brodie and Walker reported that while in Virginia they had heard directly from Cann that he had consigned his cargo to Leigh and that, if this proved a successful venture, he planned on sending much more to Leigh in the future.

All of these men were Virginians, and they wanted to leave Halifax with the *Sally* and continue on their trade. Instead of being required to give evidence at trial months later, they were able to give their testimony in the form of depositions that could be presented in written form at the trial. An order of the governor and council in 1753 made into law a practice of the courts to take depositions from witnesses, instead of requiring their appearance at trial, when witnesses were going to sea. Depositions would have to be taken before two justices, with both parties examining or cross-examining the witnesses. Once concluded, the depositions were sealed until trial.[7] The process appears to replicate what occurred at trial, but with the evidence transcribed, something that did not happen at trial. This allows us to see how trial witnesses likely presented their evidence: the men told their stories with relatively little questioning by Leigh. When he felt they had reported all he needed from them, Jones had the right to cross-examine them.

At trial, Leigh presented the four depositions and a copy of Cann's written orders to Captain Brewer. Leigh had two goals with the evidence: to prove the defamation and to demonstrate that it damaged him. Keating and Brewer's testimony did the first. The legal requirements for defamation required that more than one person hear the defaming comments and that the comments be repeated. Brodie's and Walker's evidence was aimed at proving the damage by showing that this was Cann's first trade into Halifax through Leigh and that Cann originally intended to do more business with Leigh. Leigh could show that the defamation, if successful, would hurt future business.

There is no record of Jones's evidence. His interventions in the deposition evidence, however, imply at least part of his defence. By asking Brewer whether or not the *Sally's* cargo was in the end consigned to Leigh, Jones appears to have intended to demonstrate that Leigh suffered no real damage.

The reliance on so much deposition evidence in *Leigh v. Jones* is unusual. In most cases, witnesses would be expected to appear in person. Some trials could even end up relying on several witnesses: when fisherman James Welch sued merchant Robert Campbell for assault in June 1764, thirteen witnesses were summoned by the parties to give evidence.[8]

The bench sometimes made decisions to ensure trials occurred. In 1759, the cooper Garret Nagle and Elizabeth, his wife, sued the labourer Thomas Murray, accusing him of calling Elizabeth a "bitch" and a "whore" and claiming he had had "carnal knowledge of her." This led to Elizabeth getting into "Evil Repute and Disquiet" with Garret "And other Enormities," which they valued at £20. David Lloyd's initial line of defence on Murray's behalf was to assert "the said Elizabeth in the Writt and Declaration Mention'd is not the Wife of Garret Nagle and Therefore hath no Protection under him for the Commencement of her Suit against the Defend^t." Daniel Wood, the Nagles' lawyer, clearly saw this as an attempt to avoid a jury trial. He replied that Elizabeth and Garret had been married as of the date of the defaming remarks in January, and in any case this was "a Matter of Fact and not a point in Law to be pleaded in Barr," in other words something for the jury not the judges to decide. The judges rejected Lloyd's attempt, and the dispute went before a jury at the March 1759 session.[9] While the practice in Halifax's courts meant that most actions never went to trial, when settlement was out of the question and excepting those moments when abatements and dismissals were possible, the jury trial remained at the core of the system. All litigants would assume that any action, once initiated in the Inferior Court, could end up before a jury, even if their experience told them it was unlikely.

Special Juries

All of the trials described so far were before regular juries drawn from those men summoned to serve in juries at the session. Not all jury trials were held before these juries: some trials were held with special juries, made up of jurors not necessarily drawn from a regular venire. In Halifax the term "special jury" was applied to two different cases: when a trial was held outside of a regular sitting of the Inferior or Supreme Courts[10] or when a jury drawn from those summoned by the venire was deemed inappropriate or unacceptable. By English usage in the eighteenth century, the latter use was preferred: in England, a special jury was, according to its historian, James Oldham, "a jury of individuals of higher class than usual; a jury of experts; and a 'struck jury,' that is, one formed by a special procedure allowing parties to strike names from an unusually large panel of prospective jurors."[11] The special juries called during a regular session in Halifax were juries of experts, but as will be seen below, this probably also meant they were on average of higher class or status than normal juries. As in England at the time, Halifax litigants never played a role in selecting, approving, or challenging the make-up of a jury hearing their case, and there is no example of a struck jury in Halifax in the 1750s and 1760s. Records remain of twenty-five special juries in the Inferior Court (and six in the Supreme Court). Of these, eight of the Inferior Court special juries were for trials held outside of one of the four annual sessions of the court. Most special juries were ordered by the court when the litigants requested a jury that had expertise in the matters at trial.

In November and December 1758, merchant William Ball shipped to John Franks, a merchant in Philadelphia, a variety of trade goods such as musket balls, lace, and buttons to sell. Ball wanted Franks to take the proceeds of the sale to purchase rum, sugar, and iron and ship them back to Halifax. On 30 April 1760, Franks sued Ball, claiming that Ball still owed him £115 8s 5¾d, the difference between the value of the goods he sold in Halifax on Ball's behalf and the shipment of rum.[12] Ball countersued on May 3, demanding that Franks present to him a "reasonable account" of all of his trading transactions on Ball's behalf, testing Franks' claimed debt.[13] In an action for a reasonable account, the plaintiff demanded that the defendant provide a thorough accounting of all of the business transactions at issue. If the account showed that the defendant was in arrears, then damages would be awarded to the plaintiff to balance the accounts of the two. Often, these actions arose with the dissolution of a business partnership or between the executor of an estate and the deceased's creditors or debtors.

Both Franks and Ball entered into recognizances for £230 16s 11½d to ensure their attendance at trial. Such recognizances were unusual at the Inferior Court, although appellants at the Supreme Court were required to enter into recognizances to ensure that their appeals would go ahead. The value of both recognizances was equal to twice Franks's claim in his suit.

The two actions were scheduled to be heard at the June session, but were put off until September. At the September 1760 court, it was decided between the litigants and the judges that the two cases would be tried together and a special jury would be called. On October 6, a special venire was issued, commanding that the provost marshal summon "eighteen good & lawfull Men Merch[ts] of the County of Halifax" to the courthouse on October 9 for the trial. Of the twelve jurors who heard the case, eight had been identified as merchants in other court documents. Two others had been identified as shopkeepers as well as either a brewer or auctioneer in other trials. Two jurors had no occupations listed in other appearances. Of the six jurors summoned who did not serve, four were identified as merchants in other appearances; one was a shopkeeper, retailer, and trader; and one a master mason.

The types of evidence at trial were similar to those offered in *Leigh v. Jones*: Franks presented two written and notarized depositions from men in Philadelphia with whom he had done business on Ball's behalf, along with detailed accounts of all of the goods he had received from Ball and sold, all of the goods he had purchased for Ball, and the costs of shipping everything. Ball presented a variety of written documents, including receipts, accounts, and invoices. The invoice for the November shipment read, in part, "twelve Keggs of musquette Ball, ship'd by William Ball on Board the Ship Foudryant Captain Taylor bound for Philadelphia and Consigned to M[r] John Franks & is on acc[t] & Risque of the Shipper the Return to be made in good old Jamaica Rum sugar & some Iron." The second shipment included, among other things, more musket balls, five pieces of gold and silver lace, and forty-eight dozen gold and silver buttons. When he received the shipments, Franks wrote to Ball in February 1759 that he would try to sell the musket at the London Coffee House, having been told that this was "the best way to dispose of them." By June of 1759, Franks wrote again, noting that the lace and buttons had still not be sold, although he would try to sell them all together or in smaller lots before he left Philadelphia in a couple of weeks. In the end, Franks seems to have sold the balls for £79 18s 5d and some cloth for another £42 17s 2d.

After hearing the arguments and reviewing the evidence, the special jury gave its verdict for Franks, awarding him damages of £110 13s 9¾d, not much less than he claimed. Ball gave notice to appeal the action.

The Franks and Ball actions were not unusual. Juries drawn from the regular Inferior Court pool heard similar actions between merchants involving documents like those presented in evidence at trial here.[14] The difference between when a special jury was called appears to have turned on several possible elements that made the cases special. First, the value of the action appears to have been important. The average demand and claim in actions heard by special juries were £207 8s 10d (n = 16) and £123 8s 8d (n = 19), respectively. The average demand and claim before ordinary trial juries were just over half as much: £116 18s (n = 417) and £74 8s 3d (n = 317). The median demands and claims for the two types of juries were much lower but reveal an even greater divergence between special juries and regular juries: special juries' demand median and claim median were £117 and £49 11s 8d, respectively; trial juries' demand median and claim median were £25 and £17, respectively (one-quarter and one-third the values for special juries). Second, special juries were used when there were countersuits. Third, they could be called when the disputes included intercolonial trading relationships or litigants from away. Fourth, they could be called when the disputes turned on more complex financial or trade transactions than were normally heard by regular juries or that involved covenants, agreements, or other written evidence that was not normally presented before regular juries. None of these factors on its own would necessarily lead to a special jury being called, but often several of them were in play in actions that did go to special juries. Although rarely used, especially in cases involving significant sums of money, special juries were available if the litigants could convince the judges of their necessity to the case at hand.

The second type of special jury was that called for a hearing outside of the regular court sessions. The governor in council established the procedures for special sessions in an order proclaimed in January 1751. Plaintiffs could request a special session of the court if either of the parties was expected to leave the colony before the next regular session. The matters that could be covered were restricted: in cases for debts, for example, only debts originally contracted between the parties could be litigated at a special session; the plaintiff could not sue for debts purchased or consigned through a signed-over note of hand. If the request for a special session was accepted, the court would issue a summons to the defendant and prospective jurors. The court could meet as little as forty-eight hours after the summons was issued. Executions on judgments (described in the next chapter) could be issued immediately after the judgment was issued and could be made returnable within forty-eight hours. The regulations of January 1751 at one point describe special sessions as a "special Court or Court Merchant," although at no point were the special courts described as being only for merchants or commercial matters, nor were any special or different rules of procedure (except for the time compression) instituted for special sessions.[15]

Juries of Inquiry

Introduced in 1764, the jury of inquiry did not hear the action and issue a verdict; rather, its job was to determine the value of damages in cases where the defendant defaulted. The jury would meet after the conclusion of a session with the provost marshal directing its business of reviewing the written evidence of all of the defaults of the previous session to determine the true damage to the plaintiff. The jury met in all cases of default; records remain for only nineteen juries of inquiry up to 1766, but there are no records of defaults without juries of inquiry after its introduction. It is unclear from the documents why the Nova Scotia lawmakers decided to introduce the juries of inquiry. The jurors themselves were drawn from the same pool as trial jurors. As will be seen in the next chapter, the invention of the jury of inquiry significantly increased the costs of defaults and probably encouraged defendants to choose some other process rather than defaulting.

A typical action that ended with a jury of inquiry was heard at the September 1765 session. On 8 March 1765, Daniel Hogan gave William Jeffrey a promissory note for £17 15s 10d, payable one month later. When Hogan still had not paid off the note by May 20, Jeffrey initiated an action against him. Hogan hired James Monk to be his lawyer, and at the June session, Monk successfully sought a continuance until the September session so that the two parties could come to an out-of-court agreement. No settlement was made, and in September, Jeffrey's lawyer, James Brenton, demanded that Hogan defend himself in court. Neither Hogan nor Monk made any statements "in Bar or prevention" of Jeffrey's claim, and judgment was made against Hogan in default.[16]

The court, although passing judgment for Jeffrey, claimed in another legal fiction to be, in the words of the writ of inquiry, "Unacquainted what Damages the afors^d William by means of the Premises afors^d in this behalf hath Sustained." That is, the court stated that it had not evaluated the note of hand to determine what was owed. Thus, the provost marshal William Foye was commanded to call a jury of twelve "lawfull and honest men of his Bailwick diligently to enquire" as to Jeffrey's damages and costs of court. The jury was to report back to the court at the beginning of its December session.

On 29 December 1765, at the end of the December session, the jury met and, having examined the evidence of the debt, determined Jeffrey was owed £17 15s 10d: the value of the note and exactly what he had claimed. This was typical: claim and damages awarded were equal in seven of the fifteen inquiry awards. In another two actions, the difference was a fraction of a penny, and in one more the difference was less than a shilling.

Arbitration

The jury found for Roger Hill when he sued Anne Webb in December 1761. Webb was not prepared to accept this and appealed the case to the Supreme Court of Nova Scotia (the process of appeals will be described in chapter 7). At the Supreme Court in June 1762, their dispute was tried all over again but rather than go to trial before another jury, Webb and Hill agreed to settle their differences through arbitration. On the day of the trial, Chief Justice Belcher, following a motion by Webb and Hill, issued a rule of court to refer the matter to three arbitrators: John Burbidge (Hill's choice), Bartholomew Kneeland (Webb's choice), and George Smith (the court's choice). Belcher ordered the arbitrators to meet, review the evidence, and report back to the court with their award before the end of the Supreme Court's session. When the jury heard the evidence at the Inferior Court, they found that Webb owed Hill what he claimed: £22 7s. While the arbitrators also found that Webb owed Hill money, they were not as accommodating as the jury, reporting to Belcher that they found Hill was owed only £16 10s.

Belcher accepted their award and incorporated it into a judgment of the court, as enforceable as any other judgment.[17]

In both the Inferior Court of Common Pleas and the Supreme Court of Nova Scotia, litigants could elect to refer their disputes to arbitration rather than go through a jury trial. It was a common option: one-tenth of all Inferior Court actions went to arbitration; one-fifth of Supreme Court actions did as well. Arbitration was present right from the beginning of civil justice in Halifax, as the dispute between Elijah Davis and Ephraim Cook described in chapter 2 showed. Although in that case arbitration was likely chosen in part because no civil court yet existed, it had some similarity to the arbitrations that followed. When Governor Cornwallis ordered the arbitration, he backed up his order with the assurance that he would make their award his decision and enforce it accordingly. This enforcement structure essentially remained over the next sixteen years. As in *Webb v. Hill*, arbitration was done under a rule of court. The parties would request it, and the court would order that the issue be turned over to arbitrators who would report their decision back to the court by a certain date, usually before the end of the current session of the court. In most cases, arbitration panels were made up of three men,[18] one appointed by each litigant and one appointed by the court. In a handful of cases, arbitration panels were made up of five arbitrators, and in another handful of cases, the court did not appoint the third, but left this to the other arbitrators. Once the arbitrators reported to the court, it would issue a judgment.

Arbitration ordered through a rule of court in Halifax differed from the arbitration practices in England or other parts of British North America at the time. The Halifax process was significantly easier and less expensive. Opposing litigants went to court only once, to get the arbitration begun. The arbitrators would be appointed in the rule of court and make their report back directly to the court, where it would be made a judgment of the court and enforceable at the end of the court's current session. There are few examples of litigants in Halifax entering into penal bonds for arbitration, and no examples of the other methods of enforcing arbitration found elsewhere at the same time. In England and the colonies, even when statutes provided for alternatives, arbitration was often enforced through penal bonds or other methods of securing performance of the arbitrators' award. In the seventeenth century in England and Virginia, the practice was for parties to agree to arbitration and then enter into penal bonds. The bonds committed each party to pay the other the value of any award in favour of the other.

Failure to pay would be a breach of the bond, which could be enforced for its penal value by a court. The penal value of the bonds was usually set at more than any possible expected award. In England, the courts' enforcement of the bonds was inconsistent, so that in 1697 a statute allowed arbitration to be made a rule of the court. Having reached an agreement as to who would arbitrate, the parties could ask for the rule of the court. If one of the parties failed to live up to the award made, then the other party could ask the court to rule the delinquent party in contempt of court and subject to agreed-upon penalties. The only defence against a contempt motion lay in proving that the arbitrators had been corrupted in reaching their decision. The 1697 statute specified neither who was to appoint the arbitrators nor how many should be appointed. This was left to the parties. The historians of the statute have argued that disputants made limited use of the statute through to the middle of the eighteenth century.[19]

In Connecticut, a new arbitration statute was introduced in 1753. Although it replicated much of the 1697 English statute, the Connecticut one also allowed arbitrators to present their award directly to the County Court, which could then be asked to issue a writ of execution directly. This latter provision seems to have been similar to what occurred in Halifax, but practice in the two colonies differed. Historian Bruce Mann discovered that only two-fifths of commercial arbitration and one-fifth of non-commercial arbitration was performed under a rule of court. The majority was extrajudicial, through bonds or by pledging executions, when both parties would go to court and confess judgments against themselves in favour of the other party for the value in question. If the losing parties failed to fulfil their obligations, the victors could seek execution on the confessed judgment and avoid going back to court.[20]

In the earliest cases of arbitration in Halifax, such as the conflict between Ephraim Cook and Elijah Davis, arbitration was ordered because the arbitrators, as experts, would have had the best capacity to figure out what likely occurred and what the customs of the profession were in like cases. This appears to have remained at the core of the decision to arbitrate. For example, in May 1753 mason William Hunstable and merchant Benjamin Gerrish also chose to go to arbitration rather than trial in a general court appeal of an Inferior Court jury trial. At issue between the two men was an outstanding account for goods that Hunstable had with Gerrish. Hunstable claimed that the value of the account was offset by work he had done for both Gerrish and for Phillip Knaut, who had been ordered to pay Hunstable's fees to Gerrish. Hunstable named fellow mason William Best as his arbitrator, Gerrish selected fellow merchant Samuel Shipton, and the court chose mason Henry Winn. The two masons would have the expertise to evaluate Hunstable's work and determine if he had claimed its value properly. If they agreed, Shipton could be out-voted, but if they disagreed, Shipton could choose to follow the mason who made the best case.

Shortly after the arbitrators were appointed, Gerrish's attorney moved that Henry Winn, the court's appointee, be removed. Winn lived on property owned by Hunstable, and this created a conflict of interest. The court agreed and replaced Winn with William Piggot, a tavern keeper and sometime trader. This shifted the balance in the arbitration panel from one dominated by artisans to one dominated by those in the merchant and trading community. As the sole mason, Best would be able to evaluate Hunstable's work without worrying about a contradictory opinion from another mason. Yet, he could be out-voted by the merchant and sometime trader, who could read the other evidence differently than he would.

The arbitrators made two findings. First they found that Hunstable did owe Gerrish £12 6s 1½d on a debt on account. At the original jury trial, only Gerrish's accounts were considered, and he was awarded £51 11s 7½d in damages. The difference in the awards was the value of work Hunstable had done directly for Gerrish. Second, the arbitrators rejected Hunstable's claim that Gerrish owed him for the Knaut work. Instead, the arbitrators declared that Hunstable could sue Knaut directly for the cost of that work if he had not yet been paid. Unlike the jurors at the first trial, the arbitrators had an opportunity to look at Hunstable's work first-hand. In addition, he submitted to them his own written account of the work, something he had not done for the Inferior Court jury trial.

The specific knowledge that arbitrators brought to both *Hunstable v. Gerrish* and *Webb v. Hill* – masonry in the former case and commerce and accounts in the latter – was important. In some cases, the need for expert knowledge was so apparent that the court ordered it independent of the trial. At the June 1757 session of the Inferior Court, the carpenter William Falkner sued shopkeeper Richard Tritton on account for £21 6d, the cost of a variety of carpentry jobs. The account Falkner sent to the court was broken down by time: for example, for thirty-eight-and-one-quarter-days' work from March 1 to May 17 in 1756, Falkner demanded £7 19s (or 4s 2d a day). The court appointed three carpenters, William Ingolls, Josiah Marshall, and Joseph Wakefield, "to view & survey the Carpenters work Charged by the Pl[t] and audit the Acc[t]."[21] In their report, they detailed the specific work done and its appropriate costs (for example, making a six-panel door, cutting it out, and casing it was worth £1 10s) and came to a total value of £21 6d: the same debt Falkner claimed. Once they had reported to court, a new arbitration panel was appointed to determine what was owed in the end. For the arbitration, Falkner selected Jonathan Harris, a truckman and retailer, while Richard Tritton selected William Best, the mason, and the court selected John Burbidge, another carpenter and a frequent arbitrator (including in the Hill and Webb action at the Supreme Court).[22]

Arbitration was used much more frequently in actions where expert opinion among the decision-makers could be important. For example, debts on notes of hand went to juries in the Inferior Court 16 per cent of the time, less (but not significantly so) than the frequency of jury trials altogether, which was 18 per cent. Debts on notes only went to arbitration 4 per cent of the time, much less frequently than the arbitration rate altogether, or 11 per cent. Notes required little expert evaluation in and of themselves, and so arbitration offered little relief for defendants. Debts on account or for work done, however, could benefit from expertise in evaluating the evidence presented. Deciding on the validity of competing accounts, determining the value of goods and services traded, or evaluating work done were all tasks that could benefit from the expertise of arbitrators. Account actions were more likely to go before a jury than to arbitration, although arbitration was common: 15 per cent of account actions in the Inferior Court went to arbitration, compared with 19 per cent that went to jury trials. In work and wages cases, where expert evaluation of the work completed could be the key to the dispute, arbitrations were more common than jury trials: more than one-third (35 per cent) of such cases went to arbitration in the Inferior Court, while about one-quarter (24 per cent) went to jury trial.

Other disputes between commercial men and women could also be ideal for arbitration. Upon the division of a partnership or the breakdown of some other business arrangement, if one party felt the division of assets and debts to be wrong, he or she could sue the other party and demand a "reasonable account" of the business between them. These actions turned on expectations of good business practice and required the evaluation, at times, of quite complex accounting of transactions. Not only could arbitrators apply expertise with the documents; free from the time pressures of a courtroom, the arbitrators could evaluate the evidence at a determined pace. Of eighteen reasonable account actions, eight (44 per cent) went to arbitration, compared with only four (22 per cent) defaulted and four (22 per cent) sent to a jury. Another one was confessed, and the plaintiff and defendant agreed to have their accounts audited to determine the size of damages. One of the defaulted actions was also audited. The auditing worked in a similar way to arbitration, but the defendant already accepted liability or had been found liable by the court.

Arbitration then had some similarities to the special jury process: experts could be chosen to evaluate special sorts of evidence and apply the general practices of a trade. It gave litigants greater control over the decision-makers in their cases than going to a jury trial did, but that did not ensure a better chance at success.

Jurors and Arbitrators

In jury trials and arbitration, much of the decision-making was taken out of the hands of the litigants or the judges and placed in the hands of the community. This role for community members as jurors was essential to the common law system and the ideology of British justice. The British historian E.P. Thompson described the jury and jurors role thus:

To be a juror is to have thrust upon one a temporary office, to which is attached an inherited weight of rules, practices and expectations; and this weight transforms an office into an imposed (and often internalised) role. The role is exercised for a day, a week, or for three months, and then as suddenly as it was adopted, it falls away once more. Seen in this way, the jury is less an institution than a practice, or a place amidst adjacent judicial practices: a place through which generation after generation flows, inheriting the practices of their forerunners, yet inheriting those with little formal instruction, and practising the role in the light of expectations brought with them into the jury box and shared by the public outside.[23]

This captures both our contemporary notion as well as our historical sense of juries. But regardless of how reflective it may be of the jury experience, as either lived or observed, it does not so clearly capture the experience of being a juror in Halifax in the 1750s and 1760s.[24]

Jurors and arbitrators did not make legal affairs their careers, but they were experienced men.[25] In making their decisions, they drew on their own experiences as people in trades and commerce, and on their prior experiences of serving on juries and panels. Although several individuals served both as jurors and arbitrators, overall the two groups were made up of different people from different backgrounds. This section looks at who served on juries or arbitration panels and how experienced both the individuals and the juries and panels as a whole were.

Jurors

Who could serve as a juror was prescribed in law. At first, Halifax jurors were officially expected to meet the English property qualification of having £10 of freehold property or £20 of leased property. The assembly in 1758, and again in 1759, reduced the qualifications to three months' residency in the colony and either £1 in freehold or £10 in a personal estate (i.e., property in things, not land). Writing about criminal petty juries in Halifax before 1759, Jim Phillips has convincingly argued that "those who actually served appear to have been drawn by lot from a larger list than those qualified."[26] Retroactively determining the property holdings of most individuals in Halifax in the 1750s is almost impossible, but it is clear that the net for trial jurors was cast broadly.

Juries can be divided into five categories: trial juries at the Inferior and Supreme Courts, juries of inquiry, special juries and grand juries at the Supreme Court. Juries of inquiry and special juries were specific to dealing with civil actions; the grand jury served some local governance functions, but was primarily needed for criminal prosecutions (where it would determine at the beginning of a Supreme Court session whether or not to indict each accused). The civil trial juries at the Supreme Court appear to have been drawn from the same venire and pool of sworn jurors as their counterpart petty juries who heard criminal trials at the same court. To the extent that criminal proceedings at the Quarter Sessions that corresponded with the Inferior Court of Common Pleas had juries, it is not clear if they were drawn from the same pool as the Inferior Court jurors, but it is reasonable to assume they were.

Prior to each session of the Inferior and Supreme Courts, the chief judge of the court issued a writ, the venire, to the provost marshal to summon men to appear as jurors. The 1758 jury statute set out the process for determining who would be called: the provost marshal was required to make up a list annually of all the men in the colony who met the new property qualifications. All of the names were placed in a ballot box. Ten days before the opening of a court, the clerk and either the First Justice of the Inferior Court or Chief Justice of the Supreme

Court would draw twenty-four or thirty-six names, respectively, to serve. Those who informed the court they could not serve had their names placed back in the box and replacement names were drawn. Names would be drawn from the box "from Court to Court till the whole number of Freeholders and other Persons qualified ... shall have served."[27] The jurors for individual trials were then selected from those summoned who appeared.

The actual jury venires for the period vary in length. The oldest for the Inferior Court is from 1754, when thirty men were called, and one from September 1755, when thirty-six were called. For the December 1757 Inferior Court, only seventeen men were called. Even after the 1758 statute set specific requirements, the number called could vary. In 1765, thirty-two men were summoned for the February session and twenty-four for each of the June, September, and December sessions.[28] Despite the rule that the ballot box, once filled, was to be drained until it was empty, in practice the provost marshal was commanded to draw up a new list and refill the box every year. This meant that individuals could be called many times, and in fact were. I can identify 772 different people who served on juries between 1750 and 1766. Many jurors served on several trials, making distinct juror appearances over a single court session or several years.

On most venire, there would be comments beside several names, noting they had been excused from service. This could be because they were out of the colony, too ill, or for some other reason accepted by the provost marshal. By the 1760s, a number of those summoned to serve at any session failed to either appear at all or to return to the court after they had first been sworn in as jurors for the session without providing a valid excuse. The judges of the inferior courts, in an effort to ensure attendance, began to initiate actions against these absenting jurors and people listed on the venire who had not attended at all. The 1758 statute provided for a 10s fine for every day missed, or £5 for failing to appear at all during a session. At the March 1762 session, three absent jurors were fined; at the September court, six more were fined; in September 1763, twelve were fined. At the September 1762 session, five of those fined were fined for one day, the sixth for two days. In September 1763, six were fined for ten days each – the £5 maximum – two were fined for nine days, and the remaining four were fined for one, four, five, and six days.[29]

In total, 772 different people served as a juror at least once in the 328 trial, special, and inquiry juries at the Inferior Court of Common Pleas or the Supreme Court. Each of these individuals appeared on one or more juries. To fully understand who served on juries, it is useful to study both the individual jurors and the jury appearances. For example, as table 5.1 shows, less than a third of the individuals who served on a jury only appeared on one jury. More than half of the individual jurors appeared on at least three juries, and many appeared on several more juries. Thus, while 369 individuals served on only one or two juries, they account for only 13 per cent of all juror appearances. At the other end of jury experience, 19 individuals, or 2 per cent of the individual jurors, appeared on 21 or more juries; these 19 people account for 12 per cent of all juror appearances. Overall, this meant that on an average jury, 9 or 10 of the 12 jurors had experience sitting on one or more juries.[30]

Unsurprisingly, the proportion of experienced jurors increased over time. As table 5.2 shows, by the late 1750s, first-time jurors were always less than one-quarter, and usually less than one-fifth, of the jurors appearing that year.

The system encouraged repeat jury service: in a particularly busy session, the jurors summoned could end up sitting on several trials over just a few days. But many jurors had experience over many sessions and several years. Peter Mackey served on fifty-three juries up to 1763, all in the Inferior Court. It appears he served at only one trial each of the first two sessions he served, in September 1753 and March 1755. In June of 1756, he sat as a juror on three trials; then, in 1758 and 1759, his service increased significantly. In both years, he sat on juries at two sessions (something that was, in theory, not supposed to happen). In 1758, between the March and September sessions, he was a juror for nine trials. In 1759, he was a juror at twenty-three trials over two sessions, June and December. He was also plaintiff in a trial heard by a jury in the June session. Mackey sat on the jury in other trials with all of the jurors at his trial – sitting on only three juries with Thomas Heathy that session, but on five juries with James Kidder, foreman of the jury at his trial, and on seven juries with four other jurors at his trial (Richard Knox, Ebenezer Messenger, Jonathan Panier, and Samuel Pearce).[31] Despite the crossover in jurors between his action at the session and the trials he sat on, it does not appear that the jury treated him or his case differently by either favouring or harming him. There is certainly no record of the defendant in this case or litigants in other actions challenging the results because Mackey was both juror and litigant at the session.[32]

Table 5.1: Patterns of jury service: Inferior and Supreme Courts[a]

Number of juror appearances by an individual juror	Number of individual jurors	% of individual jurors	Total number of juror appearances[b]	% of total jurors
1	242	31	242	6
2	127	16	254	7
3	68	9	204	5
4	60	8	240	6
5	45	6	225	6
6	28	4	168	4
7	30	4	210	5
8	21	3	168	4
9	21	3	189	5
10	16	2	160	4
11	16	2	176	5
12	14	2	168	4
13	12	2	156	4
14	11	1	154	4
15	13	2	195	5
16	7	1	112	3
17	7	1	119	3
18	8	1	144	4
19	1	0	19	0
20	6	1	120	3
21	4	1	84	2
22	6	1	132	3
23	4	1	92	2
24	1	0	48	1
26	1	0	26	1
29	1	0	29	1
33	1	0	33	1
51	1	0	51	1
TOTAL 772		100	3,918	100
First-time jurors			−772	
Jurors with experience			3,146	

Proportion of experienced jurors: 3,146/3,918 = 0.803

[a] Experience on a civil trial jury in either common law court would be the same in terms of whether or not the juror brings prior juror experience with him to the decision-making process.

[b] This is equal to the number of juror appearances multiplied by the number of jurors who made that many appearances (column 1 x column 2).

Table 5.2: New jurors and arbitrators

	Jurors			Arbitrators		
Year	Apps[a]	New Jurors[b]	as % of Apps[c]	Apps	New Arbs	as % of Apps
1749	0	0	0	3	3	100
1750	120	36	30	78	40	51
1751	36	24	67	112	29	26
1752	155[d]	73	47	117	30	26
1753	108	66	61	111	28	25
1754	24	15	63	64	13	20
1755	167	59	35	90	22	2
1756	107	29	27	32	2	6
1757	518[e]	71	14	42	4	10
1758	323	43	13	31	7	23
1759	395	49	12	43	4	9
1760	371	51	14	56	16	29
1761	452	78	17	30	5	17
1762	252	23	9	53	5	9
1763	294	62	21	41	6	15
1764	321	57	18	69	11	16
1765	168	11	7	5	0	0
1766	95	11	19	5	1	20
TOTAL	3,906[f]	765		982	226	

[a] "Apps" is appearances, in this case the total number of juror (or arbitrator) appearances per year for which a juror's name is known.
[b] The number of jurors (or arbitrators) appearing for the first time.
[c] First-time jurors (or arbitrators) as a percentage of the total number of juror (or arbitrator) appearances in the year.
[d] The records are not always complete or legible, and so at several times the number of jurors is not divisible by 12.
[e] The jump in the number of appearances reflects a change in the documentary record, from primarily minute books (which did not record juror names) to ephemera.
[f] This number differs from the total number of appearances in table 5.2 because one jury cannot be identified.

Prior experience as a juror had several effects. Experience brought with it an understanding of the process and expectations of what should occur during a trial. John Beattie, in discussing criminal trial juries in England in the eighteenth century, has argued that the effect of experienced jurors on jury deliberations was "surely decisive": "They would be familiar with the variety of verdicts possible under the law

Table 5.3: Individuals as litigants, jurors, and arbitrators in the Inferior or
Superior Court

Role	Individuals n	Litigants n	Litigants %	Also Appearing as Jurors n	Also Appearing as Jurors %	Arbitrators n	Arbitrators %
Litigants	2512			461	18	192	8
Jurors	773	461	60			118	15
Arbitrators	226	192	85	118	52		

and that indeed had to be considered in most cases ... They might get
some help on this matter from the judge, but obviously some familiarity with the complications of the law was an asset that would further
enlarge the influence of some jurors."[33]

Moreover, as the proportion of experienced jurors on a jury increased,
they would be able to pass their own experiences on to the novice jurors, either directly or indirectly, in the way they reacted to the trials
and made their decisions. This could lead to a more nuanced appreciation of the trial, or to rigidity in expectations and decision-making, or
even to boredom with the process. It likely led to all of these in different
combinations in individual jurors. As a whole, though, the experienced
jury pool may have lent significant consistency to the trial process and
outcomes. People engaging in trade needed to have some sense that if a
dispute arose, the rules applied to determining the result would be consistently applied. Having a significant proportion of experienced jurors
on any jury could lead to greater consistency in results, which would
provide that necessary consistency. This in turn could explain why a
much larger proportion of disputes went to jury trial in Halifax than in
other British North American jurisdiction in the eighteenth century.[34]

The jurors were drawn from the local community, from a list of men
who had at least some property. In a sense, these were the same men
who came to court as litigants. As table 5.3 shows, of the 773 different
people identified as jurors, 60 per cent were also litigants at least once.
Even if several people on any one jury of twelve had never before gone
to court, from the beginning it was probable that someone on the jury
had litigation experience, and within just a few years it is likely that every jury had several members who had sued or been sued themselves.
Moreover, the most experienced jurors were often also experienced liti-

gators. Only 49 men accounted for a little more than one-quarter (1,009 or 26 per cent) of all juror appearances. Although 7 of these men never appeared as litigants, 42 of them were litigants in 432 actions, an average of 10 actions a person. Their appearances split relatively evenly between being plaintiff and defendant, with a slight bias to the latter (201 appearances as plaintiff, 231 as defendant).

This trend slightly favouring defendant appearances applies overall: of all jurors, 383 men were defendants at least once, and acted as jurors 2,483 times (an average of 6 appearances each), while 348 men who were plaintiffs at least once acted as jurors 2,300 times (an average of 7 appearances each). Of course, many of these men (270) were both plaintiff and defendant at some time, but 78 jurors appeared only as plaintiff litigants and 113 appeared only as defendants. Sixty per cent of jurors had litigation experience (40 per cent had none) – 35 per cent as both defendants and plaintiffs, 10 per cent as plaintiffs only, and 15 per cent as defendants only. Thus the defendant experience was the most common, including among those who had never sued but had themselves been sued.

As was discussed in chapter 2, defendants were somewhat different from plaintiffs in aggregate: from typically less wealthy occupations and likely of a somewhat lower status than plaintiffs. On average, jurors may, too, have been less wealthy and of lower status than plaintiffs. This can be tested by looking at the occupational data that is available for jurors.

Of the 772 different people who served on a jury in the years 1750–66, 365 can be identified with an occupation by cross-referencing jurors to litigation records. Accounting for repeat service by many of these men, it appears that 63 per cent of all juror appearances were made by people whose occupation can be identified. The five most common occupations for individual jurors were yeoman (66), traders (60), merchants (50), retailers (44), and carpenters (39). Even accepting that the formal qualifications were not enforced in Halifax before 1758, this did not mean that the provost marshal did not try to secure people with property to serve on juries. The rules existed, and while including people in the list with property less than £10 or £20 might have been necessary, including only people with *some* property respected the spirit of the law. There is every reason to believe that the provost marshal accepted the basic ideological premise behind the property qualification: that only those men with property of some value could truly understand and be sympathetic to the questions of debt. Yeomen (as farmers) and traders and merchants (as the likely wealthier group of people involved in commerce) would be most likely to have property and so would most likely be included on a list and then a venire. The inclusion of retailers and carpenters at the end of the list of the top five points to the general make-up of the jury.

It was artisans who ended up serving on juries the most. For example, the 50 merchants who appeared as juror served on 5 juries each (240 juror appearances). By contrast, 16 tailors appeared as jurors on an average of 12 juries. As noted in chapter 2, the most frequent juror, Peter Mackey, was a tailor. Other trades were similarly represented: 9 blacksmiths appeared on an average of 11 juries each (95 appearances total), and 8 coopers appeared on an average of 10 juries each (81 appearances total). Of the 25 men who appeared as jurors most frequently, 18 can be identified with occupations, and 8 of these were artisans. The 39 carpenter-jurors averaged 8 appearances each (297 total). While the merchants averaged only 5 appearances each and traders 6½ appearances each, the 44 lower-status retailers averaged 9 appearances each (381) and the non-commercial yeomen averaged 8 appearances each.[35]

The jury lists were drawn up from property holders, which included men from widely divergent levels of wealth and status. It was those men of lower status and less wealth overall who ended up serving more frequently on juries. These are the same people who more often were defendants than plaintiffs when they came to court.[36]

The second implication of the bias toward defendants as jurors regards decision-making. It is possible that jurors' being in general of lower status and less wealthy than the plaintiffs and often being experienced defendants themselves could mean they were also biased toward, or had greater affinity or empathy for, defendants than plaintiffs in the actions they served in. Even if, individually, some were more likely to picture themselves as the defendant rather than the plaintiff in the actions they saw, it may not have had a significant effect on the jury's decision. The repeated service on the jury likely worked against such developments. This question will be taken up again below, in discussing arbitrators and again, more definitively, in chapter 6.

Arbitrators

Unlike in the case of jurors, there were no statutory restrictions on who could serve as an arbitrator. Arbitrators were selected by the litigants, or the court, because their work or experience made them appropri-

ate to evaluate the questions placed before them, or because their local status commanded the respect expected of someone entrusted to
arbitrate. In theory, the absence of a property qualification would make
the arbitrator pool larger and more democratic than that of jurors. In
practice, the pool of arbitrators was much smaller than the jury pool,
on the whole better off than jurors, with similar repeat appearances by
several arbitrators.

Between 1749 – when Captains Forester, Nevin, and Rous arbitrated
between Elijah Davis and Ephraim Cook – and 1766, 226 different
people acted as arbitrator at least once. Almost half of the men who
were appointed as arbitrators, 108, served as arbitrator only once. At
the same time, two men – one serving 64 times and the other 36 – made
almost as many appearances as arbitrators just between themselves.
Twenty-five arbitrators, serving 11 or more times each, made up half of
all the arbitrator appearances, although they amounted to only 11 per
cent of all of the people who served as arbitrators at least once.

The selection of experienced arbitrators began immediately after the
city's founding: already in 1750, half of the arbitrators selected (38) had
already served as an arbitrator once before in Halifax. Between 1749
and 1755, fewer than 30 per cent of arbitrators were serving for their
first time, and in the next ten years only 15 per cent of arbitrators were
serving for the first time.[37] As table 5.4 shows, the proportion of experienced arbitrators on an average panel was less than the proportion of
experienced jurors, but in effect this meant that most arbitration panels
had at least two, and sometimes all three of the arbitrators had arbitrated in Halifax before.

It is likely that experience played a somewhat different role on the
arbitration panel than on the jury. Like jurors, experienced arbitrators
could help novices around the technical details. Unlike jurors, it is likely
that many arbitrators were chosen because of their experience. Experience was either prized in itself or a sign of some other quality, such as
expertise or status that made the person an ideal arbitrator. In either
case, it was not by the luck of the justice's draw that they were selected
as arbitrators but the active choice of the litigants or the court, which
expected that the experience or the qualities they stood for would lead
to a better decision.

Much like jurors, arbitrators were also litigants themselves: 85 per
cent had already been or would be a litigant by 1766. More than half
would also act as jurors at some time, although 85 per cent of jurors
would never act as arbitrators. The eight men who acted as arbitra-

Table 5.4: Patterns of arbitration service, all civil courts[a]

Number of juror appearances by an individual arbitrator	Number of individual arbitrators	% of individual arbitrators	Total number of arbitrator appearances[b]	% of total arbitrators
1	108	48	108	11
2	30	13	60	6
3	22	10	66	7
4	11	5	44	4
5	8	4	40	4
6	5	2	30	3
7	4	2	28	3
8	5	2	40	4
9	5	2	45	5
10	2	1	20	2
11	4	2	44	4
12	2	1	24	2
13	1	0	13	1
14	1	0	14	1
15	1	0	15	2
16	3	1	48	5
17	2	1	34	3
18	4	2	72	7
20	1	0	20	2
22	1	0	22	2
23	2	1	46	5
27	1	0	27	3
34	1	0	34	3
36	1	0	36	4
64	1	0	64	6
TOTAL	226	100	994	100
			−226	
			768	

Proportion of experienced arbitrators: 768/992 = 0.774

[a] This table includes records for all civil court arbitrations (primarily from the Inferior and Supreme Courts).
[b] This is equal to the number of arbitration appearances multiplied by the number of arbitrators who made that many appearances (column 1 x column 2).

tors in 20 or more actions made 249 appearances as arbitrators (25 per cent of all appearances) and 324 litigation appearances (3 per cent of all litigation appearances). The least experienced litigator among them made only 7 appearances, while half made 25 or more appearances, and the average number of litigation appearances for the eight was 40! Of these litigation appearances, 254 times were as plaintiffs or 78 per cent. The eight arbitrators, however, made only 13 juror appearances, less than two per person. Even more than jurors, arbitrators often had litigation experience themselves, but it was somewhat more likely to be as a plaintiff than as a defendant.[38]

The arbitrators were distinguished by being drawn first from commercial occupations. Fifty-nine men identified as merchants made 573 appearances as arbitrators: 58 per cent of all arbitrator appearances. The three most popular arbitrators were all merchants and men of some standing in the community: Malachy Salter (64), Benjamin Gerrish (36), and Samuel Shipton (34). While 18 of the 25 most used arbitrators were merchants, only 3 were artisans. William Best, a master mason, was an arbitrator 21 times, the most of any artisan. Best was rare for Halifax artisans in being described as a master. The prevalence of merchants among arbitrators is reflective of the merchants' status. Litigants seem to have wanted arbitrators who not only had expertise but also were considered the most successful, the wealthiest, from the highest class.[39]

Arbitrators, Jurors, Litigants

Decisions in civil disputes were made by people who had been or would be litigants themselves. They were making verdicts and awards not for some other group in the community but for people very much like themselves. They had experienced the civil justice system already or could expect to do so in the future. Even when they had not yet been to court as a litigant, the people who came to court were most often their neighbours, their friends, or their acquaintances. Thus, as they made their decisions, they were deciding not about abstract disputes but about real conflicts they had experienced themselves directly or indirectly. The decisions they made had to reflect not some idealized notion of justice, but a very local, concrete sense of justice, the answer to the question, Seeing as I could be in the exact same circumstances, or ones very much like it, what result would I think just?

But while most jurors and arbitrators had experience as litigants, the reverse cannot be said. Only 18 per cent of litigants ever served on a jury, and 8 per cent served as arbitrators. Juries had property qualifications, and arbitrators often had some status in the community; such limits were not placed on litigants themselves. It is true that many litigants would see their friends and compatriots in the jury or be able to ask friends and equals to act as arbitrators, and many litigants who could have served on a jury or been asked to arbitrate simply never were. For many other litigants, however, jurors and arbitrators would have been of an entirely different class from themselves. Halifax was not so large that jurors and arbitrators would be strangers, but they would be people who moved about in different circles, people who employed and sold to litigants but did not socialize with them.

The 56 individuals whose combined litigation experience accounted for a quarter of all litigant appearances were also frequent jurors or arbitrators. Of them, 42 appeared as arbitrators, making a total of 381 (38 per cent) arbitration appearances. Fewer of these most frequent litigants appeared as jurors; the 37 who did made only 241 (6 per cent) appearances as jurors. The frequent arbitrators were much more likely to be litigants, and frequent litigants at that, than the frequent jurors.[40] Those men who accumulated a great deal of juror experience did, nevertheless, have litigation experience themselves, some of it quite substantial. The men most often chosen as arbitrators had most of their litigation experience as plaintiffs, while those men who most often served on juries had more balanced litigation experience but made more defendant appearances. Unsurprisingly, considering the size of Halifax and the ubiquity of going to law, litigants, jurors, and arbitrators came from the same groups of people, but both jurors and arbitrators reflected smaller subsets of the larger litigant community. In the next chapter, the decisions and verdicts they made will be discussed and compared with the outcomes of those actions that ended without trials.

6

Ending the Action

When Roger Hill summoned Anne Webb to the December 1751 session of the Inferior Court of Common Pleas, he demanded £27 in damages. In the declaration and the accounting of the debt he provided the court, he claimed Webb was indebted to him for £22 7s. The jury found for Hill and awarded him £22 7s in damages for the debt he proved. In addition, Webb was taxed £3 15s 3d to cover the costs of the trial, including Hill's lawyer's fees and his share of the judges', clerk's, and marshal's fees in bringing the dispute to trial. This was an unequivocal victory for Hill: Webb was ordered to pay him what he claimed he was owed, as well as the costs he had accrued in getting the case to trial.

Anne Webb appealed, and at the Supreme Court, Hill and Webb opted for arbitration. The arbitrators returned an award for Hill for £16 10s.[1] Webb still owed Hill money and still had to pay his court costs. But, in the end Hill would receive less than three-quarters of what he claimed to be owed and what a jury had found he was due. Hill still received damages for the debt he claimed he was owed, so he was still, on the face of the verdict, victorious. But Webb was ordered to pay him almost £6 less, so she may have benefited from the appeal too.

Who won the second action? In popular discussion of the law today, we are inclined to think about cases as being won or lost. This is, in the end, not particularly helpful in looking at civil disputes in the eighteenth century in Halifax, and probably not of much value generally in thinking about civil disputes. Civil litigation was, and remains, a continuation of market transactions in another forum. Unlike simple sales or work transactions today, where the price of a good or labour time is fixed, all transactions in the eighteenth century were negotiable. The price agreed to at one moment did not necessarily remain the price actually paid: the fact that most transactions began on credit meant that prices in the end could fluctuate based on the purchaser's capacity to pay, the seller's capacity to enforce the original price, and the willingness of the parties to come to continuous agreement on the cash value of labour and goods exchanged. Much of the time, this continuous negotiation would occur outside of the courts. Bringing a dispute to court, however, did not necessarily mean the enforcement of the original bargain. Rather, it meant that bargaining over price and value would occur before others, who would then determine a new, enforceable price, although not necessarily the final paid price, nonetheless.

In the overwhelming majority of actions, judgments and verdicts were entered for the plaintiffs; that is to say, the plaintiffs were awarded some damages. Some defendant victories are easily identified: they won outright when a plaintiff's action was nonsuited, abated, or dismissed, where the jury's verdict was explicitly for the defendant, or where arbitrators awarded nothing to the plaintiff. But when the verdict was for the plaintiff, determining who *actually* won the action requires comparing the difference between the plaintiff demands or claims on the one hand and the damages actually awarded on the other. When damages awarded were significantly different from those claimed, it meant that the plaintiffs did not have sufficient evidence to prove that they were owed all that they asserted. Sometimes defendants did not contest debts outright but replied that they owed something less than was claimed against them. Awards that were close to what the defendant argued, or found some middle ground between defendant and plaintiff claims, need to be interpreted not as victories for plaintiffs but maybe as victories for defendants or something else entirely.

Investigating the differences between claims and damages in light of the type of process and the type of action highlights how the choice of process could shape results. This in turn adds to the argument that the civil courts were an extension of commercial interaction and that litigation arose for a wide variety of reasons, not always conflictual. However, as will also be seen, it is unlikely that defendants always contested a claim with which they disagreed. Any fight to reduce damages, however, came with costs of court, and the middle part of the chapter turns from verdicts to the costs taxed to argue that these had a determinative effect on whether defendants tried to challenge plaintiffs' claims.

The final part of the chapter turns to the methods used to try to enforce judgments once they had been rendered. Having damages awarded was not the same thing as receiving satisfaction, and without collecting the damages awarded, victory was hollow.

Verdicts and Damages

Uncontested Actions

Only two types of uncontested action ended in damage awards: defaults and confessions. Nonsuits, abatements, and dismissals ended in verdicts for the defendant, who would receive no damages, although they would often receive awards for their costs. When an action ended in default, the value of the damages awarded was based on the evidence the plaintiff provided to the court. In debt cases, this was almost always a copy of the account or the promissory note affixed to the summons or declaration or otherwise provided to the court. It was the defendant's responsibility to contest a plaintiff's claims, and so, in defaults before 1764, the awards judges made were usually exactly what the plaintiff claimed, although not always. In almost two-thirds of cases, the awards were equal to the value claimed, and in 80 per cent of defaults where the claim and damages award are known, the award was equal to the plaintiff's claim or within 6 pence of the claim (see table 6.1). The introduction of the jury of inquiry in 1764 appears to have changed this. It appears that in fewer than half of cases were awards equal to the claim, and in only two-thirds of the actions were awards within even 1 pound of the claim. The jury of inquiry changed the very nature of the default, effectively making it like a trial even if the evidence presented to the jury was limited.

In a relatively simple case, the Halifax merchant Brook Watson sued the mariner John Rockett of Louisburg for debts owed to Watson and his now deceased partner John Slayter. Watson and Slayter had provided Rockett with trade goods worth more than £2,000 beginning in March of 1762. Over the following years, trade goods and money traded hands, but by the spring of 1766 some £65 13s 1¾d was still owed. The first writ, for the June court, was returned with the defendant not found. A second, issued in June was returned noting that the defendant was now in custody in Louisburg. Rockett defaulted at the December Inferior Court and turned the matter of damages over to a jury of inquiry that would meet in George Vanputt's house on December 16. At the inquiry, the provost marshal effectively acted as foreman

Table 6.1: Relationship between damages and claims by process

			Damages in relation to claim						
	Damages as a		Equal		Within 6d[b]			Within £1	
Process	% of claims[a]	Number of actions	n	%	n	%	n	%
Default	95	577	377	65	454	79	499	86
Inquiry	92	13	6	46	8	62	9	69
Confession	91	144	83	58	96	67	109	76
Jury[c]	75	247	80	32	106	43	129	52
Arbitration	48	173	16	9	18	10	30	17

[a] The mean of each action's damage award as a per cent of the claim made.
[b] This is cumulative, including all those already accounted in the pair of columns to the left.
[c] This includes special juries.

to the jury of twelve men, including the host George Vanputt. They evaluated Watson's accounts and issued a finding that the damages owed Watson were £65 13s 1¾d, exactly what he had claimed.[2]

A year earlier, the merchant Michael Franklin sued James Stirling, fisherman, shoreman,[3] and trader at Canso, Nova Scotia, for a debt £695 3s 5½d. The debt was owed for "sundry stores &c. for the fishery," which Stirling promised in writing to repay. When the action first came to the Inferior Court in December of 1765, Stirling's lawyer, William Nesbitt, sought a continuance so he could imparle, that is negotiate, with Franklin. This was granted, but nothing came of it. When the court heard the action again in March of 1766, Nesbitt offered "Nothing to Bar or to Obstruct the action," and so judgment was made against his client in default.[4]

The court ordered a jury of inquiry to investigate the damages. The note was presented, and this, in most cases, would have been proof positive of a debt to the value claimed. In this case, however, the inquisition was provided with Franklin's accounts as well. At the bottom of one of the accounts, but not noted on the promissory note itself was the comment, "to his credit on his note of hand dat^d 26th Decr 1764 for £695.3.5 ½ £104. 4. 9." Taking all of the evidence together, the jury found that Stirling owed Franklin £590 18s 8½d.[5] Although it is possible that the judges would have found for the same amount if this case had come before the development of the jury of inquiry, clearly one of the roles of the jury was to properly investigate all of the evidence available. For some defendants who did not dispute the debt but disputed the value claimed, the jury of inquiry shifted the focus from the trial to the inquisition, where evidence could be presented and interrogated but matters relating to the actual existence of liability could be ignored.[6]

Unlike in the case of defaults, when defendants confessed, they had some power to determine the damages to be awarded against them. It appears that plaintiffs had to agree to the value confessed, so defendants could not confess to only a nominal debt. The confessed debt was likely the result of negotiations, and failed negotiations could lead to a trial or arbitration instead. The patterns of confession awards were not very different from those of defaults: most defendants confessed to the plaintiff's claim, as table 6.1 shows, yet some confessions were for significantly less than the claimed debt.[7] For example, when Nathan Nathans confessed to a debt of £106 14s 3d owed to Mathias Van Aelslyn and Judha Hayes for a debt on a penal bond discussed in chapter 4, Van Aelslyn and Hayes claimed £254 15s 2d, the penal value for

Nathans's failure to pay the bond on time. Nathans confessed to all he owed on his original debt but not the penal value of his bond with the New York merchants, and they agreed. The core concern for creditors was repayment of the specific debt. The penalty in the bond was to encourage payment, and when Nathans made a serious effort to repay on a schedule, Van Aelslyn and Hayes would have been willing to accept the confession and would have had little desire to enforce the bond to its full value.

Contested Actions

Jury trials and arbitrations both routinely ended with damage awards. As with defaults and confessions, awards could be equal to what the plaintiff claimed, but, as table 6.1 shows, in practice both juries and arbitrators routinely deviated more consistently from plaintiff claims. This is, of course, to be expected: the very nature of a contested action means that there were different positions in dispute. John Beattie, in studying the eighteenth-century criminal trial in England, drew historians' attention to partial verdicts, where juries would find defendants guilty of lesser offences than those charged. Partial verdicts saved many an accused from death while punishing them nonetheless.[8] In determining simultaneously if a litigant was at fault and what the damages owed should be, civil juries and arbitrators had powers analogous to their contemporary criminal juries' partial verdicts. The patterns in assessing damages differ considerably between jury trials and arbitrations. The patterns themselves can be explained by what sorts of disputes went to each, the methods of determination, and the people who acted as jurors and arbitrators.

JURY TRIALS

When Roger Hill and Anne Webb took their dispute before a jury at the Inferior Court, the jury awarded Hill exactly what he claimed he was owed. In just less than a third of actions did juries award what was demanded. For debt actions, like the dispute between Hill and Webb, juries were often more likely to award the plaintiffs' claims, but not by much. As table 6.2 shows, only 37 per cent of awards in debt on account trials were equal to the claim, and only 45 per cent were within 6 pence or 1 pound. Nevertheless, half of all jury awards in debt on account actions were equal to at least 98 per cent of the claim, even though in more than half of jury awards on debts, the awards were more than a

Table 6.2: Jury trials of debt awards in relation to claims

	Number of actions	Aggregate awards[a]		Equal		Within 6d		Within £1	
		Avg %	Median %	n	%	n	%	n	%
Account	78	78	98	27	37	33	45	33	45
Note	29	107	100	15	52	18	62	19	66
Work and Wages	13	57	63	2	17	3	25	3	25

[a] The mean or median award as a percentage of its claim. 100 is equal to claim.

pound different from the claim. In other words, while juries frequently deviated from the claims plaintiffs made, the final awards for half of them were not significantly less than the claim. In debts on notes, juries were less likely to deviate from the claim: in more than half, they awarded what was claimed. The note was evidence of a debt for a specific value and a promise to pay, and it was significantly more different for defendants to call into question the claim or produce contrary evidence. In contrast, for debts for work or wages, juries were positively inclined to significantly discount the claimed debt. Although there are only thirteen cases where claims and awards are known for work and wages cases, the differences between these cases and other debt cases are so stark they demand some analysis. Of the thirteen cases, in only two were the awards equal to the claims, and in only one more was the award within 6 pence. In the other ten cases, the award was at least a pound different, in fact less, than the claim. The median award was for less than two-thirds of the claim, and the average award was even less.

For debts on accounts and for work or wages, defendants could expect to discount the claims. Table 4.2 shows that only 13 per cent of note actions went to jury trial, compared to 19 per cent of account debts and 24 per cent of work and wages suits. The pattern of damage awards for the plaintiffs corresponds with this trend: note cases where defendants might be required to pay more and had little success in discounting went to trial least often. Work and wage debts, where defendants could on average get the greatest discount, were most likely of debt actions to go to trial.

Other sorts of disputes were more likely to go to a jury, especially actions for defamation and assault. There are two explanations for these actions going to trial. First, the very personal and subjective nature of the wrongs in question meant that the parties likely had significant differences in opinion about what happened, differences that needed to be aired in a trial or arbitration. Second, because of the sort of evidence provided and the nature of the demands for damages made (see chapter 3 of this book), decision-makers had much greater leeway in determining damages than in debt cases. Defendants in these sorts of actions were very successful in reducing damage awards from the value demanded.

As noted in chapter 3, damage demands in defamation suits were often very high: £50, £100, even £500. The damages that juries granted were always lower, usually substantially lower (in one case, the jury awarded the plaintiff only 1 shilling in damages). In the ten defamation actions at the Inferior Court where both the demand and the jury's award are known, the median demand was £500, while the median award was only £12 10s, and the two largest awards were £100. The awards were on average only 9 per cent of the value of the demands, and no award was more than 20 per cent of the demand. The differences for assault actions where demand and award are known were significant but not quite as stark: awards were, on average, 19 per cent of the demand, and in all but one case the award was less than 25 per cent of the demand.[9] Juries were reluctant to award all the damages claimed in disputes where the harm done could be difficult to clearly quantify, a tendency on the part of plaintiffs in defamation and assault cases to inflate their demands, or a pas de deux as plaintiffs demanded excessive damages, knowing that the jury would reduce, and the jury reduced damages in awards, knowing that plaintiffs inflated demands.

In some of these suits, juries were prepared to grant significant damage awards to plaintiffs. The defamation action *Leigh v. Jones*, where Joseph Jones was accused of defaming Benjamin Leigh to one of the latter's Virginia clients, was described in chapter 5. Leigh demanded £500 in damages. As the evidence at trial showed, Leigh was not actually harmed by Jones's defamation, but such defamation *could* cause serious economic hardship to Halifax merchants like Leigh. Jones's comments not only defamed Leigh, but they could have cast a bad light on the Halifax merchant community as a whole. The case was tried twice before juries: at the Inferior Court and on appeal at the Supreme Court. The jury at the Inferior Court awarded Leigh £100; at the Supreme Court, the jury awarded £300. These damages did not so much compensate Leigh for a real loss as they punished Jones for his words and warned others in the community against trying something similar.

In other cases, juries were reluctant to award any damages, even if the facts showed that the plaintiff had been defamed. The tavern keeper and wharf owner James Quin was sued by Richard Gibbons, Junior, for an incident in the summer of 1763. In his capacity as proctor of the Court of Vice Admiralty, Gibbons and his father, the deputy provost marshal, had gone to Quin's tavern to demand money that the Court of Vice Admiralty had ordered Quin to pay Gibbons Junior as part of a protracted dispute over the schooner *Seaflower*. Gibbons claimed that ,instead of turning over the money, Quin had berated him in front of several bystanders, saying, "Law you ... do not know Law you ... do not know the meaning of the word Law[.] It is Your ... profession is it[?] Oh,

I wish you ... Joy of your ... profession." This public calling into question of his capability as a lawyer, Gibbons averred, had done serious harm to his ability to make a living. Gibbons Junior asserted that his reputation had been so badly tarnished by Quin's outburst that he was no longer able to profitably practise law in Halifax.

Quin was clearly as angry with Gibbons. He explained how angered he was by the disservice the Gibbons had done to him by coming to collect from him during the dinner hour. Quin claimed he felt "provoked ... to ask [Gibbons] whether he thought such proceedings were Lawful[.] He said Yes[.] I then asked him whether he understood the word Law, he said Yes[.] I then pulle'd of[f] my Hatt and said y^r Servant Mr Lawyer[,] did you receive your Education at the Temple[?]"

Although Quin and Gibbons remembered the exchange differently, in both accounts Quin clearly was disputing Gibbons's ability as a lawyer. Quin's own recollection is, if anything, more defamatory in its wit: Gibbons, like that other lawyers in Halifax, clearly had not trained at any of the Inns of Court (of which, in the eighteenth century as now, the Inner and Middle Temples were among the most famous).

The action finally went before a jury in the autumn session of the Inferior Court in 1764. The jury returned a verdict for Gibbons, finding that Quin had defamed him. Gibbons had demanded £100 in damages; the jury awarded him 1 shilling (the equivalent of receiving a nickel in damages in a suit for $100).[10] Although the jury found that Quin's words were, in their content defaming, their token damages suggested they found that neither did the words do Gibbons any direct damage nor did such talk offer a threat to the economy more generally.

Despite the caution above against easily assigning winners and losers in these cases, some plaintiffs did suffer complete losses at the hands of juries. Juries did find outright for the defendant more often than either judges or arbitrators did. This was especially the case for special juries: of the 25 special jury trials where the verdict is known, 9 (36 per cent) verdicts were for the plaintiff. Regular trials juries found for defendants in almost a quarter of cases, 124 of 540 (23 per cent). In certain types of actions, juries were more willing to find for the defendant outright as well: 13 of 41 (32 per cent) ejectment actions and 8 of 35 (23 per cent) assault actions ended with verdicts for the defendant. These disputes were particularly likely to turn on competing accounts that were irreconcilable and open to vexatious suits. It is perhaps, then, not surprising to see significant defendant victory in these sorts of cases.

When juries found for defendants, often the evidence of the matters in dispute was open to interpretation. For example, in 1762 the shop-keeper Joseph Jones sued Joshua Mauger for a debt from a lengthy account dating from May 1751 to July 1760. Jones claimed a debt of £40 14s 5d and produced a note of hand from Mauger for an additional £9 3s. At trial, Mauger presented an account showing Jones as owing him £52 2s 9d. Sorting through these competing accounts and the oral evidence given to explain them, the jury returned a verdict, "We finde for the Def[t] his costs."[11] When evidence presented competing versions of the truth, juries could find some middle ground, or, as in this case, they could find completely for one party or the other.[12]

In other cases, the litigation appears to have been vexatious. At the June 1761 session of the Inferior Court, Patrick Kennedy, a truck-man and labourer, sued William Easton, a fishculler and trader, for a debt on account for the remaining value of a contract to haul wood from a lot inland to the shore in late fall and early winter 1760. Easton defaulted. At the same session, however, with writs dated after the March 1761 writ Kennedy had taken out to sue Easton, Easton and the merchant William McGee both sued Kennedy. Easton sued Kennedy for breach of contract, asserting that he had contracted with Kennedy to bring some 285 cord of wood from land called "McGee's Lott" down to the shoreline in the previous fall and early winter. Easton claimed damages of £145. At trial, Kennedy presented evidence that he was to be paid 30 pence a cord, or £35 12s 6d in total. In February of 1761 he received £22 from Easton and the purser for the commodore in Hali-fax. McGee sued Kennedy for trespass, claiming that Kennedy had cut down and sold 55 cord of wood from McGee's land near Dartmouth on the eastern side of the harbour. McGee claimed damages of £10 6¼s. Other than evidence showing the original grant of land to McGee, nothing from this trial remains. In both cases, however, the jury found for Kennedy.[13]

Although plaintiffs fared better when actions ended in default or with a confession, in most cases juries were prepared to accept the plaintiff's position despite the defendant presumably mounting a de-fence. In debt cases, particularly debts by notes, but even on account, plaintiffs received awards from juries that matched their claims. Rather than being a source of instability, for most plaintiffs a jury trial led to the same or almost the same result as if the defendants had not de-fended themselves. Juries seem, on the whole, to have been more sym-pathetic to plaintiffs than defendants.

ARBITRATION

Arbitration awards were the most likely to diverge substantially from plaintiffs' claims: fewer than one-fifth of arbitration awards were within even 1 pound of the claim, while the average award was less than half of the claim. This suggests that defendants had the greatest success in arbitration, which in turn raises the question of why plaintiffs would accept arbitration as an option at all.

Arbitration was most preferred in cases of debts on account or for work and wages. In many of these cases, the litigants would present opposing accounts of what was exchanged and what the value of the exchange was. Arbitrators, like jurors, would then compare and evaluate the evidence. Unlike jurors, arbitrators were often all drawn from trading professions or the artisanal class directly involved in the dispute. The arbitrators also had much more time to interrogate the evidence: days or weeks rather than the minutes jurors frequently had.

The action between Roger Hill and Anne Webb which opened both this chapter and chapter 5 is a good example of this process. When the jury heard the action in the Inferior Court of Common Pleas, it found that Webb owed Hill what he claimed and what the account he provided appeared to show. Webb appealed the verdict, and at the Supreme Court of Nova Scotia, they decided to refer the dispute to arbitration. The arbitrators still found that Webb owed Hill, but they found she owed him £6 less than the jury had found and what Hill had claimed.

Of 105 actions sent to arbitration where records include both claims and awards, 87 were for debts of one sort or another, and 71 were for account debts in particular. Of those, only 7 arbitration awards were equal to the claim, and only 15 awards were within £1. On average, the awards arbitrators gave for accounts debts were less than half the value of the claim (46 per cent, with a median of 53 per cent). Workers and artisans did only slightly worse as plaintiffs in arbitration for their work or wages (awards in these 13 cases were on average 45 per cent of the claim with a median of 52 per cent). As table 6.1 showed, this was the general trend.

Although defendants controlled whether or not an action would be contested or not, parties were required to agree to go arbitration. If plaintiffs did better on average in jury trials over arbitration, why then were they willing to refer disputes to arbitrators? In situations where the plaintiff had a clear claim, as in a note debt or in many account debts, most defendants did not contest the action. Although a few defendants contested to delay debt collection, most appear to have done so because there was a real disagreement between the parties over whether the plaintiff had any legitimate case or if the defendant owed as much as the plaintiff claimed. *Hunstable v. Gerrish*, described in chapter 5, arose over a conflict between a mason and merchant over each man's account with the other. Arbitration offered a chance to have third parties, who could understand the documents and the value of goods, labour, and construction exchanged or done, review everything and try to sort out who was correct or what middle ground would appear best. If litigation was not necessarily a zero-sum conflict with winners and losers but a continuation of the market, then choosing arbitration could make sense even for plaintiffs who stood to likely receive awards significantly less than their claims. In commercial disputes, plaintiffs launched actions because they needed some greater security that they would be paid. In disputes like *Hunstable v. Gerrish* or *Hill v. Webb*, this could simply mean that without interference from a jury or arbitrator, the parties would be unable to agree on who owed what to whom.

DISPUTES OVER VERDICTS AND AWARDS

Having juries or arbitrators resolve disputes, however, meant doing this under the supervision of a bench, which would hear the same evidence at trial or see at least some of it before arbitration. Judges almost always accepted what the juries and arbitrators ordered, but not always. Even in these rare cases, however, juries and arbitrators were reluctant to change their minds.

In a 1752 action, John Webb and Robert Ewer sued John Franks for £403 12s 2¾d to balance a trading account. The account was for a wide number of goods in wholesale volumes: for example, six striped waistcoats and breeches for 8s 3d each, twenty-five white shirts for 5s each, and 55 pounds of tea for 4s 6d a pound. Franks appears to have attempted to repay the debt several times: by conveying a piece of land to Webb and Ewer, then by returning a significant amount of tobacco they had previously sold to him. At trial at the Inferior Court, the jury returned a verdict for Franks, ordering Webb and Ewer to pay costs. The clerk then recorded the following: "The Court was of Opinion that the Verdict was Contrary to Law, and the Evidence given them, and ordered the Jury to reconsider the Case again, the Jury Inclosed, and in a Short time returned and brought in their Verdict as formerly, the Court Passed Judgment for the Defendant."[14] Required to reconsider, the jury did – and repeated its verdict. This time, the court accepted the verdict and made it the court's judgment. Webb and Ewer appealed and won at the Supreme Court.

Arbitration under a rule of court meant that the litigants knew that any award could be enforced like any judgment. The award had to be acceptable to the judges, but judges almost never rejected a proffered award. In the 1761 defamation action *Heffernan v. Murray*, the Inferior Court judges refused to accept the arbitrators' initial award. Scrivener, trader, and self-described gentleman Daniel Heffernan sued Garret Murray for £50 for defamation, claiming Murray had told two merchants, "Daniel Heffernan is a Rogue a Thief and had Stole his [Murray's] wood ... and that ... Daniel Heffernan kept or Hired people to Steal Wood and take other peoples Wood where ever they could find it." The arbitrators' first award was unique: "We the Subscribers do hereby award that the Defendant Garrot Murry [sic] at a proper time in presence of Jonathan Gifford and James Creighton and others before whom the Slanders ... were expressed; shall make a public acknowledgment of his fault and pay Costs of Court." The public apology was not a common feature of Halifax civil practice at the time. The court refused to accept the award, returning it to the arbitrators with the instruction to reconsider and return a new award to the court at the next session. There is no written document remaining that explains the court's problem with the award. The new award, when presented, was virtually the same, calling once again for a public apology in front of the people to whom Murray had first slandered Heffernan. The only difference was in the costs: now each party would be required to pay his own costs. The judges accepted this award.[15] Heffernan received only the apology: he received no monetary damages, and more importantly, was left responsible for his own portion of the cost of litigation.

Costs

Eighteenth-century courts, although created by the government to serve the needs of the colonists, were effectively paid for by user fees. At every court, fees were attached to every piece of paper filed, signed, or processed, as well as to the tasks and appearances of marshals, criers, clerks, jurors, judges, arbitrators, and witnesses. At the Inferior Court of Common Pleas, litigants paid their own fees along the way to judgment, but usually one party was made liable for all costs in the end and charged with reimbursing the opponent. The decision-maker, judge, jury, or arbitrators assigned who would be liable for costs as part of the verdict, award, or judgment. In most cases, the putative loser was made responsible for the victor's court costs. A plaintiff claiming £50 who was awarded only £1 in damages or who was awarded £50 would still, in most cases, receive costs.[16] The burden of potential costs could play an important role in any litigant's decision to initiate an action or to default or defend against an action.

Costs for all of the actions with verdicts or decisions rendered at a session were taxed by the court clerk at the end of that session. The bill of costs would list each item that would have to be reimbursed along with the fee. Most of the bill would include only the opponents' costs, as most of the fees owed by the litigants being taxed would have been paid as the tasks or stages were done, and the payment of the litigants' own lawyer's fees would be a matter between litigant and lawyer. The value of each element was assigned by the governor and council at first, and then by the elected House of Assembly.

The value of the costs assigned would depend on the way the action was resolved and, to a degree, on who was the nominal victor.[17] Table 6.3 shows the differences in average, median, minimum, and maximum costs based on specific processes at the Inferior Court. Unsurprisingly, costs were lower on actions that did not go to trial than on those that did. Costs taxed in withdrawals, abatements, confessions, and defaults all averaged at less than 2 pounds an action. The means for all four of these categories were as much as one-quarter pound higher than the median cost awards: while there were high outlier cost awards, for all four, the costs in half or more of cases were close to 1 pound. Additionally, withdrawal and abatement costs were so much lower than confessions and defaults because defendants typically received costs in these cases, and their personal outlays to the courts up to this point would be somewhat lower than the plaintiffs'. Defaults and confessions, where plaintiffs usually received costs, had higher costs awards, as would be expected, considering the paperwork the plaintiffs had to use to introduce litigation.

Costs in arbitrations, and jury and special jury trials were higher, averaging between 2 and 3¼ pounds; while costs assigned when a jury of inquiry was used were significantly higher, with both average and median around 8 pounds. It should not be surprising that costs for jury trials and arbitrations should have been substantially more expensive: each involved more than just sittings of the court, and there were many more people to pay. The very high costs of the jury of inquiry are the most important outlier here. Based on costs, the inquiry should have

Table 6.3: Costs in the Inferior Court of Common Pleas

Process	n	Mean	Median	Minimum[a]	Maximum[b]
Withdrawal	18	1/1/4	0/15/3	0/7/4	4/12/5
Abatement	16	1/5/2½	0/9/6	0/9/0	7/14/9
Confession	206	1/6/5½	1/2/4	0/12/9	8/8/2
Default[18]	802	1/9/4	1/2/0	0/12/9	7/14/9
Arbitration	150	2/2/6½	1/14/7	0/5/0	11/17/10
Jury trial	289	2/8/0½	1/19/4	0/1/0	9/19/9
Special jury	11	3/5/6¾	2/1/5	0/11/0	14/2/0
Inquiry	11	8/2/9¾	7/19/10	6/17/5	10/1/2

[a] These are usually set by an action where the plaintiff was assigned the defendant's costs.
[b] In some actions, multiple processes would be initiated before the final resolution (for example, a jury might be impanelled and then the action withdrawn).

radically altered the landscape of civil justice by making defaults suddenly significantly more expensive than any other process. The precipitous decline in records for the Inferior Court just after their introduction does not make it possible to test if the introduction of the inquiry significantly altered defendant behaviour, leading, for example, to many more confessions of debt or more reliance on summary proceedings. It would not be surprising if it did.

There were cases where the litigants would be responsible for their own costs or where the putative winner was assigned to cover the loser's costs. The examples of *Heffernan v. Murray*, where each party paid his own costs, or *Gibbons v. Quin*, where the "victorious" plaintiff had the defendant's costs assigned to him, were unusual. In these cases, it appears the decision-makers were making cost orders to reflect their opinion about the matter as litigation and penalizing plaintiffs for whom they had no sympathy.

Assigned court costs did not cover the full cost of litigation. Lawyers could charge more for their work. In 1763, Daniel Wood sued Daniel Heffernan for his legal fees accrued over several years. Wood's account shows, for example, that the lawyer demanded a 10-shilling retainer simply to take up an action, and then charged fees for every stage.[19]

It would be unsurprising for litigants to make decisions that were at least to a degree affected by the cost of litigation. A defendant facing a small claim might see no value in paying the cost of a lawyer and arguing the matter, even if the claim was for more than the defendant actually believed was owed. As the value of the claim increased, however, the relative value of the costs would diminish, making litigation more and more sensible. As argued in chapter 4, the threshold seems to have been claims of £20 or more. Nevertheless, the effect of costs at the Inferior Court in Halifax was likely similar to that described by John Dickinson in writing about civil courts in New France in the eighteenth century: "Although most suits could cause temporary financial difficulties for a peasant or an artisan, they were not out of reach, and it would seem to be an exaggeration to say that they were ruinous. For a merchant, the outlay of capital would not be of great concern."[20]

Satisfaction

Plaintiffs began legal actions because they had some debt that needed to be repaid, some injury that needed to be remedied. In other words, plaintiffs needed satisfaction. In some cases satisfaction could be an apology or some other act taken by the defendant. For most plaintiffs, however, satisfaction would mean being paid money. Victorious defendants at least desired satisfaction of their costs. The Inferior Court of Common Pleas in Halifax had a system of ensuring satisfaction was made. The court could issue writs of execution demanding payment. If those failed, litigants could initiate the new action of *scire facias* or seek enforcement of an execution through imprisonment or sale of the losers' property.

Execution

The process of getting payment was called execution. After litigants received judgments in their favour and costs had been taxed at the end of the session, the litigants could ask the clerk and chief judge of the court to issue a writ of execution. The writ commanded the provost marshal or his deputy to find the named party and to demand and collect the awarded damages, court costs, and the clerk's and marshal's fees for service of the writ. The writ would have a return date, usually immediately before the next session of the court, and the marshal was expected to attempt to serve the writ and then return it to the court before or on the return date. When returning the writ, the marshal would record whether any payment had been made, and if so, how much and when.

If a writ was returned unsatisfied or only partially satisfied, the litigant could ask for a second or additional writ(s). Each new writ (sometimes called an alias) was similar in language, form, and rules to the original, but only for the value outstanding, as well as any new execution fees charged by the marshal and clerk. Multiple writs were often necessary to get some satisfaction. For a majority of actions only one writ remains in the record. Nevertheless, in half of the actions where writs of execution exist, there is no record of any satisfaction being made. This could mean any of three things: that a significant number of writs of execution no longer exist, and satisfaction was made in a greater percentage of cases; that a great number of actions were satisfied without resort to executions; and that many times, successful litigants were never able to collect on their awards. It is likely that each of these explain some of what occurred.

Scire Facias

In chapter 3, Anne Webb's action against William Fury in November 1761 was introduced, and in chapter 4, Fury's default was discussed. Fury's default may have signalled to Webb that he did not contest her claim. It turned out to also show that he had no intention or perhaps no ability to repay her. Fifteen months later, in February 1763, Webb returned to the Inferior Court and took out a new writ against Fury, a writ of *scire facias*.

The writ of *scire facias* demanded that defendants appear in court and show why the court should not issue of writ of execution against them for an earlier judgment. If the defendants could prove no cause, then the plaintiffs would have a new judgment for the total damages and costs of the original judgment and the costs for the new action. Between 1750 and 1766, forty-five writs of *scire facias* were issued by the Inferior Court of Common Pleas.[21]

Fury defaulted on Webb's *scire facias*, just as he had originally. This was common: of the thirty *scire facias* actions where the process to judgment is known, twenty-nine ended by default. If the plaintiff could prove the earlier judgment, there was very little defendants could do to mount a defence.

Scire facias had a very specific purpose: the one time an action went to trial, the plaintiff was attempting to use the writ to enforce provisions in a bail bond. The value of the bond, £130 for each of the two defendants, was significantly greater than the £40 debt it secured. The jury found for the defendants, either because they felt the claimed damages were disproportionate to the actual damages owed the plaintiff, or because they found (or had been directed to find) that the requirements of the writ were not made out because there was no prior judgment on the bond.[22]

No records remain showing if William Fury satisfied Anne Webb's *scire facias* judgment. Writs of *scire facias* were issued because a person had, to date, been unwilling or unable to make satisfaction. For litigants already willing to ignore a court order on the original action, the *scire facias* offered little added incentive, while increasing the total owed by adding more in court costs. The writ may have been used to revive old judgments that had not been executed earlier, but there is no evidence, outside of the use of the writ, to show that the Halifax courts placed time limits on the enforcement of judgments.

Sales of Property

When the deputy provost marshal received a writ of execution, he was given the power to sell the property of the person upon whom he served the writ. After at least sixty-five Inferior Court actions, the provost marshal held a sale of property to secure payment.

Ephraim Cook had legal troubles throughout the early 1750s. In 1750, Stephen Theodore Janssen of London was already in correspondence with the Board of Trade concerning his claims against Cook and his schooner, the *Baltimore*.[23] In June of 1755, Janssen came to Halifax with the intention of collecting on debts Cook owed to both Janssen and several other creditors. Janssen initiated an action for the incredible (in Halifax) sum of £8,000. Cook lost.[24] At the same time as Janssen's suit, and probably prompted by fears that if successful, Janssen would clear out all of Cook's assets, four local litigants also initiated actions against Cook.[25] Cook lost all of the actions against him: in total the judgments against him added up to £8,401 1s 3d, including the full £8,000 claimed by Janssen.

On 2 September 1755, deputy provost marshal Richard Gibbons held a public auction in Halifax to sell some of Cook's personal property to cover the various debts. The total value of this sale was £2,342 1s 5¼d. This fully satisfied three of the June actions against Cook and left John Baxter due £38 13s 2d and Janssen due £6,020 6s 7¾d. On 23 October 1755, a second auction was held in Lunenburg, collecting £1,000. At another auction recorded on the same writ, Cook's slave Edward and other property were sold for an additional £327. A third writ issued 27 December 1755 led to another sale in Lunenburg of spades, pots, saws, and similar goods, for £31 1s 1d. Six months later, in July 1756, a fourth writ was issued for £4,694 4s 10d. This writ was returned *non est inventus*, meaning that neither Cook nor his property could be found by the provost marshal. A final writ issued 12 November 1756 was also returned unsatisfied, with the note that neither Cook nor any of his property could be found. No further attempt was made to collect.

Janssen's attempt at satisfaction was only partially successful. By the time Cook disappeared from the colony, Janssen had collected about £3,000, less than half his £8,000 damages. Cook's local creditors who were successful in June 1755 completely collected on their debts. It is not clear why the money collected from the sales was divided as it was. In cases with multiple creditors, the order of satisfaction may have been by some lawful sequence of creditor entitlements, but none is specifically identified in the documents. In Virginia in the eighteenth century, debts held by people who resided outside of the colony were satisfied only after debts made to Virginians and claimed within a year had been satisfied.[26] Considering how Nesbitt was frozen out of the division of the returns from the sales and how both local John Baxter and from-away Janssen received money from the proceeds of the first auction, it does not appear that this rule transferred to Halifax.

In some cases, sales of property did not even partially satisfy claimants. In 1755, William Piggot lost to plaintiff Silvanus Cobb at the Inferior Court and lost again on an appeal to the September Supreme Court. Cobb was awarded £45 14s 2d in damages and costs of £2 16s 4d by the Supreme Court. The first execution of 9 February 1756 was returned unsatisfied. A second was issued on 16 October 1756. When he returned the writ ten days later, William Foye the provost marshal noted, "By Virtue of this writ I took a house & Land Shown me by the Defendant to be his Estate which I exposed to Sale at publick Auction and as no purchaser appeared I Return this Execution in no part satisfied."[27]

When William Hunstable, a Halifax bricklayer, lost his appeal against New England trader David Gleason, his house was put up for auction. No one appeared to bid, so the execution also remained unsatisfied. A second execution was issued, and the deputy provost marshal attempted to imprison Hunstable, but "he made a forceable Escape from me and I have not been able to take him or find out where he is Ever since."[28] Failed auctions might have reflected a lack of interest in the property. It is also possible that in some cases other Haligonians chose, or were convinced, not to purchase the property put on sale, either to spite the claimant or to assist the defendant. In any case, unless they were prepared to bid for the property themselves, claimants could not guarantee that public auction would secure them full, or even partial, satisfaction.

The failed sales of Piggot's and Hunstable's property were special for another reason: in both cases, their homes were put up for sale. The apparently easy recourse to selling real property for the satisfaction of an execution was peculiar to Halifax in the mid-eighteenth century, at least in comparison with other parts of the common law world. In 1732, the English Parliament had made the selling of property to settle debts available in the colonies, although limiting execution against real property to the same as applied to specialty debts in England.[29] Bruce Mann has argued that in the Thirteen Colonies prior to the revolution, land could not be executed against in the South, while in the North land could be put up for sale only if the debtor pledged it as security.[30] After the conquest, rules similar to those in the northern colonies were contemplated for Quebec.[31] The first elected assembly in Nova Scotia similarly provided for the forced sale of property, capturing local practice in a statute.[32] In England, no such options existed. The successful creditor could execute only against the debtor's goods or against the debtor's person. Any sale of property could be difficult, as debtors with goods seizable for auction could either hide them through gifting to friends and family or rely on, through living with several generations of adults in the same family, being able to confound identification of the debtor's own property. Thus, Margot Finn has concluded that in England in the last half of the eighteenth century, "compelling payment through extended (or indefinite) periods of imprisonment [was] more appealing to many creditors than seizure of the debtor's goods."[33] New South Wales, which was founded later in the eighteenth century than Halifax, did not officially allow execution on real property held in freehold until 1814, although there were some executions against real property in the first decade and a half of the nineteenth century despite the absence of positive law to allow for such actions.[34]

The forced sale of real property to satisfy an execution seems to have been the law in Halifax from the beginning. For instance, William Ewer initiated his suit against Robert Ewer and Anne Webb in August of 1757 with a writ of summons, so no security was required from the defendants. The action was split so that William sued Robert and Anne separately at the June 1758 Inferior Court. Victorious in both actions, William had execution issued against Robert as soon as he could: July 5. An auction of Robert's house and lot, along with a separate garden lot was held on July 18. William bought the house and its lot, while the garden lot was bought by James Monk.[35]

EQUITY OF REDEMPTION

The ease with which a person's house could be sold in Halifax was, however, matched by the importing of the equity of redemption. Over the sixteenth and seventeenth centuries, the English Court of Chancery developed the equity of redemption to allow mortgagors the right to redeem property lost due to default on a mortgage so long as they paid the principal owed, as well as interest and costs. Seventeenth- and early eighteenth-century precedents established that the equity could be exercised years after the mortgagor originally gave up the property, even past the point of the mortgagor's death. By 1750, Lord Mansfield ruled in *Burges v. Wheate* that "the equity of redemption is the fee simple of the land," not the land as passed to the creditor.[36] British legal historian William Holdsworth described the mortgagee's powers thus: "The fact that the mortgagee had sold the property to a purchaser without notice could not affect the mortgagor's rights – he was the owner, and as the mortgagee merely held the property as a security for the debt, he could only convey it subject to the mortgagor's rights."[37]

Moreover, it seems that, because under the theory of equity of redemption the new owners of the land held it as security only until the debt was paid off, the land could return to the original owner for only the value of the original debt and interest; the new owner would not be compensated for any improvements made to the land.[38]

The doctrine was a part of Nova Scotian law. Debtors would give up their property to creditors, signing over the deed to the land but often remaining tenants in possession. They could then pay off their debts to the creditor in rents, while the creditor held the property as security for the debt. If the debtor failed to make sufficient payments, the creditor could go to court to eject the debtor and thus take possession of the property. If, on the other hand, the debtor did pay off the debts, then he or she could exercise the equity of redemption to regain title. There was no right to redeem other kinds of property, or to redeem property lost in Vice Admiralty actions.

A 1751 proclamation by the governor and council allowed that real estate taken in "execution," that is to satisfy a court judgment, could be redeemed within two years by payment of the debt, court and execution costs, and lawful interest. The debtor could apply any profits the creditor earned from the property, less "necessary repairs and improvements," against the outstanding debt. If the debtor died within the two years, his or her heirs would have two additional years from the date of the debtor's death to redeem the land.[39]

Equity of redemption was an issue for land owners seeking to extinguish possible challenges to their title. In an August 1752 action, Boston merchant William Gordon won an action against Halifax attorney William Nesbitt for £100. Gordon accepted the deed to Nesbitt's home and lot in full satisfaction of the debt. Nesbitt remained a tenant in possession of the land, though no longer its owner. Here the exchange of property was not through a court-ordered sale, but the effect was the same. In December 1757, Gordon sued Nesbitt to eject him from the property.[40] In actions like this, creditors and debtors like Gordon and Nesbitt used the right of redemption to extend the time of payment on a debt while providing the creditor with security. In satisfaction of his original suit, Gordon took ownership of Nesbitt's property as security on the debt. Gordon and Nesbitt expected in 1752 that Nesbitt would pay back Gordon and thus exercise his right of redemption. Until the redemption period passed, Nesbitt remained in possession of his land; while title changed in law, possession remained the same. All the rent Nesbitt paid as Gordon's tenant was to be deducted from his debt. At any time after the end of the redemption period, if the creditor was still owed money, he or she could sue the tenant in an action of ejectment, as Gordon did in 1757. Because the creditor had received title to the land, the debtor would lose the ejectment action, and the creditor could foreclose, remove the tenant, and either take the land or sell it to collect on the debt. A number of ejectment suits follow the same pattern as *Gordon v. Nesbitt*, suggesting this was a common practice in Halifax.

This last practice is similar to the English process of *elegit*, whereby a creditor, after receiving judgment in his or her favour, could have a moiety of the debtor's land while the debtor remained in possession and paid off the debt.[41] The fundamental difference in Halifax was that full title actually transferred to the creditor, and the debtor could permanently lose the property without any legal process for recovery. The rules about the sale of property were designed first and foremost to secure repayment of debts. The concerns both in England and in other colonies, particularly the plantation colonies like Virginia, to protect landowners simply did not take hold in Nova Scotia. The colony was reliant on trade, not agricultural produce: it was better to ensure that merchant transactions were secured than to create and protect a nascent aristocracy, or even a small-holder agricultural class.[42]

Imprisonment

In addition to mandating the sale of property, a writ of execution allowed the provost marshal to imprison someone who failed to pay what they owed. Between sixteen and twenty imprisonments are documented for the period covered in this book, all arising from actions at the Inferior Court.[43] Eight of the imprisonments concluded actions for debts by note or account, one for a replevin action, and one for desertion. The last one, although an unusual action in the Halifax civil courts, is an excellent example of imprisonment on execution of a civil action.

On 27 October 1759, Elisha Reed made a verbal contract of service with Nathan Nathans "as servant to the said Nathan in such Employ as he the said Nathan should have or require."[44] Nathans promised to provide Reed with "sufficient Necessaries during the said Term." Almost immediately after, Reed absented himself from work and refused to return. On 12 November 1759, Nathans swore out a writ of trespass upon the case against Reed, demanding £10 in damages, but claiming only £4. Neither Nathans's declaration nor his oath of debt actually explain the demanded and claimed sums: they may have been the value of advances in pay Nathans had made, but nothing was specified.

Reed was attached to be tried at the December 1759 court but defaulted. In assessing the damages, the court passed judgment on the default for £2 10s. On 21 February 1760, Nathans swore out his first writ of execution against Reed. It was returned by deputy provost marshal Richard Gibbons with the following note: "I have taken the def[t] and for Want of Goods Chattels or Estate have Committed him to his Maj[s] Jail in s[d] Halifax." Unable to make satisfaction immediately, Reed was imprisoned until he could make satisfaction or arrange for someone else to pay for him. A second note on the execution, dated 12 March 1760, recorded that Nathans had received payment in full.

Imprisoned debtors do not appear to have been in prison long. For five actions, dates of both imprisonment and receipt of full satisfaction are available. These dates mark the maximum period of imprisonment in the actions, though in each case the debtor may have been released from prison before making complete satisfaction. In one action, the period was seven days; in two actions ten days; and in *Nathans v. Reed*, fourteen days. In the fifth action, the imprisonment could have been much longer: 126 days – from November 28 to April 2. Based on jail returns from 30 October 1764 and 4 June 1765, it appears that two debtors, John Tongue and Francis Wroughton, were imprisoned for at least 217 days, although it is possible that either man could have been imprisoned twice for different debts and thus appear in the two jail returns.[45]

Nevertheless, the extant legal records *may* for some reason significantly undercount imprisonments. In the 1752 census of Halifax, there were eight criminals in jail, but nineteen debtors.[46] The census does not identify if these men (all of the prisoners were men) were imprisoned awaiting trial or after trial. In either case, if the census is accurate and did not catch an exceptional moment, then imprisonment for debt was more common than the other evidence suggests.

Those imprisoned included traders like Israel Abrahams, labourers like Reed, and craftspeople. Six were traders, retailers, or tavern keepers. Seven were identified as carpenters, tailors, coopers, bakers, fishcullers, carters, or labourers.

Imprisonment was not an automatic result of failing to make satisfaction when it was demanded. Although empowered by the writ of execution to imprison, the provost marshal would do so only at the claimant's specific request. The claimant was responsible for the costs of imprisonment. While imprisoned, the prisoner may not have been required to stay in the prison during the day, and so may have been able to work to earn the money owed: the records are unclear. Imprisonment offered several potential advantages to claimants, however. Compelling the imprisonment of one debtor might convince a creditor's other debtors to pay their debts and help persuade the debtor's family and friends to pay the debt on his behalf. By having the deserter Reed imprisoned, Nathans could impress upon his other employees the necessity of staying on the job. To avoid making satisfaction, some debtors could hide or deny the existence of assets or property from the provost marshal. Neither the marshal nor the claimant was required to prove that no property sufficient to pay the debt existed, only that the debtor had not made such property available.[47]

The evidence presented here suggests that in Halifax lawmakers and decision-makers had much greater sympathy for creditors than debtors. Nonetheless, many creditors were themselves debtors at times and may have been disinclined to imprison debtors because they feared imprisonment themselves. More importantly, however, the ease with which execution could be taken against property probably limited the need to rely on the prison. Halifax and Nova Scotia were also small communities. Unlike in London, many of the larger cities in England, or even well-settled New England, it would have been difficult for debtors to hide their property or transfer it to a third party undetected. The creditor's biggest worry would be the debtor's flight from the colony, but exercising execution against property quickly could prevent this as easily as imprisoning the debtor.

Conclusion

Although a judgment might state that a defendant owed a plaintiff something, who – if anyone – won or lost the action depended more on the relationship between the award and the plaintiff's claim or demand. But if an action ended with a defendant owing anything, then the legal system invested the plaintiff with significant power to ensure payment was made.

It appears that relatively few actions ended with fully satisfied writs of execution, but the vagaries of historical record survival rates seem to explain this, at least in part. Like so many of the other pieces of paper produced in the course of a legal action, it is likely that many writs of execution were not kept. In many cases, however, writs of execution may never have been issued. Having received judgment in their favour, many litigants may have held onto that as security and made private arrangements to be paid back. Although executions could be issued as soon as the session was over and costs taxed, they did not need to be. The threat of execution, and with it, forced sales of property or imprisonment, could have been enough for many litigants to come to agreements.

The alternative that some executions were satisfied in cash before or after a term in prison or by auction, while most actions simply went without satisfaction, seems untenable. The frequent recourse to litigation by some many people in Halifax – essentially the investment by litigants, jurors, and arbitrators in making the system work – seems to imply that plaintiffs and the community as a whole had some expectation of it working all the way through to the end of an action.

The Inferior Court of Common Pleas was not, however, the only court. Actions that came to an end there could be appealed to the Supreme Court of Nova Scotia, and from there, through the process of injunction, appealed again to the Court of Chancery. Running parallel to this system, too, was the Vice Admiralty Court. It is to the appeal process and these other courts that the next chapter turns.

7

Appeals and Other Courts

Roger Hill's action against Anne Webb was tried twice: first at the Inferior Court of Common Pleas and then at the Supreme Court of Nova Scotia. The first time the action was tried before a jury, and the second time Hill and Webb turned it over to arbitrators. Although most actions initiated in the Inferior Court ended there, litigants did have the opportunity to appeal to the Supreme Court, and then, in effect, to appeal again to the Court of Chancery. Borrowing from English law and North American practice, the appeals process in Nova Scotia was, nonetheless, a colonial creation.

In addition to the Supreme Court and Chancery, two other courts heard civil disputes in Halifax: the courts of Vice Admiralty and Prohibited Marriage and Divorce. Each of these had distinct jurisdictions and neither was part of the appeal structure. None of these four courts did business on the scale of the Inferior Court, but they each had important roles in the civil court structure. This chapter begins with the appeal process, and then delves into the non-appeal function of Chancery and the uses made of the remaining two courts. Finally, two cases from Vice Admiralty are presented to show how the jurisdiction of the courts was challenged.

The Supreme Court and Appeals

Along with the County Court, the precursor to the Inferior Court of Common Pleas, the governor and council created a General Court over December 1749 and January 1750. The General Court, modelled on those in Virginia and other North American examples, was in its civil jurisdiction to be a court of appeal for the county and later Inferior Court. In principle, actions involving a member of the court could be initiated at the Supreme Court, but this does not seem to have been the practice. Actions to enforce earlier judgments of the court (e.g., *scire facias*) were initiated at it as well. It would meet twice annually, in spring and autumn sessions, following the pattern of the Assizes in England. The governor and council would act as the court's judges. By 1754, it became clear that the court could not be effective without someone trained in law, both to maintain its own legitimacy and as a court of review for the Inferior Court, which was also staffed by amateurs. London appointed a chief justice, Jonathan Belcher, to preside over the colony's court, now reformulated as the Supreme Court of Nova Scotia.[1] Belcher was the court's only judge until 1763 when two assistant judges were appointed to the court, one of whom was Charles Morris, the long-time chief judge of the Inferior Court.

Chief Justice Belcher, like Charles Morris, hailed from Massachusetts. He was the son of a merchant who served as governor of Massachusetts in the 1730s and of New Jersey between 1747 and 1757. Having studied at Harvard College, Belcher moved to England where he studied mathematics at Cambridge and law at Middle Temple. After being called to the bar in 1734, he failed to develop a successful career in England. He moved to Dublin in 1741 where he was appointed deputy secretary to the Lord Chancellor of Ireland in 1746. Although a New Englander by birth, Belcher was schooled in the law in England and had compiled an abridgement of the Irish statutes just prior to his appointment to Nova Scotia. Susan Buggey has asserted,

Both his English training and his Irish experience equipped him to oppose the Massachusetts precedents which had dominated the Nova Scotia courts prior to his arrival. In accordance with the instructions to the governor that the laws of the province should be "as near as may be Agreeable" to the laws of Britain, Belcher promoted English precedents and laws. As a result of his work they became more widely applied in Nova Scotia.

Belcher was certainly used to English law. In his first charge to the Halifax grand jury he relied on published English models. Yet too much can be made of the return to English practice under his rule. Paul Craven has shown that in writing Nova Scotia's master and servant legislation in 1765 Belcher relied on the Irish and Virginian statutes. Despite Buggey's assertion, little in the civil procedure of Nova Scotia changed with Belcher's arrival, including its American appellate practices.[2]

The Legal History of Appeals

The English common law courts of the eighteenth century did not have a well-defined hierarchy of inferior and superior courts. This meant that there was no structural design to allow appeals from one level of court to another. There were differences in jurisdiction and powers between summary jurisdiction, Quarter Sessions, Assizes, Nisi Prius, and the Westminster Hall-based courts of King's Bench, Common Pleas, Exchequer, and Chancery.[3] While the judges of the central courts certainly held themselves and their courts to be above the Justices of the Peace and their hearings and courts, the individual forums were not clearly ranked from lowest to highest. By the mid-eighteenth century, a variety of writs allowed some judicial review in England. A party to an action could seek a writ of error if there was manifest error in law in a court's acts that was apparent on the written record or if facts that would have called into question the very validity of the action were not tested in the original action. Normally the writ was issued by another court, in most cases the King's Bench, and ordered that the issues in question be examined by the original court or by the court that issued the writ. The hearing would determine if the errors, once proven, were sufficient to reverse the original decision. A second writ, *certiorari*, would remove the records of an action from a summary hearing, the quarter sessions, or another juridical body and have the action tried at King's Bench. While the writ of error could be sought only after an action had concluded, *certiorari* could be sought at any stage of a proceeding, even prior to trial. The purpose of the two writs, however, was to determine whether a court's ruling was unlawful, not to retry an action or even appeal in a twenty-first-century sense. In addition to the writs, if a trial judge certified that the jury's verdict was contrary to the law as he stated it or to the evidence presented, if affidavits of juror or judicial misconduct were produced, or if the trial judge erred in explaining the law to a jury, then litigants could move for a new trial.[4]

There were courts in England based on Roman traditions that had more hierarchical structures. The ecclesiastical courts developed a doctrine of appeal that allowed for the rehearing of actions from one level of church hierarchy to the next. Admiralty and military courts followed the ecclesiastical structure and had their own doctrines of appeal. The model was also adopted by the directors of English chartered companies in the sixteenth and seventeenth centuries to deal with the legal jurisdictions they were granted, especially when the companies operated outside of the British Isles. Local courts would deal with concerns in their areas, but their decisions were appealable to higher, central company courts. The 1619 and 1620 *Orders and Constitutions* of the Council for Virginia adapted this system, devising a hierarchy of courts so that inferior court rulings could be appealed to superior courts, with the final right of appeal resting with the governor and council. This structure replaced the common law writs of error and *certiorari* within the court structure.[5]

At the founding of the British colony at Annapolis Royal in 1713, the governors were instructed to refer to Virginia's statutes as the model when making the new colony's statutes and legal structures.[6] The Board of Trade's 1749 instructions for Governor Cornwallis repeated the command to use Virginia as a model, and then further specified that all actions tried in Nova Scotia could be appealed from the highest local court to the Privy Council. Moreover, appeals on cases in which damages exceeded £300 could be demanded of Common Right, meaning the Privy Council was required to hear such appeals if made, but could refuse to hear other appeals.[7] The Virginian model provided for a hierarchical structure and the 1749 instructions assumed one would be established in the colony. Until 1764, the civil jurisdiction of the Supreme Court, originally called the General Court, primarily heard appeals from the Inferior Court, while after 1764 it also began to hear some matters at first instance. The Inferior Court of Common Pleas was itself the appellate jurisdiction for summary actions, although it was most often a court of first instance.

To appeal the jury verdict at the Inferior Court, Anne Webb simply had to make a motion to the court within five days of the end of the December 1761 session stating she intended to appeal. She did not have to lay out any grounds in law or fact for her appeal. All she had to do, having made the motion, was provide a recognizance and two sureties confirming that she would, indeed, follow through with the appeal. In most cases the recognizance was at least £20, and sometimes much more if the damages awarded were significantly greater. The sureties were made by two other people who pledged to guarantee the appellant's appearance. Their pledges were each half the value of the recognizance, usually £10. The appellant typically made the recognizance bond and his or her attorney was often one of sureties. This, however, was not always the case and anyone could act as a bond or surety. Once the motion to appeal was made it was impossible to execute on the original judgment unless or until the appeal was withdrawn.

Appeals in Halifax

Following the ecclesiastical and American models, appeals in Halifax were rehearings of actions. A complete copy of all of the records of the initial trial was prepared by the clerk of the Inferior Court and this was forwarded to the Supreme Court. The Supreme Court followed the same basic procedure as the Inferior Court. The parties again determined how to proceed. As table 4.1 shows, while a handful of actions were withdrawn and there were singular instances of confession and default, most went to a jury, special jury, or arbitration. Of those three, jury and special jury trials were more common at the Supreme Court than at the Inferior Court. As a proportion of the three options, at the Inferior Court, more than a third of actions went to arbitration, while at the Supreme Court less than a quarter did. Roughly a tenth of actions were resolved by a special jury at the Supreme Court, so it is possible that the smaller panel of experts in arbitration was eschewed for the larger panel of experts on a special jury by some litigants.

The procedures for jury trials and arbitrations were essentially the same for the two courts, which is why jurors and arbitrators in both courts were grouped together in the analysis in chapter 5. Once jurors or arbitrators had arrived at a verdict or award, the court would make it into a judgment and execution would proceed in the same manner as in the Inferior Court. This system of appeal completely distinguished the Halifax common law courts from the English ones. There are no records of *certiorari* sought in the Halifax civil courts before 1766. There was, however, one instance in which a writ of error was issued and used to seek review of a Supreme Court action by the governor and council.[8]

Not every judgment could be appealed. The rules of court proclaimed in December 1749 restricted appeals from the then county court, which would later become the Inferior Court, to cases where the damages claimed were greater than £5. In December 1752, the governor and council altered the rule so that appeals would only be allowed if the damages *awarded* in the Inferior Court exceeded £5. If a plaintiff in a trespass action demanded a greater sum, but received less than £5 in damages, no appeal would be allowed.[9] There is no record of a motion to appeal from the Inferior to the Supreme Court being denied before 1766.

When Anne Webb appealed the judgment against her and in favour of Roger Hill from the Inferior Court it is unclear exactly what she wanted. The jury at the Inferior Court awarded Hill all of his claimed damages. At the Supreme Court the arbitrators returned an award that still saw Webb owe Hill, but they found she owed him less. When Benjamin Leigh sued Joseph Jones for defaming his character as a merchant he won at the Inferior Court, but he only received £100 in damages, much less than the £500 he demanded. He appealed and in the trial at the Supreme Court his damage award was increased. Both appeals were successful at least in so far as the new awards favoured the appellants more than the initial awards. The two appeals fit into a general pattern: of the 74 appeals for which the judgment is known, 56 confirmed the judgment of the lower court. But, as in *Webb v. Hill* and *Leigh v. Jones*, the value of the awards could differ: the value of the original award was confirmed in fewer than half (24, or 44 per cent) of the 53 appeals for which the value of the award is known in both the original and appeal. In 15 appeals the value of the award was increased, and in 14 it was decreased.

Both Anne Webb and Benjamin Leigh appealed jury verdicts. Of the 112 Inferior Court judgments appealed to the Supreme Court, 102 (91 per cent) were from jury trials. There were only 589 jury and special jury trials at the Inferior Court from 1750 to 1766, so 17 per cent of jury verdicts were appealed. Arbitration awards were much less likely to be appealed: only 4 were appealed, accounting for only a little more than 1 per cent of arbitrations.

The greater willingness to appeal jury verdicts coupled with the greater use of juries at the Supreme Court deserves some explanation, especially in light of the arguments made about jury trials in chapters 5 and 6. Two things set juries apart: first, they were more willing than arbitrators to find fully for the defendant; and second, they were willing to award damages of a different value than that claimed or demanded by the plaintiff, although not as willing to depart from the claim as arbitrators were. In the first case, this meant that losing plaintiffs or defendants who believed in the justness of their position and that there was no middle ground, no possible shaving of damages one way or the other, could appeal in hopes that a new jury would see things their way. In the second, litigants like Anne Webb who were confronted with a jury verdict that was not sufficiently alert to the differences in accounts could appeal in the hope of securing a better reading of the accounts.

The evidence of practice in the two courts does not suggest that there was litigant frustration with jury trials as a whole. The coupling of a greater willingness to appeal jury verdicts with a greater use of juries and special juries in the Supreme Court suggests that litigants were looking for the right jury rather than an alternative to juries. The evidence also suggests something about the arbitration procedure. It is possible that, unlike juries, arbitrators spent some time talking to both parties as they made their determinations. In some cases, arbitrators likely came to a mediated solution, one that both parties could, perhaps grudgingly, agree to accept. Thus, the likelihood of appealing the award was lower in arbitration than in jury trials. Juries, even though they were made up of the litigants' neighbours and sometimes their friends, came to their verdicts without negotiating with the litigants. Thus, the likelihood of a litigant being disappointed by and unaccepting of a verdict was high. Appeals of jury verdicts would be more likely than appeals of arbitration awards, but not because juries, were on the whole, becoming unacceptable to litigants.

The Injunction and the Court of Chancery

Appellants or respondents (appellees in the language of the time) were not always happy with the results of their appeal to the Supreme Court. Dissatisfied appellants had one remaining option: to go to the Court of Chancery and seek an injunction against the judgment. Mary Sarah Bilder, the historian of the origins of appeals in North America, has argued that lying behind the ecclesiastical appellate system was a doctrine of equity, which required the application of good conscience to judgments so that they would be both lawful and just. She argues that these principles were borrowed by the English Court of Chancery so that by the end of the seventeenth century it had a developed a doctrine of "appeals in equity" over common law judgments.[10] Through the injunction, these hearings would allow the Court of Chancery to review common law decisions and stop execution of common law judgments where the result, however lawful, was demonstrably inequitable or unconscionable.

The Nova Scotia Court of Chancery was established by at least 1751, although it was probably contemplated earlier. In this court, the governor would act as chancellor with members of his council assisting. As with the Inferior Court bench, this meant that in its earliest years there was no one with legal training sitting in the court. As well as being Chief Justice in the common law courts, Jonathan Belcher was a master of Chancery. As a master, he could support the court in its work and sometimes make findings for the court, as he did in 1756 when taxing costs in a Chancery dispute.[11]

Chancery courts were unusual in North America in the 1750s; several of the older American colonies never established them or only established them in the eighteenth century or after the American Revolution.[12] In Halifax the Court of Chancery court met at the request of a complainant. For much of its history, Nova Scotia's Court of Chancery dealt mainly with foreclosures and other property actions.[13] In its earliest years, however, it was most often used to secure injunctions against common law actions and thus acted similarly to an appeals court. It was not used as often as the Supreme Court: as table 4.1 shows, the court heard on average only about one case per year.

One of the historians of the court, Jim Cruikshank, has demonstrated that the court likely followed the Irish Court of Chancery's Rules of Procedure. He explains this in part by the influence of Belcher and Bryan Finucane, the first two Chief Justices of the colony, both of whom were members of the Irish bar. The earliest case Cruikshank analyses for procedure is from 1782. Similarly, the other historians who have discussed the eighteenth-century court have discussed cases much later than the era discussed here.[14] Nonetheless, the procedures he outlines seem consistent with Chancery procedure throughout the 1750s and 1760s.[15]

The use of the Court of Chancery to have one more hearing of a case can be seen clearly in the actions between John Grant and William Piggot. On 21 July 1755 the surgeon John Grant took out a writ of attachment against Piggot, a trader, tavern keeper, and wharfinger, for a debt arising from a breach of contract. Grant claimed to have rented Piggot a wharf and buildings for £25 per annum in 1753. Two years later Grant claimed Piggot owed him £34 in back rent.[16] Piggot's attorney, George Suckling, replied to the attachment with a plea of demurrer on September. Demurrer, like abatement, was a plea contesting the legal basis of an action. Suckling maintained that in his declaration Grant had improperly quoted the length of his contract with Piggot. William Nesbitt, Grant's attorney, argued that the error was not significant to the matter at hand, and the justices agreed. In theory, if a defendant pled demurrer and failed, the defendant lost and could not then plead the issue and go to trial. In this case, however, the demurrer was actually treated as a plea of abatement and the action continued on its merits.[17]

Piggot decided to fight Grant's claims completely, and a jury trial was held at the same session of the Inferior Court. He maintained that Grant had approached Piggot to rent the wharf. When Piggot refused, citing the insufficiency of the pilings and lack of a gallows, Grant had promised to fix these as inducement to rent the wharf. Piggot was convinced of Grant's good intentions and entered the contract, but only after having secured a signed covenant from Grant to pile and build the gallows. In essence, Piggot's argument was that because Grant had failed to do the work on the wharf, he was under no obligation to pay the rent. The trial jury found for Grant and awarded him the whole £34 damages he claimed.

Suckling immediately moved to appeal the action to the Supreme Court where another jury affirmed the Inferior Court's judgment and damages.[18] In December 1755 Piggot applied to Chancery for an injunction against execution of the Supreme Court judgment, arguing that he had been treated unjustly in the common law courts.[19] On 30 January 1756, the court met with Suckling and Nesbitt. To avoid added expense, Nesbitt agreed to forestall execution of the Supreme Court judgment without a formal injunction. Nesbitt did require, and received from Suckling, an assurance that Piggot would provide the clerk of Chancery with security equal to the Supreme Court judgment. With the consent of both parties, Chancery stayed the execution of Grant's common law victory until the court could make its final decree.

Although the hearing in January was done orally, the argument and evidence in Chancery had to be presented in writing with very few hearings. Over the next several months both parties submitted a variety of petitions to the court laying out their positions and evidence. Witnesses' testimony was recorded by a clerk before a single member of the court at an examination and then submitted in writing to the court. On 19 June 1756, a hearing was held to review the testimony and allow the parties to present any final arguments. Two weeks later the court issued a provisional order declining to rule on the issue for the time being. Instead it ordered that a new common law trial be held to determine what damages Piggot had sustained by Grant's failure to pile the wharf and erect a gallows. The refusal to rule seems more like an unwillingness to find Grant's victory both legal and just, even as they understood Piggot may have a counter-claim.

The new trial was held at the September 1756 session of the Inferior Court, one year after Grant's first Inferior Court action against Piggot had been tried. At the new trial the jury found Grant owed Piggot £12 10s in damages.[20] Grant moved to appeal to the Supreme Court and simultaneously petitioned the Chancery for a retrial. Nesbitt maintained that the jury's verdict was "Erroneous as proceeding upon an Iregular order was given without the Support of proper Evidence & not agreeable to the Directions of the Inferior Court." Chief Justice Belcher, acting as a master of the court, agreed with Nesbitt's claim. He reported to the governor and other members of the court that the trial jury "had not proceeded regularly according to Evidence & the directions that were given them." On 7 January 1757 the Court of Chancery ordered a new trial forthwith by a special jury. On 18 January 1757 the special jury was charged:

Gentlemen, Your Issue is to try whether any and what Damages have been sustained by the said William Piggot the Plaintiff by the said John Grant the Defend[ts] not performing the Promise Contained in the [18 July 1753 note promising to pile and build a gallows] annexed to the Order of the Court of Chancery and return your Verdict accordingly.

Unlike the original jury, the special jury returned finding "no damage proved."[21]

Having received the verdict of the special jury, the Chancery met and on February 9 issued its final ruling on the matter:

Upon reading the Bill answer & depositions of the witnesses produced for the pltf[s] [and] Def[t] and also upon reading the order & verdict of the Jury reported by the first Justice of the Inferior Court of Common Pleas, with his Certificate that the same was regular & hearing what could be further alleadged by the Soll[rs] on both side the Court do order that the Injunction to stay proceedings at Law formerly ordered in the case be now desolved and dismissed ... that the Bill be Dismissed with Costs to be paid by the plaintiff to the deft as the same shall be taxed by the Honble Jonathon Belcher Esq[r] as a master in Chancery.

In total Piggot owed Grant the original £34 and costs of £11 15s 4d. In addition, he had his own costs to cover; halfway through the Chancery action he already owed the court £4 8s, so it is possible he could have paid Chancery alone another £9 in costs. Piggot's attempt to fight Grant through the Inferior, Supreme, and Chancery courts probably cost him at least £50 in damages and court fees.

Piggot's case is exemplary of appeals and the role of Chancery. His argument before that court that the damages awarded against him at the Inferior Court were unjust speaks to the very heart of equity jurisdiction. Piggot's rental agreement with Grant contained no written provisions regarding the piling of the wharf or the building of a gallows. At common law Piggot was liable for the rent, and the Inferior and Supreme Court juries found him so. He seems to have hoped that the Court of Chancery would recognize in Grant's covenant factors that would mitigate his debt for rent. The Chancery was prepared to accept that Grant's failure was a mitigating factor. Unfortunately for the tavern keeper, the court was unprepared to attach a value to his loss and referred it back to the common law. The covenant had no penal clause and so there was nothing in it to allow a claim at common law for Grant's failure to pile the wharf.

Litigants seeking injunctions were seldom successful. The process did, however, offer an extension of the litigation. In the litigation between John Grant and William Piggot, Piggot was able to postpone payment for seventeen months from the time of the first Inferior Court judgment. Appeals, whether in the common law or to Chancery, provided litigants a chance to postpone execution. To those, like Piggot, who may have believed the judgments of the lower courts unjust, the appeal structure offered an opportunity to retry actions and to make arguments in Chancery that would be impossible in common law.

Chancery also served other functions, even in the 1750s and 1760s. One was to administer certain sorts of property disputes, like those over the equity of redemption introduced in chapter 6. On 22 June 1752, George Taylor, a baker, entered into a bond with the merchant Thomas Saul for £80, payable 22 June 1753. As security, Taylor mortgaged two lots in Halifax. The bond laid set out that if Taylor was unable to meet the payment condition, he would forfeit his land to Saul. The bond acknowledged that Taylor would have right of redemption for one year following his forfeiture. By this right of redemption, Saul would be unable to sell the property for the year and Taylor would have the right to redeem it by paying off the bond. If Taylor could not redeem the property within the year, he would lose it outright and Saul would have absolute fee simple ownership. In effect, the bond gave Taylor two years to pay back his debt, one year while enjoying his property, and one year with Saul having use, or usufruct, of the land.

Taylor did not repay the bond by 22 June 1753 and passed the land over to Saul. Nor did he redeem the land by 22 June 1754. Sometime after June 1753, in fact, Taylor left the colony "in his Majesty's service," according to later legal documents. In April 1757, almost three years after Taylor's contracted right to redemption had expired, Saul sold the lots to John Anderson. Anderson took full possession of both lots, refurbishing an existing house on one lot to serve as his own. Sometime after, Anderson's house burned down, destroying all of his deeds and records of his transactions with Saul. Anderson then built a new house on the property. In 1760 George Taylor returned to Halifax and began expressing an interest in his old property. At common law, failure to meet the conditions of the bond was final; the year-long right to redemption was simply a contractual obligation between parties. Without it, the property and rights thereto would have transferred completely to Saul in 1753. Having lost his land due to the bond and without trial or execution, Taylor's claim would seem to have expired with the right in the bond in 1754.

But what of the equity of redemption? Seventeenth- and early eighteenth-century precedents established that the equity could be exercised years after the mortgagor originally gave up the property, even past the point of the mortgagor's death. Taylor sought to redeem his title, and Anderson turned to Chancery to prevent this. *Anderson v. Taylor* reveals that in practice in Nova Scotia the equity of redemption was restricted in ways impossible in England. In England the mortgagee could foreclose on a piece of property. This would nominally end the right to redeem the property, but in fact a foreclosure could be overturned if the mortgagor could repay the debt. There appears to be no such foreclosure option open to someone who subsequently purchased the property from the mortgagee as Anderson did.

During the sixty-eight months from the initiation of Anderson's action to final decree, at least fifty-two documents were produced by the two parties. Anderson began with James Brenton as his attorney, but switched to James Monk during the trial. Taylor used Daniel Wood as his attorney. The attorneys were responsible for filing petitions, outlining their cases, introducing written evidence and responding to the evidence and arguments presented by the other side. When witnesses gave evidence they were questioned by a judge of the court in the presence of the clerk and attorneys. The questions posed would come from the lists of questions the attorneys presented the court in writing prior to the hearing. Anderson demanded his tenure be confirmed and argued against any equity of redemption. If, however, Taylor was able to exercise his right to redeem, Anderson asked that he be compensated for all improvements to the lots he had made, including his new house. All told, he claimed to have invested £1,300 in the land.

Taylor claimed he deserved a right of redemption limited, at most, to the £80 he originally owed Saul. He argued that even the £80 was too great, as the rents Saul earned from the land should have long ago covered most, if not all, of the value of the mortgage. Taylor argued he owed Anderson nothing for the new house or other work done on the property. Taylor had not been responsible for the fire, nor should he be held responsible for paying for a third party's improvements. Further, Taylor maintained he had not been given an opportunity to exercise his right of redemption prior to Saul's sale of the land. As Saul had failed to offer Taylor his due, it should not fall on Taylor to pay for anything Anderson did subsequent to the impugned sale.

On 9 August 1763, the Chancery assigned Charles Morris, who was one of the governor's councillors and had recently been appointed as an assistant judge on the Supreme Court, to investigate the deeds, evidence, and laws material to the action. Morris did not make his report until 1 February 1764. He did not declare whether or not Taylor should have a right to exercise his equity, but he wrote that if the court was to recognize the right, it should only be for a reasonable and restricted time. After reviewing all of the accounts for the land while under Saul and Anderson's control, Morris concluded that exercising his right of redemption would cost Taylor £949 in addition to his original £80 bond. Morris found that Saul and Anderson had made improvements to the property valued at £979, but he also found they had collected £30 in rents over the years.

Taylor entered a motion taking exception to Morris' report on a number of points, but his motion failed. On 14 June 1764 the Chancery Court decreed that Taylor would have six months to exercise his right of redemption. Exercising it would cost £1,029, inclusive of both his original debt and the costs of improvements. If he failed to exercise his right by 14 December 1764, he would give up all legal claims to the property.

On 13 May 1766 Anderson petitioned the court a final time. He argued that Taylor, having failed to exercise his right of redemption, had ceded any claim to the property. Anderson sought confirmation of his title from the court. The court agreed, confirmed his tenure to the two lots, and also awarded him costs for the entire action.

The legal principles in *Anderson v. Taylor* were very different from those of the common law debt cases discussed above, although the decision rendered was not. To explain the importance of equity of redemption in eighteenth-century England, David Sugarman and Ronnie Warrington have argued:

In addition to being an important instrument for preserving and consolidating landed wealth, the equity of redemption was also a set of political and cultural codes. It was a repository of stories signifying the central importance of the landed aristocracy and gentry to English society. It assumed a certain ordering of preferences and rights: of what was proper and what was illicit; and who and what should be recognized, protected, or excluded.[22]

The doctrine of equity of redemption came to Nova Scotia, but its inherent conservatism posed a problem for the colony. Preserving a landed class was not as important to the colonial elite as making a strong colony, and this required supporting the merchants, traders, and others who were building the colony's economy. To do so meant, as in the common law courts, advancing the interests of creditors over debtors. It also meant encouraging improvement to the land and ensuring that those who built something in the colony were paid what they deserved for the improvements they made. The Nova Scotia Court of Chancery ruled equity of redemption existed in Nova Scotia, but unlike in England, the equity could expire after a specific time and the creditor had the right to be compensated not only for the original debt and interest, but also for the cost of any improvements made. This severely restricted the equity.[23]

Although the *Anderson v. Taylor* action is an outlier with total costs exceeding £122, all Chancery cases were costly, time-consuming, and labour intensive. The volume of written materials meant that what could take several minutes in a hearing would take weeks or even months in back and forth letters, entreaties, and other writing between lawyers and the court. With each piece of paper, the costs would rise. As table 7.1 shows, the average cost of a Chancery trial was three times greater than that of any other court, and more than ten times greater than that of trials at the Inferior Court. While the high mean for the Chancery in table 7.1 is due in part to one outlier, even median costs are more than five times those of trials at the Inferior Court. The Chancery was available to litigants in Halifax, but unlike the Inferior Court, it was not a court that many could consider using because of the high cost.

In the 1750s and 1760s, the Court of Chancery was primarily a court of appeal, which heard actions aimed an enjoining some action by the common law courts either already taken, as in *Piggot v. Grant* or likely to be taken, as in *Anderson v. Taylor*. It did not grow into the full range of its authority until sometime later. Rather, it was essentially the method by which the governor and council, including the judiciary on

Table 7.1: Costs in other courts

Court and Process	n	Mean £/s/d	Median	Minimum	Maximum
Supreme					
Withdrawal	4	5/0/9¼	4/8/2	2/15/0	8/11/9
Arbitration	3	5/11/5½	5/0/5	5/0/5	9/6/5
Jury Trial	21	4/12/4½	4/10/4	1/13/4	10/11/3
Chancery					
Trial	7	31/9/4	9/8/8	7/0/11	122/1/7
Vice Admiralty					
Trial	19	10/12/8	5/13/6	2/7/10	43/13/5

council like Belcher and Morris, could exercise final supervision over the courts.

Vice Admiralty

A whole range of disputes could not or were not supposed to be heard by either the common law courts or Chancery, and so other courts were put into place or created to deal with these. The most important of those courts was Vice Admiralty, which had jurisdiction over actions that arose at sea. For instance, a suit for damages brought when one vessel struck and damaged a second vessel would fall under Vice Admiralty, even though the issues might be similar to an action on land between two colliding carts. Vice Admiralty jurisdiction was divided into "instance," which encompassed most disputes like wages, trade, negligence, salvage, or insurance, and "prize," which covered captured enemy vessels. In the 1750s and 1760s, Vice Admiralty tried the following actions, listed in declining importance: prize; wages; illegal trading, often, although not always, with the French; salvage; insurance; and negligence.[24] Prize will not be discussed in much detail here as it concerns questions more related to war and diplomacy on the sea.

The Court of Vice Admiralty in Nova Scotia predated the founding of Halifax; it was first established in the British colony at Annapolis Royal in 1720. Edward How, the first Vice Admiralty judge in Halifax, was appointed in 1737. A second court was established in Cape Breton after it was taken from the French by New Englanders in 1745. After the founding of Halifax, How became the judge for the Court of Vice Admiralty, and Benjamin Green became his assistant. After How's death in 1750, Green took over as surrogate judge until 1753 when he was replaced by John Collier. Collier remained the judge of the court until 1769.[25]

Benjamin Green, like both Charles Morris at the Inferior Court and later Supreme Court, and Chief Justice Jonathan Belcher, was born in Massachusetts. He first came to Nova Scotia in the mid-1740s with the New England forces at Louisburg. Green was appointed to the governor's council in 1749 and remained on council after he resigned his post as Vice Admiralty judge. In 1760 he was commissioned as a Justice of the Peace for Halifax. While in England in 1761 and 1762, Green was forced to go before the Board of Trade to face accusations from Robert Sanderson, speaker of the Nova Scotia House of Assembly, that he had ensured Malachy Salter was awarded two government contracts in exchange for a portion of Salter's profits. Green acknowledged he had business ties to Salter, but denied the charges. The board sent him back to Halifax with only a reprimand. John Collier, his replacement at Vice Admiralty, was born in England and came to Halifax with Cornwallis. He was given charge of one of the original divisions of the town and appointed one of the first Justices of the Peace in July 1749. In 1764 Collier was appointed, along with Morris, as an assistant judge of the Supreme Court. Neither Green nor Collier appears to have had any legal education before being appointed to their positions in Halifax.[26]

Unlike the Inferior Court, almost all Vice Admiralty actions went to trial. Additionally, Vice Admiralty actions often took very little time and could lead to much larger damage awards than in the other civil courts. From initiation to satisfaction, actions often took less than a week to complete. Satisfaction there, unlike in any of the other courts, virtually always resulted in almost immediate court-supervised sale of property. The litigants had little time to reach out-of-court agreements or to use the court processes to delay payment. Vice Admiralty defendants facing imminent property loss had much stronger motivation to go to trial, even when they faced almost certain loss, than did common law court defendants. Any chance at victory or at least mitigating damages through evidence at trial had to be taken because the cost of judgment against a defendant could be so high.

Vice Admiralty procedure was quite different from that in either the common law courts or at Chancery. Trials were in front of only a single judge, with most evidence presented orally and recorded by the court's registrar. Wage disputes were the most similar to common law court actions, but even in these the procedures were very different. The court had an advocate general, a lawyer appointed to prosecute all of the actions in the court. While defendants could get legal counsel of their own, plaintiffs had no need to do so, because their cases were pled on their behalf and all the advocate general's fees were charged as part of the court costs at the end of the trial.

The first action heard in the Court of Vice Admiralty after it relocated to Halifax was a wages case, initiated 3 October 1749 by Michael Handly against Ephraim Cook. Handly appeared before Edward How, judge of the court, demanding wages owed him for service on the ship *Baltimore*. Cook, master of the ship, had hired Handly in London, England on 2 May 1749 for £1 5s per month. After arriving in Halifax, Cook sent Handly aboard a brigantine to Louisburg. While in or around Louisburg Handly "was Order'd by the said Ephraim to go on board the London and that by Force they carried his things along side the London and ordered him on board." Handly refused to be transferred to the *London* as it was "contrary to the Agreement of his Voyage." He returned to the *Baltimore* and continued to work. But, due to "ill useage" at Cook's hands, on 14 September 1749 Handly "left the said Ship Baltimore & entered on his Majestys Ship of War call'd the Sphinx." Handly claimed Cook owed him wages of £6 16s as well as his bedding chest and clothing.[27]

The trial was held at ten the following morning, October 4, at assistant judge of the court Benjamin Green's house. Both Cook and Handly presented arguments, and both parties appear to have called witnesses. All of the pleadings were oral, and the registrar of the court, Charles Morris, did not record their content.

On 5 October, Judge Edward How made his decree. How found that Cook Shipd the Complainant Michael Handly according to the act of Parliament,[28] for a voyage to Chebucto in his Ship Baltimore in his Majestys Service and after the Arrival of said Ship in said Port Ephraim Cook Esqr aforesaid acknowledges to have sent the Defendant in a Brigantine in the same employ on a Voyage to Louisburg and at the Return of the said Brigantine further acknowledges to have agreed to discharge the Complainant in Order that he should go on board the Ship London and altho^g the said Defendant did not proceed in said Ship London looking on this to be a dif^t mission from said Ephraim Cooks Service more especially since the Complainant enter'd soon after on board of his Majestys Ship Sphinx Capt Loyd Commander.

Having made this finding, How determined that Handly was due wages from the day he shipped with the *Baltimore* until he began with the *Sphinx*. He also ordered that Handly's bedding and clothing be returned to him.

Comprising almost a quarter of the court's work, wage disputes were almost always decided in favour of the sailors demanding wages. The speed with which Vice Admiralty trials occurred, the fact that sailors could join suit together, and the greater possibility of forced sales of property than in the common law courts (see below), made wage cases in Vice Admiralty more likely to result in a positive outcome for sailors and a more threatening to employers than wage cases at common law.[29]

Most actions in Vice Admiralty concerned monetary damages, but calculating the value of the award differed depending on the type of action. In debt actions, like sailor's wages disputes, the damages would generally be a specific monetary award. In *Handly v. Cook* for instance, Handly was awarded £1 1s 2d, little more than a sixth of his demand of £6 6s. Eighteen sailors' wages actions ended with a decree for the complaining sailor. And while a few received close to what they demanded, on average, sailors received in awards only 44 per cent of what they demanded.[30] The ratio between wage claims and damage awards in Vice Admiralty was similar to the ratio in the common law courts. Unlike in the common law courts, however, the work of sailors was not inspected, rather the reduction in damages awarded could have been due to money or goods already paid, a finding of bad service, or different accounting of time at work.

Damages in Vice Admiralty actions, like salvage, prize, or illegal trade, were different than damages in common law courts. For those convicted by the court for illegal trade, the penalty was essentially capital punishment applied to the vessel: the forfeiture at public auction of the defendant's vessel, its "tackle, apparel, furniture, stores, boats and appurtenances," and all of the cargo. The auction was conducted by the marshal of the court, who kept 2 per cent of the gross to cover his costs. The remainder was divided into thirds: the first went to the informant or party who captured the illegal trader, the second to the governor, and the third to the King. All assessed court fees were deducted from the King's third. Prize actions also ended with the forced auction of the vessel, equipment, and cargo, and the proceeds were divided among the captor of the vessel, the crown, and the court.[31]

In salvage actions, the master who salvaged any or all of the crew, cargo, equipment, or vessel would sue the salvaged vessel and its master. The court would determine the rescuer's expenses and award him and his crew an appropriate sum. The salvaged goods would then be auctioned. The rescuers' award would be deducted from the gross proceeds of the auction then the court costs would be deducted. Any remainder would be turned over to the master or owners of the salvaged vessel.[32]

Trials at Vice Admiralty were much more expensive than those at the common law courts. Actions cost an average of £11 10s 5½d, although the median costs were only £6 7s (see table 7.1). Because costs, like damages, were secured against the impugned vessel or its cargo, even though costs were significantly higher than at the Inferior Court, working class sailors were willing and able to use the court.

Prohibited Marriage and Divorce

The non-criminal court with the least business in Halifax in the 1750s and early 1760s was also the court most peculiar to Nova Scotia: the Court of Prohibited Marriage and Divorce. Divorces were difficult to secure in eighteenth-century England, and the authority to grant divorces was fiercely protected by those who had it. Couples or individuals wishing to divorce had to turn either to the ecclesiastical courts or to Parliament. In cases where a marriage should not have occurred in the first place (as between siblings), the ecclesiastical courts could award a complete divorce (*a vinculo matrimonii*), but in other cases, such as abuse or desertion, the courts could only award a divorce from bed and board (*a mensa et thoro*) which allowed the couple to live separately but did not allow either to remarry while their spouse was alive. Parliament could award a complete divorce in cases of adultery through a private bill. This effectively placed divorce out of the hands of a vast number of people who could not afford the ecclesiastical courts or the private bill, and did not have access to Members of Parliament to make the case for them. Alternatives, like the process of the sale of wives, developed for working people, only worked if there was agreement within the community about what was occurring and if people of higher classes were kept in the dark.[33] In the seventeenth century, civil courts in Massachusetts heard petitions for divorce, but after 1692 that power was reserved to the governor and Council. In Connecticut, divorces were first granted by the General Court and after 1666 the Court of Assistants, which later became the Superior Court. In the other New England colonies, similar practices for administering divorce were created.[34]

It was in this context that on 15 May 1750, Lieutenant William Williams petitioned the governor and council to grant him a divorce from his wife. He complained that he had proof that during a recent absence from Halifax his wife Amy "lived in a habitual Course of Adultery with Mr Thomas Thomas." He wanted the governor and council to grant him a divorce. The council first decided that it could hear the petition because, with no ecclesiastical courts in the colony, someone needed to be able to grant relief in cases such as this, and they were the best positioned to do so.

The council then held a hearing at which William and Amy were called to present their cases. Three witnesses were called and examined under oath. The council decided, based on the evidence provided, that Amy had had, or was even still having, an adulterous relationship with Thomas. The secretary of the council was ordered to draw up an instrument of divorce in the style produced by ecclesiastical courts. With this instrument, William was told he could remarry. Amy, however, was not allowed to remarry while William was alive and she was exiled from the colony, given ten days to leave.[35] By the 1752 census, William Williams was listed as living with a woman over the age of sixteen, although whether she was a wife, daughter, or servant is not specified. Thomas Thomas was not listed in the census, nor was Amy Williams listed as a woman living alone.[36]

The governor and council's decision here seems more aimed at resolving the Williams's problems than in following England's, or New England's, laws and practices of divorce. The council justified taking carriage of Williams's petition because there was no ecclesiastical court or other already existing process to which he could turn. But, in granting him a divorce so he could remarry, they gave him a divorce the English ecclesiastical courts could not have given in the same circumstances: adultery might be cause for divorce, but it did not make the marriage prohibited, and so the ecclesiastical courts in England could not grant a complete divorce in this case.

Following Williams's petition, the governor and council decided that they needed to regularize how they would deal with such petitions. They began to characterize themselves as, when necessary, a Court of Prohibited Marriage and Divorce, much as they characterized themselves as a Court of Chancery when so required. The idea of being a court and the names used seem to suggest they were using the Massachusetts process as their model, offering both complete divorces and divorce from bed and board. In doing so, they stipulated that they made determinations as a court rather than in their capacity as an analogy to Parliament.[37]

In 1758 the first assembly passed a statute conferring jurisdiction on the governor and council for prohibited marriages and divorces. Originally, divorces could be granted on a number of grounds including impotence, marriage between kin, adultery, and desertion for three or more years. After 1761, desertion was removed as a cause, but cruelty was added.[38] Between the time of its creation and 1766, the council as a Court of Prohibited Marriage and Divorce heard six actions. It had a narrow jurisdiction, and was called upon infrequently. It was, however, special. In disputes at the court, women were integrally involved as litigants: contracts of marriage were contracts to which they were always parties and they could petition the court in their own right without their husband's approval or agreement. In the common law courts that decided all other matters of contractual and tortious liability, women were much less frequently litigants, and married women were often present as co-litigants with their husbands or as unnamed people who contracted debts, extended credit, or provided labour and services in their husband's name. In most disputes, married women were present as members of a family unit defined by their husband and his name, but at the Court of Prohibited Marriage and Divorce that very unit was in question and they appeared as individuals on their own.

Sorting out Jurisdiction: The Example of Vice Admiralty

With effectively five different courts that handled different non-criminal legal disputes, questions of jurisdiction could be expected to be a problem. The clearest place where overlap was possible was between Vice Admiralty and the common law courts. Although the difference between land and sea appears on its face to be pretty obvious, this was not necessarily the case. After all, very little that happened on sea occurred without some element having occurred before or after on land. A sailor on a fishing boat who was not paid his wages could sue in Vice Admiralty, but if the same sailor signed on for the value of a portion of the catch and did not receive his portion, then he had an action demanding a reasonable account in the Inferior Court of Common Pleas.

Ryan, the boatswain of the private brig *Edward*, after two months of service, was impressed to a Navy man of war. He sued for his wages due from the *Edward* in Vice Admiralty. The attorneys for the *Edward* sought an injunction against this in Chancery. They made four arguments against Vice Admiralty's jurisdiction. First, because Ryan's employment agreement was made on land in Portsmouth, Great Britain, it was not a maritime contract and so not under Vice Admiralty's jurisdiction. Second, being an action for wages, it was an action for damages, and was thus "a proper subject of Trial by a quantum merit [sic] at Com. Law." Third, impressed onto the man of war without finishing his employment contract, the boatswain "ought not to be paid for his Services." Fourth, the original libel to the court to initiate the action did not specify that the substance of the action occurred at sea (super altum mare) or otherwise fell in Vice Admiralty's jurisdiction (infra jurisdictionem maritimam); without such proof of jurisdiction, it should be assumed that the court had none.[39]

Jonathon Belcher wrote a long decision on behalf of the Chancery rejecting the attempt to remove the action from Vice Admiralty. Belcher's decision relied on a number of precedents, but was essentially a restating of established Admiralty law in other jurisdictions.[40] Citing Lord Chief Justice Matthew Holt's ruling in Clay v. Sudgrave,[41] Belcher acknowledged that if a legal error had occurred originally in awarding Admiralty jurisdiction over sailors' wages, the error was so old and practice for determining such suits so developed that Admiralty's jurisdiction should be recognized. In reply to the Edward's lawyers' first two points, Belcher cited Holt's four policy reasons for allowing Admiralty to continue to hear the cases regardless of the law. First, unlike the common law, Admiralty allowed several sailors to join together in a single action. Second, in Admiralty sailors would have two securities: the master and the vessel. Third, the debt arose not from a contract for service signed on land, but "from their Merits & Services" done on vessels at port and on the sea. Fourth, if a vessel was lost at sea, sailors forfeited their wages at Admiralty; thus they should be allowed to go to Admiralty to collect wages in other instances. Belcher added a fifth argument: as sailors were transient the speed with which Admiralty cases could be tried and satisfied made them much more convenient to sailors and masters than having to wait in port for the next scheduled common law civil sessions. To support Holt's ruling and the policy considerations, Belcher cited a number of subsequent cases that followed Holt in confirming Admiralty's jurisdiction over sailors' wages actions.

Belcher then addressed the third argument for injunction: that, having not completed his contract, the boatswain could make no claim for partial work. Belcher cited precedent and policy to allow sailors wages for partial completion of contracts. First, although the boatswain was an officer, Belcher ruled he was still a mariner, and subject to English admiralty statutes and rules regarding wage recovery.[42] Thus, the common law rules regarding non-performance of contracts of employment did not apply. Second, Belcher noted that the boatswain quit the *Edward* for "the service of the State to which every private man must give way."

In concluding, Belcher explained the length and detail of his decision in terms of the importance of maritime labour to Halifax:

I have gone at large in the reasons & resolutions relating to Mariners Wages because Halifax is a Country where the Fishery & the Seamen ought to be indulg'd & protected, & that it may hereafter be known, that unless a downright Common Law Agreement takes the Suit for Wages out of the Admiralty, where the remedy is easier cheaper & more expeditious than in the temporal Court, if any Prohibitions are mov'd for again in Suits for Mariners Wages, I will deny them with exemplary Costs.

This was a strong statement in support of the jurisdiction of Vice Admiralty. It also underlined the differences of law in practice between Vice Admiralty and the common law courts. Belcher asserted the special importance of Vice Admiralty, and its different practices and decisions.[43]

Unlike the common law courts, Vice Admiralty often worked against the interests of merchants and traders in the enforcement of trade laws, in the more equitable application of wage recovery rules than the common law courts, and in the division of property from salvage and prize rulings. The power interests in Vice Admiralty law were those of imperial shipping, often contrary to the wishes of local merchants, traders, and others who might profit from international trade but saw their local needs as pre-eminent.[44] While Chief Justice Belcher may have defended Vice Admiralty's jurisdiction over wages, its jurisdiction in other matters was not as certain.

On Wednesday, 5 December 1750, Captain John Rous, commander of the sloop of war *Albany* and senior naval officer in Halifax, brought information to the Court of Vice Admiralty alleging that Thomas Power's sloop *Catherine* had landed at Halifax a variety of goods of foreign manufacture, including brandy and wine, in contravention of the *Navigation Acts*. Benjamin Green, now surrogate judge of the court, issued an order to arrest the *Catherine*. Copies of the order were delivered to Thomas Power and affixed to the mainmast of the sloop. The trial would be at three in the afternoon on Friday. The court would meet in Charles

Morris's house. Power and any others concerned were expected to attend.[45]

The first day of the trial progressed much like other Vice Admiralty trials for breaches of the *Navigation Acts*. Several witnesses described Power's summer activities. The *Catherine* and another ship he owned, the *Francis*, sailed from Halifax in March 1750 to fish on the Grand Banks. In August both vessels put in at Louisburg. After leaving Louisburg, the two vessels met in a bay along the Cape Breton coast. Power transferred from the *Francis* to the *Catherine* "[cherry] Brandy, seven loafs of sugar a large scuare box contents unknown and some Quantity of Silk and Worsted stockings," while other goods went to the *Catherine*. All of these goods, according to the witnesses from the *Francis*, were taken on at Louisburg. John Owen, master of the *Francis*, claimed that only a seventh of the total Brandy taken at Louisburg remained on the *Francis*, and it was the only thing taken at Louisburg for the use of the crew: in other words, all of the other goods were taken for trade.

The *Francis* separated from the *Catherine* on the fishing banks after leaving Cape Breton, and was eventually forced to sail north to St. Peter's Bay in Newfoundland for reprovisioning. It returned to Halifax sometime after Power and the *Catherine*. Members of the *Catherine*'s crew testified that some of the goods taken from the *Francis* were consumed, but that some of the brandy, wine, and sugar were taken ashore when the *Catherine* returned to Halifax in September.

Although not officially at war, diplomatic tensions between the French and English remained high. Although many fishing vessels from Halifax put in to Louisburg, this was often cause for suspicion of smuggling. Reprovisioning there was acceptable under the *Navigation Acts*, but only if the goods purchased in Louisburg were consumed on board the ship before it came into port in Halifax or elsewhere in British territory.[46]

The trial resumed on Saturday afternoon and took an unusual tack. Joshua Mauger appeared before the court desiring "leave of the Court to offer a Paper in behalf of" Power. Mauger brought with him a letter addressed to Judge Green from the merchants of Halifax in support of and written at the request of Power. Mauger's letter, a defence of Power, was an indictment of the colonial government and the enforcement of imperial statutes. The letter and Mauger's presentation cast merchants, fishers, and others who invested in trade and production as the true builders of the colony. Allied against them were their servants,[47] governing policy, and agents of the Crown. Mauger, Power, and their fellow merchants were quite clear in their belief that their interests were most important for the colony as a whole. Unfortunately, Power's prosecution seemed to demonstrate that the security of their investments and activities was not of great enough concern to the colony's courts. In their mind, justice required the law of the colony to change.

Mauger first complained about the use of informants. Although Captain Rous was formally listed as the informant in this case, Mauger asserted that Rous had learned of Power's trip into Louisburg and the liquor from loose talk among common sailors. To allow the chief naval officer to make arrests based on such information put all owners of vessels for the fishery or trade "at the Will and Pleasure of Drunken Idle fishermen or Sailors." Mauger argued about the relative importance of different groups in the colony. The idea that merchants and other capitalists could be threatened by vexatious court actions launched by or based on information from their subordinates was anathema. The fact that colonial officials would accept the word of such people only exacerbated the problem.

Mauger then questioned the timing of the suit in an argument that predicted the judicial limiting of the equity of redemption. For merchants to be able to invest and expand their activity in the colony, they needed to know their investments were secure. But in this case, the *Catherine* had been arrested more than two months after it had returned to Halifax. Mauger asserted:

no Person will be safe in purchasing vessells in this Settlement, as the property cannot be made good to him, whilst it is in the Power of the Captains of his Majesty's Ships to take Cognizance of past Offences … I am almost Confident that every Vessel belonging to America have more or Less Clandestinely rund Goods or Merchandise for their Own Use.

The effect of illicit trade was less important than protecting investments. If the crime of illicit trade allowed for the arrest of the vessel and not the human perpetrator, then no one would be willing to purchase vessels for fear that they would lose their investment. Likewise, if the vessel could be arrested months after an alleged act, then no investor could be sure of the security of their purchase. The colonial government and Court of Vice Admiralty should "Assist the Poor rather than distress them,"[48] and encourage investment rather than add to investors' uncertainties. One way to do this would be to secure merchants' property regardless of past infractions. Mauger's premise was partly inapplicable to Power's case: Power was, and remained, owner of the *Catherine* so he was not faced with losing his property for some prior owner's misdeeds. Yet, while he was being prosecuted, the *Catherine* remained under threat of court-ordered auction.

Mauger then returned to the specific facts of Power's case, defending Power's actions on the grounds of good economy and bad crews. He argued that Power went to Louisburg, not with the intention of illegal trade, but because he needed to reprovision his schooners. Until that point the catches of both the *Francis* and the *Catherine* had been poor, "owing to ill success and in some Measure to the ill behaviour of the Crew of the Francis." Louisburg was much closer to the fishing grounds than Halifax, and Power did not wish to expend more resources than necessary on a time-consuming and unproductive provisioning run. Once in Louisburg, not only did Power provision the ships with brandy and wine, but also with bread and meat, a fact not previously introduced into evidence. The volume of provisions, including the alcohol, was no more than would be expected to provision two schooners with a total complement of sixteen men. His actions were not those of the wily smuggler but those of the good businessman, concerned as he was to earn as high a return as possible on his investment. His intention was not to cheat the imperial government, but rather to acquire necessary provisions.

The need for provisioning does not explain why all but one of the half-anchors[49] of brandy were transferred to the *Catherine* instead of being divided evenly between the two sloops. Mauger explained that the crew of the *Francis* "made bad use of Liquor and thereby neglected their Duty." Power intended to have the two schooners fish together, and he would pass alcohol over to the *Francis* as it was required. The two vessels separated on the Banks, however, and thus Power was left, upon the *Catherine*'s return to port, with eighteen gallons of spirits as well as wine and sugar. He carried these ashore "in Order to secure it from the Crew of the Vessel who would probably have bad of it if it had been left on board."

Mauger then addressed whether even entering Louisburg to trade should be assumed a breach of the *Acts*. He argued that a man, "under Necessity of pursuing his Lawfull business for a livelihood for himself and Family," should be given leeway. In provisioning his vessels it was better to trade, even with a foreign nation, than to steal his necessities. In fact, Mauger stated, this sort of trading is "lawfully allowed to be done in all Parts of the known World."

In closing, Mauger appealed directly to Green and more broadly to the governor and Green's fellow councillors. He complimented Green on the good principles and leniency that he had so far demonstrated in his tenure. Mauger then prayed Green,

and all other Gentlemen who are in the Legislature of this Infant Colony will prove Fathers to the Poor Inhabitants who all greatly stand in need of Favours or at least Indulgences and not to suffer any of them to be oppressed by evil minded men who (as the vulgar saying is in our Mother Country) care not who sinks if they can but swim.

So as to be clear who the evil minded men were, Mauger then described the crew of the *Francis*

who have not caught fish enough in the whole Season to pay their Wages and now are so Vile as to Strike at the Root in Order to Compleat the Poor oppressed Man by their Malicious and badly grounded Informations and making mountains of mole Hills.

This conclusion returned to the class politics that Mauger used to open his address. The merchants of Halifax, like Power and himself, were "Poor Inhabitants" striving to make a better colony. They faced off against "evil minded" fishers and other labourers who acted selfishly and greedily to the detriment of both the merchants and the newly reorganized colony.

Unnamed, but implicitly implicated in Mauger's indictment were a number of colonial officials, including both Green and Captain Rous. As an anti-merchant institution, the Court of Vice Admiralty allowed sailors to sue for unpaid wages and ensured a quick resolution through the court-ordered sale of vessels to pay the wages. Rous, more than anyone else, brought illegal trade actions to the courts, while the *Albany* and other vessels under his command patrolled the Nova Scotia coast, making breaches of the *Acts* more difficult and dangerous.

Otis Little, advocate general of the court and thus the prosecutor of Thomas Power, was unmoved by Mauger's appeal. The case, he argued, was simple and proven. Power had imported goods illegally into the colony. Nothing else was material.

When Benjamin Green issued his decree on Monday, 10 December 1750, he showed much more sympathy than Little for the merchants' position. He began by acknowledging Power's defence that he went to Louisburg not out of any attempt to deceive the government but rather to acquire necessities. Similarly, he recognized the feelings behind the merchants' plea against "rigorous Execution of the Law for any inconsiderable and inadvertent Violation thereof." But Green was troubled: ruling in favour of Power (and Mauger) was not necessarily as favourable a policy position for the colony as Mauger had implied. Green commented,

if any one then every one of the Fishing Vessels belonging to this Place may with Impunity upon the Plea of Necessity either fictitious or if real perhaps owing to negligence or misconduct make Lewisburg the Magasine and Market from whence to furnish themselves ... and the Merchant here may shut up his storehouses whilst french Brandy can be purchased cheaper then [sic] English rum.

The solution for Green was to refrain from deciding. Power was commanded to give a bond with two sureties to satisfy a ruling of the court to be made within twelve months. In the meantime, Green "determined to transmit the Case with the Evidence Pleas and Memorial to the Honourable Board of Trade and High court of Admiralty and to pray advice thereon."[50]

Judge Green and other colonial officials found themselves caught between local interests on the one side and imperial expectations and orders on the other. Faced with a challenge from an organized merchant community and presented by one of the most prominent of that group, Green backed down. Local enforcement of the *Navigation Acts* tapered off in the months that followed. Of the fifteen prosecutions for illegal trade in Halifax's Vice Admiralty courts prior to 1766, five occurred between 1749 and 1750, three more between 1751 and 1752, two in 1757, and only five between 1758 and 1765. Not only did the intensity of prosecutions decline after Power's prosecution, the focus of prosecutions changed. After 1750, only two *Navigation Acts* prosecutions included Haligonians among the defendants, although in total Haligonians made up slightly more than one-quarter of those prosecuted between 1749 and 1765. It is possible that the prosecutions in the early years convinced would-be smugglers to forgo any breaches of the *Acts*. Yet, historians have not found this to be the case in other jurisdictions.[51] It seems more likely that breaches of the *Acts* continued, but with less rigorous enforcement against local vessels than those owned by outsiders.

Mauger's involvement was not simply out of concern for Power or even the merchant community as a whole. Mauger, along with many merchants from both New England and Britain as well as officials settled in Halifax, had been among those occupying Louisburg during the last half of the 1740s. When Louisburg was returned to the French, the vacating occupiers were given some time to dispose of their property there and remove all of their possessions. Mauger appears to have used this loophole in the otherwise strict trading regulations to import wine, rum, and other goods from Louisburg in 1750 and 1751. In November 1751, James Monk, acting on the governor's orders, searched several of Mauger's warehouses in Halifax and impounded French rum. Mauger argued that when he closed accounts in Louisburg in 1749 he was forced to grant a great deal of credit that, even in 1751, could only be paid back in goods like rum and molasses. The Court of Vice Admiralty accepted his argument and allowed him to keep the seized goods.[52]

Mauger's defence of Power was part of this longer, and more personal, fight with the governor and others in government over trade law and policy in Halifax. It was a fight Governor Cornwallis was unable to win. One historian concludes that Cornwallis's "inability either to impress Mauger with the majesty of the law or to establish any principle against smuggling is mute evidence of the hopelessness of the cause which attempted to combat the practice."[53] The Power case was special in a number of ways. Power's illegal goods were brought to Halifax not with the intent to smuggle but because of a combination of problems with his fishing expedition. This was true for at least some of the goods, although there was no defence proffered for the stockings. Having not consumed the goods at sea he could either order them destroyed or hope to make some use of them in Halifax despite the trade ban. Conceivably innocent of the intention to smuggle when he went to Louisburg, Power made for a sympathetic example of the problems the trade laws posed to legitimate capitalists in the colony. In his defence of Power, Mauger also attacked trade policy directly, not simply relying on the facts of the case to make an exception to enforcement.

Conclusion

The Inferior Court of Common Pleas was by far the most frequently used court: it had the widest jurisdiction and provided justice inexpensively. But litigants did have the option to appeal Inferior Court rulings, and those who could afford it could appeal twice. While William Piggot was ultimately unsuccessful at the Chancery, appellants like Anne Webb and Benjamin Leigh were at least partially successful. Plaintiffs were able to win, and were able to secure verdicts, awards, judgments, and decrees that matched or came close to their demands. Defendants had many opportunities to make their cases through trials, arbitrations, and appeals: at times they won outright, and often they could use these processes to reduce the awards against them. The civil courts provided a structure that in practice favoured plaintiffs, but gained added legitimacy by allowing defendants significant options to prevent abuse at the hands of unscrupulous plaintiffs.

Although the use of trespass upon the case allowed plaintiffs to introduce a wide variety of non-criminal disputes into the Inferior Court of Common Pleas, the court could not hear all possible disputes, nor was it the court best suited for all cases. Matters of divorce were beyond its power as were disputes over illegal trading or salvage at sea. Other disputes, like sailor's wages or securing tenure over land could be tried in the Inferior Court, but the resolutions available in other courts might be better. Sailors could sue for wages in Vice Admiralty knowing that their suit would be heard immediately and that the court could quickly order the sale of their masters' vessels if cash was not forthcoming. Likewise, John Anderson could have proven his tenure through a suit of ejectment in the Inferior Court of Common Pleas, but that judgment would not have prevented George Taylor from seeking to use the equity of redemption to displace him. A ruling in Chancery in Anderson's favour would and did forestall Taylor.

But, in having so many courts with potentially overlapping jurisdiction, there was a risk that justice could be denied through contesting the jurisdiction of any one court. In defending Vice Admiralty's jurisdiction over sailors' wages actions, Chief Justice Belcher noted the importance of both the imperial navy and the merchant marine to the continued growth of the colony. Supporting sailors was thus important, and so the Vice Admiralty doctrines concerning wages were transferred to Halifax unimpeded. Joshua Mauger argued that the practices in Vice Admiralty that enforced the *Navigation Acts*, in contrast, called into question merchant capital investment and thus impeded colonial growth. While the court was unprepared to rule specifically in his favour, practice in the court appears to have changed to protect local merchants from interference with their trade.

By way of contrast, in deciding John Anderson's action against George Taylor, the Court of Chancery was presented with no coherent argument defending the importance of debtor landowners for colonial development, but arguments could be made as to the importance of their creditors and the improvers of land in encouraging development. Without a rationale to preserve it, and with strong reasons to curtail it, the equity of redemption did not transfer to Halifax intact.

The Inferior Court of Common Pleas could deal with most disputes in law, but not all. A Court of Vice Admiralty was placed in Halifax to deal with maritime disputes, and from the Inferior Court's inception as a county court, the governor and council created a general and later Supreme Court to oversee it and hear appeals from it. When disputes arose that could not fit within that structure, the governor and council were prepared to take on new roles, as the Courts of Chancery and Prohibited Marriage and Divorce, rather than be accused of letting injustice or illegality persist within the colony.

8

Conclusion

When Roger Hill sued Anne Webb in November 1761, he wanted to be paid back for the things she had bought from him. They went before a jury that December and its verdict found Webb owed Hill everything he claimed. She appealed to the Supreme Court, where the arbitrators found for Hill, but awarded him less than the Inferior Court's jury had. When, at the same November Inferior Court, Webb sued William Fury, William Meany sued Roger Hill, and Malachy Salter sued Joseph Pratt, the defendants all defaulted. In these four actions, a truckman sued a trader, traders sued a truckman and a distiller, and a merchant sued a shipwright. These actions are remarkable only in their being so typical. These seven people, and many more like them, sued and were sued in Halifax throughout the 1750s and well into the 1760s.

The argument at the heart of this book is that the processes of the courts and the patterns of practice they sustained can explain why Salter, Webb, Hill, and people like them engaged in litigation, often with an abandon that was unusual for its time. Accounting for the decisions in the litigation at the most general level is remarkably easy: people sued because they determined that it was the best alternative they had at the time. Accounting for each litigant's individual specific decision to sue is impossible: no litigant's thoughts about suing remain. What lies between these, and what can be offered here, are the conditions that made the choice to sue easier in Halifax than elsewhere. These conditions are rooted in Halifax's colonial circumstances, in the processes and practices of the courts, and the intersection of these with mid-eighteenth-century settler ideology.

Halifax's legal structure was not a unique invention unto itself. The elements of civil law in Halifax were drawn from common law sources on either side of the Atlantic. Even in areas like divorce, the colonial lawmakers did not often invent new processes but simply applied them with variations to the colony. Likewise, Halifax's litigation rates were accentuated but linked to other parts of the common law and Atlantic worlds. The litigation rates can be accounted for by Halifax's place within Atlantic trade, the absence of alternative methods of resolving many of the conflicts that arose in daily life in the colony, the willingness of the courts to respond to litigants' desires to have the courts provide resolution for their problems, the conservative, consistent nature of their outcomes, and the engendering of acceptable, predictable plaintiff victories and defendant defeats.

The studies of litigation in other parts of the Atlantic world in the seventeenth and eighteenth centuries have found that litigation rates are higher for traders and merchants, especially those who traded over both short and long distances, than for others in their community. William Nelson argued that in Plymouth, Massachusetts in the eighteenth century, "about 3 percent of the people – many of whom were engaged directly or indirectly in commerce and were among the town's elite – took their disputes to court with great frequency, usually as plaintiffs and often with success."[1] Craig Muldrew found that Bristol's litigation rate in the 1750s remained higher than it was in other parts of England, despite a widespread decline in litigation because of its prominence in Atlantic trade.[2] In the 1750s and 1760s, Halifax was a town with a limited local hinterland, but was also part of the British Empire's Atlantic trade. Although it continued to suffer a trade deficit, between 1749 and 1755 exports from the colony averaged £96,400 per year, and between 1756 and 1763, £65,400 per year. British spending in the colony in the same period averaged £117,100 and £123,000.[3] Much of these goods and moneys flowed into Nova Scotia and then out again, travelling through Halifax before returning to Britain or moving on to other parts of the British Empire. In the process, merchants and traders in particular managed the movement of goods and currency in and out of the colony and up and down the class scale, in the process engaging in a great deal of litigation with all sorts of people in the colony. Plaintiffs were part of a network of trade within and beyond Halifax that impelled them to sue; in a less connected Atlantic community it would not have been necessary.

In the 1750s and 1760s, Halifax was also a community in flux. The colonists who came to Halifax after 1749 emigrated from both sides of the Atlantic. While many may have come with the intention to stay, for many others Halifax was only a temporary stop in a peripatetic life in the Atlantic world. In its earliest years, Halifax was a community whose members had few ties to one another: commonalities in church, guild, heritage, or even language did not necessarily exist. There was also a common expectation that the people one dealt with daily could leave the colony soon. Simultaneously, business and government elites struggled publicly with each other for control in the colony, to the point that it was difficult for anyone in a position of even nominal power to actually maintain the sort of respect they needed to exercise personal authority over the population.[4] Without the bonds of trust between people or the sorts of institutions that could cement them, a fast, effective alternative was necessary. The civil courts offered just that: a creditor knowing a debtor was on the way out could obtain a judgment quickly and seek execution immediately. Even when a debtor's departure was not apparently immanent, a judgment would provide a creditor with security. Thus, the litigation rates can partly be explained by the need for security and the absence of alternatives. Plaintiffs turned to the courts to protect their credit in the face of uncertainty.

Such an easy or frequent resort to formal law has been noticed in other new colonial communities as well. In explaining similarly high litigation rates in the Prévôté de Québec in the 1660s and 1670s, John Dickinson writes:

Ces premières années d'activité intense sont aberrantes. Elles correspondent à une période de transition et commandent de ce fait une approche nuancée et prudente. L'exceptionnelle mobilité géographique de la population forçait les commerçants à n'accorder que du credit à court terme et à réclamer leur dû dès l'échéance du prêt, de peur de voir disparaîleurs débiteurs ... La normalization des rapports sociaux s'accompagne d'une dimunitionet d'une stabilization du nombre de litiges.[5]

In her discussion of civil litigation in the gold rush communities in 1860s British Columbia, Tina Loo noted that "[a]mong strangers, formal law was particularly important in constituting social relationships between different groups of people – that is, in setting out the duties and obligations that bounded and shaped relationships." She argues that people "turned to the law to resolve their conflicts in the absence of the necessary familiarity to deal with them informally, and because they valued the predictable rationality of the formal legal process."[6]

Third, the settlers who came to Halifax were already inclined to think about the law and the courts as a forum open to all. Christopher Brooks, the historian of English litigation rates, asserts that in the early modern era

all kinds of English people, ranging from wage-labourers and seamen to better-off tradesmen and small farmers, regularly used legal instruments as a way of recording many life experiences from the cradle to the grave ... The use of courts of all kinds as a means of collecting debts, settling disputes between landlords and tenants, defending reputations through actions of slander, or indeed challenging the authority of local officials, took place on an astonishingly large scale.[7]

Building on this tradition and a North American tendency to broaden the available forms of law, Haligonians became accustomed to thinking that all manner of problems could be resolved in the courts. Justices and judges in the courts and lawmakers in the council and later in the assembly responded by trying to make it so. To cite two examples, litigants demanded and lawmakers developed practices and then laws that gave the courts much greater control over arbitration and divorce than elsewhere in the British Empire. In both cases, the courts and the governor in council began to act without local statutes or ordinances to guide the proceedings. The arbitration process, first tried by the council in the summer of 1749, developed into rule of court arbitration that permitted faster and easier recovery than allowed by the late-seventeenth-century legislation still in force in England. When marriages began to dissolve in the colony the response by wives and husbands was to petition the governor and council. The council responded by legalizing divorce in a way unheard of in England and beyond even the more liberal practices of New England. Plaintiffs turned to the courts expecting them to accommodate the law to their specific needs.

Fourth, the volume of litigation reflected the consistency of results. Litigants knew what judgments to expect, and so plaintiffs could plan on winning and defendants could plan, when possible, for the best possible result given the circumstances. In the exceptional *Webb and Ewer v. Franks*, discussed in chapter 6, the jury found for the debtor-defendant John Franks, and refused to change its opinion when the bench demanded it reconsider. Usually, juries found for plaintiffs, and in most cases their verdicts did not significantly depart from the plaintiffs' claims (see table 6.2). The bench sought rules that would limit successful abatements and make it easier for plaintiffs to win despite formal errors in their pleadings. Only arbitration consistently produced results that diverged from the plaintiffs' claimed losses, but these were decisions made by "experts" who were drawn from the leading people in their fields in Halifax. Their decisions did not undermine the expectations of plaintiffs so much as lead to end results that seemed most consistent with the evidence and the practice of trade and craft in the colony. Plaintiffs turned to the courts expecting to win, and they usually did, regardless of court or process.

Finally, the law buttressed merchant and trader, that is to say, bourgeois, power in the community through a legal structure that encouraged debtor-defendants to accept their inevitable defeat early. It is true that defendants had the power to fight in court, to choose the method best suited to resolving an action against them. But for many, that choice seems more chimerical than real. Defendants overwhelmingly chose to avoid trials: to confess, to satisfy the plaintiff in advance of the trial, and most importantly through default. Defendants of all sorts defaulted and defendants of all sorts sought jury trials or arbitrations. Yet, as was discussed in chapter 4 and presented in table 4.5, in aggregate, defendants who were craftspeople or labourers defaulted while merchants, traders, and other commercial litigants were more likely to challenge suits brought against them. When defendants defaulted it may have reflected their awareness that they could not win, or could not win enough to offset the cost of litigation. This would not necessarily be an awareness that they were in the wrong, but an awareness that because *other defendants were wrong* they would not win either; that justice precluded, in most cases, the debtor-defendant's success. Knowing that a jury would find for the plaintiff would encourage most defendants to acquiesce and default, confess, or satisfy. As more people defaulted, the inevitability of that result would compound and the defendant would be under greater pressure to default as well. Plaintiffs turned to the courts because they expected the defendant to default and thus secure their loans with little fuss.

Yet, to the degree this legal system favoured plaintiffs, it did so with the apparent agreement and even acceptance of the broader community. People certainly came to court expecting justice was possible, whether as plaintiff or defendant. This was preserved on the one hand by the rule of law: people had access to trial by jury if they wanted it, the ability to hire an attorney, the chance to produce evidence, and the opportunity to present or contest both fact and law and have the differences resolved in public by jurors or arbitrators drawn from the community. On the other hand, justice was preserved by the experiences and expectations of the litigants, jurors, and arbitrators. At the Inferior Court, 1,647 different people were summoned or attached at least once as a defendant. Of these, 664 (40 per cent) appeared in the same court at least once as a plaintiff. Although jurors often experienced the courts as defendants, they almost as often experienced it as plaintiffs; arbitrators experienced litigation from both sides too, but were more often plaintiffs. Litigants, jurors, and arbitrators defined justice in terms of what they, as plaintiffs, would have expected. The results of litigation were just, because the people involved believed them to be so.

Like so many people in the colony, defendants, jurors, arbitrators, and even plaintiffs were debtors. At the same time, however, they were also creditors to others. As U.S. colonial historian Allan Kulikoff has argued, borrowing and lending became "a strongly ingrained custom, a necessary part of economic and social life" for settlers in British North America.[8] Merchants and traders may have been the greatest creditors (and debtors), but even lowly Roger Hill credited some people. Julian Gwyn, in arguing against the demonization of merchants in pre-Confederation Nova Scotia has pointed out that the "merchant capitalists, who dominated political and economic life before the 1870s ... merely accomplished, with greater or less skill, what a capitalist elite always attempts: to aggrandize as much wealth as possible through the highest profits the market could withstand and to distribute as little of their incomes as possible in the form of taxes or wages." Rather than rise against the merchants, most Nova Scotians "hoped ... for a modest competence from their labours on the farm or for steady work and more remunerative wages if they were otherwise employed. They wanted customers who paid their accounts and returns sufficient to keep them free from either the poorhouse or imprisonment for debt."[9] They need not have believed they would someday be as wealthy as merchants, but they thought they saw, even in their smaller transactions, interests that paralleled those of the merchants. The legal structure established in Halifax in the 1750s and 1760s did not cause the merchants to achieve hegemony over the colony, but it certainly helped. It helped in that those other Nova Scotians who were looking for paying customers and to avoid imprisonment willingly accepted that in court their interests were aligned with creditors rather than the debtors.

Their decisions as jurors were based on the likelihood that they too had been a creditor in court, or might need to be one day. That the merchants and traders just happened to be the pre-eminent creditors, so sued and won more often, was immaterial to the colonial borrower-lender ideology. The size of a person's debts to the merchants and traders, coupled with the possibility of losing everything if they could not collect themselves, would compel the population of Halifax as a whole to define justice in terms of the creditor's expectation of being paid fair value for what was owed. If creditors could not expect to be paid, then the jurors who ruled against their peers might not be extended credit as easily or be able to pay their own debts on time.

This principle did not ensure that all debts were treated equally. In practice it led to a greater discounting of wage claims than accounts or notes of hand and allowed for the forced sale of property and the imprisonment of those who could not readily pay their debts, either from their assets or from squeezing specie out of their own debtors. In the end, this served to promote the greater concentration of wealth in the bourgeois merchant class that would dominate the colony through to Confederation. Historians of the Maritimes, and of Nova Scotia in particular, have argued over the relative importance of merchant capital and merchants as organizers, boosters, and politicians to the region's economic development or underdevelopment.[10] The legal system of early colonial Halifax benefited merchant capital and merchants and traders over all others.

In supporting creditor-plaintiffs, the legal structure supported the merchants in more insidious ways as well. The rules allowed for easy and quick court enforced property sales, including those of real property, and restricted the extent of the equity of redemption. These rules limited the ability of craftspeople and farmers to invest in expanding production and profit from those investments. Certainly the poor agricultural prospects of eastern Nova Scotia and its relative remoteness from most of the raw materials used in eighteenth-century manufacturing would have made the rise of significant capitalist alternatives to the merchants and traders difficult. The law did not so much hold them down as provide a means to undercut those who struggled to convert debt into greater profits in areas other than trade.[11] The one area in civil law in which wage disputes were particularly successful for workers were disputes over sailors' wages that occurred in Vice Admiralty. There too, merchants could lose their investment in ships through litigation gone awry, despite Mauger's work to prevent this.

It was the small fisher or coastal shipper who owned only a single vessel, however, who stood to lose the most. Effectively this was a legal system in which a broad range of people believed their need to be able to collect from their own debtors was more important than protecting debtors like themselves from creditors who could go after them next.

Finally, this leads us to a discussion of what the specificity of Halifax's legal history in the 1750s and 1760s might tell us about economic development and the law in the eighteenth century more generally. The ways in which civil law became imbricated in the merchant capitalist economy in colonial Halifax were not identical to those in other eighteenth century settings. The law does not need to have its efficiencies maximized to be effective; it needs to have its sufficiencies maximized. The forms the legal system takes in becoming imbricated with the economy can differ radically and still be effective so long as the results support wealth maximization and aggrandizement are met for those with the power to gain the most from the system. The form developed in Halifax, with its reliance on a great deal of litigation, was only one way in which the law could have developed to support the nascent merchant capitalist class in the colony. In other colonies, and in other times and places, litigation might be much more difficult, or plaintiffs might find winning much less likely. So long as the legal system sufficiently meets the economic needs of the established or premier capitalist class in the colony, however, it will have performed its role from the perspective of the ruling class.

Halifax, like all colonies, had unique elements in its legal system; the combination of what was brought over from elsewhere, how it was put into practice, and what innovations would develop locally, meant that each colony was different. That uniqueness, however, was only relative. The North American colonies hardly developed on such divergent paths as to make their laws unintelligible across boundaries.

Roger Hill, as a truckman, and Anne Webb, as a woman trader, were not part of Halifax's ruling class in the 1750s and 1760s. Merchants Joshua Mauger and Malachy Salter were. In the formal language of the courts, the rule of law, and the legal structure, however, they were all equals. Despite this formal equality, Mauger and Salter were able to consistently grow their businesses through the ruthless enforcement of Halifax's civil legal system, while others, lower down the social hierarchy were compelled to pay for this growth with what little currency, goods, or land they had. For all of its distinctive details, this in the end does not distinguish mid-eighteenth-century Halifax, Nova Scotia and its law from the law at other times and in other places.

Appendix 1
Sources and Methods

The material in this book is based on the analysis of a large volume of court records and other primary materials. This appendix describes the collection and analysis techniques I applied in going through the available sources.

Sources

I collected the documents in a database. Each database entry allowed me to record as much information as possible for the action. This included the names of all participants, separated out by the roles they played, the value of the demands, claims, and damages, the dates of different documents (writs of attachment, executions, etc.). The database program I used allowed the form to be constantly changed, so when I came to records that had new information, I could add fields to my database. When recording names, occupations, the forms of action, and other such information, I quoted the material directly rather than interpret it at the collection stage. This has meant, for instance, that instead of simply "case" suits, I have had "action upon the case," "trespass upon the case," "upon the case," and "case" (as well as other variations such as replacing "upon" with "on" or "in"). Essentially, these all mean the same thing. In later analyses these terms have been consolidated. For other categories of information (the court, the list of documents, the date), I used my own terms or forms; for example, dates were recorded as single 8-digit numbers (YYYYMMDD) that could later be easily sorted into chronological order.

The court records that provided the source base for much of this book came from two types of sources: minute books and case files. Each of the five courts studied here left different sorts of records, all of which are kept by Nova Scotia Archives and Records Management in Halifax, Nova Scotia.

Inferior Court of Common Pleas

The Inferior Court of Common Pleas left the most records. The primary source for the entire period of study was the file records, taking up twenty-one archival boxes. File records would be made up of paper prepared for an action and saved. These included copies of summons and attachments, declarations, accounts, promissory notes, defence pleadings, affidavits by witnesses, witness summonses, jury lists, court orders for arbitration, arbitrators' reports, bills of cost, notices of appeal, writs of execution, and other papers. Most individual actions would have only a portion of these records. Below I have described each of the most common pieces of paper and the information they routinely contained:

Writs of summons or attachment: The text of the writ itself would include the names of the plaintiff(s) and defendant(s), sometimes their occupations (or a status term), and their places of residence, the form of action (e.g., trespass on the case), sometimes a brief description of the incidents that led to the action, a specific value of damage (the claim), the date of the court to hear the action, and the demanded damages. In addition, these could be signed by either the plaintiff or the plaintiff's lawyer. The deputy provost marshal would often record if and when the writ was served and specify what was taken in attachment (if relevant). The deputy provost marshal or the clerk would often also record on the writ if the action had been defaulted or satisfied prior to trial or confessed.

Declarations: The declaration was a longer description of the incidents that led to the action. The plaintiff would plead to specific details. The details were shaped to meet the requirements of the action. But the declaration also included a more detailed description of what the plaintiffs alleged had actually occurred. In one 1759 case, for example, the assault in question is described in the following way. I have underlined those passages that describe what the plaintiffs' claim actually occurred. The rest is included because it was (or was believed to be) necessary to sustain the cause of action at law (although keep in mind that it was also necessary to include some of what "actually occurred," like dates and places):

John Woodin in the Twentyninth day of December In the Year of our Lord one Thousand Seven Hundred and fifty Eight In the thirty second year of the Reign of our Lord the now King &c at Halifax in the province aforesaid with force and arms to witt with Gunns, Swords, Bayonets, Staves, fists and knives on them the said Jonathan Harris and John Bath at Halifax aforesaid did make an assault and then the said Jonathan Harris and John Bath did then and there accost wound imprison and ill treat and then the said Jonathan Harris and John Beth there in prison, without any reasonable Cause and against the Law a long time to wit for the Space of Eighteen hours did detain and cause to be detained untill the same Jonathan Harris and John Bath expended and laid out and were Oblidged and compelled to expend and layout Several large Sums of money for their Deliverance from the Imprisonment of aforesaid and other Outrages to them then and there did, to the great damage of the said Jonathan Harris and John Bath, and against the peace of our said Lord the now king &c Whereby they say that they are prejudiced and have sustained Damage to the Value of One Hundred pounds (*Harris & Bath v. Woodin* NSARM RG 36 hx vol. 6 #8).

Every form of action had its own boilerplate. Debts on account, for instance, would include language to the effect that on a specified day the defendant promised to pay the sum in question and had failed to do so, although payment had been demanded several times. While it is possible, even likely, that in many cases creditors asked debtors for payment several times before turning to litigation, the specific pattern of promise, request, and demand laid out in the writ likely did not occur. The day of the promise was usually one of the last dates on the account, the day a promissory note was written or the day the note came due (if such a date was included). Like a writ, a declaration could include occupation or residency data for the plaintiff or defendant.

Accounts: An account for account debts could be short or run to several pages. For goods, it would often be specific, listing so many stockings and so much sugar, although at times it would just list "sundries." For labour, it would list either the days worked or the tasks completed or both. Each line would be dated and have the cost of the item or work. At the end of a page or at the end of all of the pages, the counter-account would be included (that is, what was paid back) and sometimes, but not always, a new total would be listed.

Promissory notes: A note of hand or promissory note would include a promise to pay a specific sum immediately, on demand, or at some specified later date for "value received," and the signature of the debtor. Sometimes the creditor signed as well; sometimes witnesses signed. When a signatory could not sign, a mark was made. The mark would be between the signatory's first and last name, with "His" (or "Her") written above the mark and "Mark" written below. In cases, where notes were passed from one person to the next, the back of the note would include a signed endorsement showing who had received the note.

Defence pleadings: A plea was usually very brief. The plea from the assault case above reads simply, "And the Defent by his attorney comes into Court and for plea saith that he is not Guilty In manner and form as the plf^s declare and puts himself on the Country." This would be the standard form: rejecting the plaintiff's description "in the manner and form" provided and putting oneself on the country, that is, to stand trial. The plea would sometimes be on its own page and sometimes written on the bottom or back of the writ or declaration. Usually it would be followed by a plaintiff's pleading to "do likewise" (that is, to be willing to go to trial).

Affidavits by witnesses: Other descriptions of the events at trial are very rare. An affidavit by a witness would be prepared for an Inferior Court trial only if the witness could not attend.

Witness summonses: A summons would briefly ask the witness to attend court on a specific day regarding an action identified by the names of the parties. The deputy provost marshal would record on the writ if it could *not* be served, but otherwise there would be nothing else on such a writ.

Jury lists: A jury list was a single long page that would identify the action by the name of the parties at the top and usually have the date of the trial. The jury would be listed in two columns, usually with the foreman listed first. Sometimes the foreman was identified in the list, but not always. Beneath this would be a brief charge. In the assault case above, the charge is: "Gent^n Your Issue is to try whether or not the P^{lts} are Endangered by the Def^t in manner & form as laid in the Declaration and Return your Verdict according to Evidence." This is a longer charge than most, which usually included "manner & form said" for the passage "manner & form as laid in the Declaration" and which usually did not include the admonition "according to Evidence." Below this, usually written and signed by the jury foreman, would be the verdict, which was almost always in the same form as in this case "We find for the plantives the Sum of fiveteen pounds: with Coast of Court."

Court orders for arbitration: Such an order would identify the parties, note that the court was referring the matter to arbitrators to make the final determination, name the arbitrators and who they represented (plaintiff, defendant, or court), specify that all three or two of them had to come to a decision, instruct them to meet as they chose, and request a report by the last day of the court so it could be rendered as the court's judgment.

Arbitrators' reports: This could be on its own piece of paper or written on the rule of court. It could be brief, simply identifying who owed whom how much money, or it could be more detailed, especially if the facts demanded it. Here are two examples. First, a brief one:

Halifax 27 June 1757
    We the Subscribers being appointed Arbitors in the above Rule of Court having had the Evidence sworn to give us just information concerning the matters controverted and having maturely considered the same do find Mr Roger Hill indebted to Robert Ambrose in the sum of five pounds eight shillings and Eleven pence witness our Hands
                            {sgnd} Jos. Fairbanks Lewis Piers Henry Ferguson
    (*Hill v. Ambrose* and *Ambrose v. Hill*, NSARM RG 39 (hx) vol. 4 #2, #3)

Now a more detailed one (just the body of the award):

Pursuant to the above Rule of Court we the subscribers having met the parties and heard and thoroughly considered their Several obligations and evidences do award that the defendant shall pay to the Plaintiffs the Sum of Eight pounds thirteen shillings Halifax currency and Cost of Suit to be taxed by the Court and that the Plaintiffs deliver up the Boat mentioned in their writ and declaration with her tackle and appurtenances as she now is to the defendant and that neither the Plaintiffs nor defendants shall have any further demand against each other on account of anything preceeding the 8.th march last {1757} in witness whereof we have hereunto subscribed our names the 14.th day of May 1757 and in the Thirtieth year of his Majestties Reign

(*Atkinson & Shaw v. Clarey*, RG 36 (hx) vol. 3 #46)

Bills of cost: Here, for example, is the bill of costs from a 1760 action that went to a jury trial and where the verdict included the defendant paying the plaintiff's costs:

writ seal service oath & fee	10/4
fee	3/8
affidavits before the Justices	4/–
2 Continuances	1/4
Jury & Court dues	16/10
pltf & 4 witnesses attendance	7/6
filing papers	–/6
	£ 2/2/2

(*Shay v. Brewer*, NSARM RG 37 (hx) vol. 6 #74)

The plaintiff was responsible, as the action went along, for covering the costs of the various elements of the process, like getting a continuance order or paying for the jury. When a plaintiff was granted costs, these fees would then be charged to the defendant. The defendant's costs, when they were granted costs, were usually less than the plaintiff's. Here is a bill from 1764 in an action won by the defendants:

warrant of attorney	3/4
appearance	2/6
plea to the Issue	3/6
Attendance on tryal	13/4
Copy of the Decon	2/
Copy of papers to file in this cause	11/
attendance to tax costs	3/4
	£ 1/18/10

(*Wood v. Heffernan*, NSARM RG 37 vol. 13 #71)

These costs include the defendant's fees for the various papers issued by the court (the warrant, the copy of papers or the "Decon," which was shorthand for the defendant's plea) and the lawyer's fees (attendance costs).

Notices of appeal: The clerk would record a litigant's intention to appeal and list who paid the bond, who were sureties, and the value of each.

Writs of execution: The writ commanded the provost marshal or his deputy to find the named party, and demand and collect the awarded damages, court costs, and the clerk's and marshal's fees for service of the writ. The writ would have a return date, usually immediately before the next session of the court, and the deputy marshal was expected to attempt to serve the writ and then return it to the court before or on the return date. When returning the writ, the marshal would record whether any payment had been made, how much, and when.

In addition to these file records produced for the Inferior Court, if the action was appealed, a case copy would be made by the clerk of the Inferior Court for the Supreme Court. The case copy included a transcript of all of the documents prepared or presented at the Inferior Court. It did not include transcripts of oral arguments or witness testimony.

The records at Nova Scotia Archives and Records Management have been organized on an action-by-action basis. In collecting the documents, I followed the collection's organization as best as I could. When it was clear that actions had been grouped together, I separated them out. After my collection was complete, I reviewed all of the documents, looking for actions where the same litigants were involved. Once I found such actions, I reviewed the information. If the court and dates corresponded, I grouped the documents together into the same action, unless there was intrinsic evidence showing them to be two separate actions (for example, two distinct causes of action, or two different claims for damages). Following this analysis, I found 2,563 distinct actions for the Inferior Court initiated between 1750 and 1767 in the case files.

The other major record of the Inferior Court of Common Pleas is its minute book. There are two periods of minute books, separated by ten years, for the period studied in this book. The minute books were kept by the clerk of the court. The 1750–5 minute books are divided by session, day, and plaintiff's attorney. They include all actions to be tried on a particular day, including some actions that were withdrawn or satisfied before the trial date. Each entry lists the names of the litigants, the plaintiff's attorney, the damages claimed and awarded, and the process by which the action was determined (for example, by default or by jury trial). The 1765–6 minute books are slight, recording only that the court was opened but not listing the actions tried.

I collected information from the minute book in a modified version of the file record database. Each entry received its own record in the database. When I had completed collecting the records, I went over them looking for actions where the parties were the same. Several actions were continued from one court to the next, and I linked these records into single actions. Where the evidence was clear that actions with the same litigants were distinct, I left the records separate (e.g., there were two entries in the same session for actions with the same litigants or if two actions appeared in subsequent sessions, but the action in the first appeared to have come to an end, by default, trial or some other measure). In total, the minute books from 1750–5 contain 2,564 entries for 2,079 separate actions.

Neither set of records for the Inferior Court is complete, although the minute books for the period 1750–5 seem the most complete. I compared all of the actions in the two sets of records by names and date and determined that 1,865 of the actions in the minute books did not have file records and that there were twelve file records from the 1750–5 period that I was not able to link to an action in the minute books. Table A1.1 provides information on the records available for each year. The range of actions in the minute books is between 219 and 559 per year (with the exceptions of 1749, before there actually was a court, and 1756, when the record books cease). During the same years, the file records only amount to between 3 and 86 actions per year. Between 1759 and 1764, the number of actions in the file records per year was considerably greater: between 201 and 387. During the years 1750–5, the ratio between file and minute book actions ranged from as wide as 1:104 in 1751 to as narrow as 2:5 in 1755. Assuming the minute book reflected all Inferior Court actions, and using the smallest ratio of two file records for every five actions, the total number of actions in 1763 would equal 967, and even in 1760 the number of actions would be 598. This would be a very large caseload unless there was considerable shift in population. The last two columns of table A1.1 offer a way to evaluate this. Based on the population estimates offered in the historical record or by various historians, the number of actions initiated in the early 1750s ranged from 61 to 132 per 1,000 people per year. The action rates based

Table A1.1 Records of Inferior Court actions by year

Year	Files	Minutes	Total[a]	Population[b]	Actions per 1,000 people
1749	0	3	3	2,500	
1750	81	420	426		
1751	3	314	314	3,200	98
1752	19	559	561	4,248	132
1753	78	317	321	5,250	61
1754	16	244	244		
1755	86	219	273		
1756	49	3	51	1,755	29
1757	170		170	3,000	57
1758	138		138	6,000	23
1759	201		201		
1760	239		239	3,000	80
1761	324		324		
1762	237		237	2,500	95
1763	387		387	2,500	155
1764	305		305		
1765	146		146		
1766	41		41		

[a] These numbers are based on both "file" records, that is, kept copies of writs and/or other materials, and "minute" records taken by the clerk of the court for the years 1750–56.
[b] The sources for the population numbers are from Fingard, Guildford, and Sutherland, *Halifax the First 250 Years* (1758, p. 6 and 1760, p. 18); Alan Marble, *Surgeons, Smallpox and the Poor* (1751, p. 27; 1753, p. 33; 1757, p. 52; and 1762, p. 70); Akins, *History of Halifax City* (1752, p. 261; 1756, p. 58; and 1763, p. 69).

only on the file records in the early 1760s range between 80 and 155 per 1,000 people. Although both sets of ranges are broad, they are relatively congruent. If the file records of the early 1760s represent only two-fifths of the total actions, however, then the action rate in 1760 would equal 199 per 1,000 people per year, while in 1763 it would reach an incredible 387 per 1,000 people. Even though the litigation rate fluctuated in the early 1750s, such high rates would deviate too much from other rates. The evidence in table A1.1 suggests that, while the file records of the inferior court in the 1750s and 1760s are inconsistent, in the early 1760s they probably reflect most, if not all, of the litigation in the courts, while throughout most of the 1750s and again in 1765 and 1766 they represent a smaller proportion of the total caseload of the court.

Table A1.2 Process types by Inferior Court records

Process	Files only		Minutes only		Both	
	N	%[a]	N	%	N	%
Default	591	50	636	37	68	33
Nonsuit	11	1	27	2	5	2
Confession	25	2	220	13	31	15
Withdrawn	112	10	280	16	15	7
Abatement	4	>1	46	3	0	0
Dismissed	3	>1	90	5	5	2
Jury Trial	275	23	235	14	50	24
Special Jury	12	1	12	1	0	0
Arbitration	129	11	167	10	30	15
Other	13	1	8	>1	1	>1
Total known Processes	1175		1721		205	

[a] Percentage of actions with known process, not of all actions.

The differences between the volume of file records and minute records for the 1750–5 period may be accounted for by selective record-
keeping on the part of the clerks of court. For example, they may have
chosen or have been required to keep records of cases that ended in
trials but not those ending in in defaults. Table A1.2 addresses this possibility. Defaults and jury trials make up a greater proportion of the
file-only records than of the minute books. Confessions, withdrawals,
abatements, and dismissals make up a significantly greater proportion
of the minute book records (although, as shown in chapter 4, the pau-
city of file records for abatements and dismissals may reflect changes in
legal practice). The differences in the record-keeping can be explained
by legal practices. By the mid-1750s, would-be defendants had to in-
form the court before the beginning of the session of their intention to
defend, or they would be marked in default. Thus, immediately prior
to session, the clerk would go through all of the writs for the upcoming
session, mark the defaults on the writs, and set them aside until costs
were taxed. At trial, jury trials, arbitrations necessarily produced more
paper in the forms of orders, verdicts, and awards. Nonsuits, because
they resulted in judgments for the defendant, would at least lead to
bills of costs. All of these new pieces of paper would point to the process that brought the action to an end. Withdrawals and confessions

need not have created any new paper (including costs which the parties could have agreed to outside of court), so the the final process would be recorded only if the clerk marked it on the writ at the time. Although there are 1,175 file-only records where the process used to resolve the action is known, there are 1,170 where the process is not recorded. It is possible that withdrawals and confessions are over-represented in the unknown records and under-represented in the 1,175 actions in the first column of table A1.2. For 83 of the 205 actions where both file and minute book records exist, the process is known only because of the minute books.

The Other Courts

The records for most of the other courts are primarily case files: the Supreme Court, Chancery, and Prohibited Marriage and Divorce Courts all left file records that the archivists at Nova Scotia Archives and Records Management have grouped into apparently distinct actions. Vice Admiralty trials were recorded in a minute book that appears to be complete. The Court of Chancery generated both a minute book that recorded the names of litigants and the dates of hearings, and file records that contain a great deal of paper from the submissions and petitions of the litigants. Because all Chancery motions had to be in writing, the case files could include more than ninety separate pieces of paper. All but one of the Chancery actions listed in the Chancery minutes has a corresponding file record. The Vice Admiralty minute book and the Chancery Court files appear to afford a fairly complete picture of both what happened in the courtroom, and to some degree, of the negotiations outside of it. The Court of Prohibited Marriage and Divorce was composed of the same men as the Court of Chancery and seems to have followed similar procedures relating to written documents. The files are less complete, however, and the earliest cases, dating from before the court's creation by local statute in 1758, have no written files at all, only references in the council's own minute books. It is possible that I did not find all of the court's cases, but considering how rarely the court was used, it is impossible to estimate how many, if any, cases are missing.

The Supreme Court's civil jurisdiction in the 1750s and 1760s was limited to primarily acting as a court of appeal. Civil actions were not recorded in its minute books for the period; instead, only file records exist of these actions. In some cases, the Supreme Court files include records of trials at the Supreme Court level. In other cases, I inferred appeals trials from the existence of case copies and other documents produced in the Inferior Court for the purpose of a Supreme Court appeal. It is likely that several appeals, once initiated, were withdrawn prior to a hearing or nonsuited at the court (although, because of the appeal bonds and sureties required, this latter course of action would be costly). Recording appeal actions where no record of the appeal trial exists is nonetheless valuable because it shows how often cases were *initiated* in the court. Considering how many actions in the Inferior Court were withdrawn, defaulted, or nonsuited, it is possible to assume that at least some actions in the Supreme Court would be abandoned in one way or another. Recording the information of the appeal where the evidence of outcome is missing is useful in paralleling abandoned cases from both levels of the common law court.

The actions in all of these courts were recorded in the same database as the files records from the Inferior Court of Common Pleas.

Other Sources

Although the court records for the period are voluminous, there are only limited other sources from the period. I have consulted the official correspondence between Halifax and London and the *Halifax Gazette* for the time period. There is a printed diary from the first few years that is useful in piecing together parts of the Justices' Affair and elite interpersonal relationships. Some of Chief Justice Belcher's personal papers are collected in a descendant's collection at the University of British Columbia archives. I found no other usable personal papers (business records, lawyer's notes, judicial bench books, or related materials) with which I could supplement or test my analysis.

Analytical Methods

Much of the analysis presented in chapters 3 through 7 is built up from a quantitative base, with qualitative data and narratives laid over it to deepen the descriptions and analysis. To develop the quantitative base, I have exported data from the original collection database into a relational database, which has many tables that are interconnected by shared data. The relational database is composed of several unique tables. Each table is built around sets of congruent data and linked to other tables by common data.

For instance, I created a table titled "person." This table contains a row for each distinct person from the data records. To create the table, I assembled from my collection database a list of all of the people, ranging from litigants, clerks, or jurors, to the deceased whose estates were involved in litigation of some sort. I then pared the list down to individuals. I did this by sorting lists of unique names by surname and given name, looking for differences in spelling that could be sounded out as the same. Where other evidence (such as similar occupations) supported combining different individuals into one, I would look for any evidence that would preclude such a grouping, such as a death or a radical change in occupation. I would balance the evidence pro and con combining the individual. I then assigned each person a unique number. All of the information I had about each individual was then entered into the table: first, middle, and last names, aliases (Anne Webb and Anne Martin), name prefixes or suffixes (e.g., sergeant or junior), all listed occupations, all listed homes, and gender.

By the number assigned to each individual, the "person" table is connected to the table "role." Each row in role has a person's number, an action number, and code for the role played by the individual in the action. The action number in turn links the role table to a variety of tables that all deal with different aspects of a particular action, such as the type of action, the processes and dates of each process, and the monetary value of the action.

To understand the day-to-day practice of the civil courts in Halifax, my first step was to develop as complex and quantifiable a picture of litigants and actions in the period as possible. The assumption contained within the structure of the database is that understanding legal practice requires studying the working of the law through the constituent parts of litigation: the litigants, the actions, the processes, the money, and the other human actors (attorneys, jurors, and others). I have assumed that, independent of the personal justifications individuals may have used to explain to themselves or others why they used the courts, similar practices can be described as patterns and that the patterns speak to one or more generally held understandings of how the courts worked, for what purposes, and more.

I have assumed that the different ways in which an individual came into contact with the civil courts mattered for that individual and, in turn, for the society at large. In other words, part of understanding how the courts worked involves understanding that Roger Hill was a litigant many times or that Peter Mackey was a juror many times before he ever became a litigant. I assume that they learned from their prior experiences, learned not just how the courts worked (as they perceived them) but also how the courts were supposed to work. This latter bit is particularly important in the explanation I offer for jury verdicts: despite the fact that, on the whole, jurors were more likely to be defendants than plaintiffs, they favoured plaintiffs because they had been taught to by other jurors and by the general atmosphere of the court room.

One method of analysing this was to compare frequent and infrequent litigants, jurors, and arbitrators. To create the categories of frequent and infrequent, I ranked everyone from fewest appearances to most appearances in each role. For the infrequent litigants, I counted up individuals' appearances, starting from those with the fewest until I reached 25 per cent of all of the appearances. I reached this with the litigants who appeared three times or fewer. I then put all of the litigants who appeared three or fewer times into the category, which amounted to 2,672 appearances. Starting at the other end, the most litigious, I began counting up all of the appearances until I reached roughly the same number and percentage of appearances, which took me to twenty-seven or more appearances (2,655 appearances in total). These fifty-six individuals were the frequent litigants. I followed the same basic process to determine who were the frequent and infrequent jurors and arbitrators.

Two assumptions underlay this division: first, that frequency mattered; those people who appeared in a role frequently would have a disproportionate effect on the court's business and practice in different ways than those who appeared infrequently. Second, having two blocks of people responsible for roughly the same number of appearances would allow for comparisons that could help understand who used the courts and how. My analysis suggested that litigation rates were high and that litigation was spread through the community. Understanding the high litigation rates required understanding, I believe, the actions of those who litigated frequently. Understanding the breadth of litigation through the community required understanding those who ended up in court, but only once in a while. Both were necessary for understanding litigation in Halifax.

I employed other generalizations in my analysis to help understand legal practice and the relationship between law and society.[1] One of the key generalizations is based on occupation data, which is discussed in appendix 2. I have also grouped people by gender and place of residence. I did the latter on the assumption that a person's place of residence, and more importantly the relationship between the places of residence of both sides in an action, can reveal something about the people, the action, and the legal system.

The division of the population by gender is more problematic. Despite a great deal of philosophical and historical work that argues that gender is not a simple binary, I have divided the population of Halifax into only two categories: male and female. This is probably not an accurate reflection of the range of gender identities in Halifax at the time, but it is reflective of legal rules regarding use of the courts, and these are the only two genders identified in the court records. To the extent that people with other gender identities were present in Halifax, questions or even evidence of their gender did not appear in the civil court records which form the basis of my study.

Gender was not often identified in the court documents. Where pronouns, adjectives, or other markers were present in the text, I identified people accordingly. At the conclusion of collecting, I began with the assumption that, unless I found otherwise, a person I collected would be male. I made this assumption based on both what I had already intuited from the records and what I had learned from other legal histories of the time period regarding the roles women could play in the common law legal system. I went through all of the names and identified those where the first name was, at the time, a woman's name or a name that was used for both men and women. I then reviewed the evidence of these individuals in the court records and elsewhere to see if there was anything I had missed that might confirm the person's gender. It is possible that I was not able to correctly identify everyone's gender (at least vis-à-vis the male-female binary), but I am confident that I was able to achieve the best possible division, given the available information.

Appendix 2
Interpreting Occupational and Status Data

Occupation data is tantalizing, but there are significant complexities to using the occupational and status data. As W.A. Armstrong suggested in the 1970s, social historians using occupational data often attempt to allocate "individuals according to two main principles, (a) by *industrial grouping* – so that we can trace the economic contours of a society and the bases on which these rest, and (b) by social ranking." In linking these, Armstrong continues, "[A] carpenter (occupation) is likely to be employed in a wide variety of *industries,* and this is the important economic variable. But all carpenters, in whatever industry, constitute an *occupational* group, and persons of that occupation are generally viewed as falling under the heading of skilled manual workers, in the hierarchy of social class."[1]

This appendix explains in greater detail the specifics of the data available in the sources and the decisions I made in my analysis of it.

Issue 1: Source
Most occupational terms come from the writs or the declarations, that is, from documents dictated by plaintiffs or their lawyers. Defendants did not self-identify their occupations, and the occupations ascribed to them were chosen by their opponents.

Issue 2: Absence of occupation and status terms
Because such terms were not essential to the documents, many litigants

never had terms applied to them. Sixty-five per cent of all defendant and 68 per cent of all plaintiff appearances had no occupation listed. The more frequently individuals were plaintiffs, the less likely they felt the need to identify their occupation or status. So, among infrequent litigants, the percentages of defendants and plaintiffs with no occupation listed were 62 per cent and 64 per cent, respectively; among frequent litigants, the percentages were 63 per cent and 72 per cent, respectively. Of the fifty-six frequent litigants, three had no occupation or status term applied in any of their appearances; of the 1,886 infrequent litigants, 1,093 or 58 per cent had no occupation or status term applied to them.

Issue 3: Multiple occupations

Over several appearances, several different terms could be applied to a single litigant. Of the fifty-three frequent litigants who had occupational or status terms applied to them, only five had one occupation, eleven had two occupations, and fifteen had between six and eleven distinct occupation terms applied to them. Of the 1,886 infrequent litigants, more than a third (705, or 37 per cent) had one occupation only; but of the 400 litigants who appeared only two times, one-tenth (40, or 10 per cent) had a different occupation label applied at each appearance as a litigant; of the 193 who appeared three times, 43 (22 per cent) had two occupation terms applied, and 5 (3 per cent) had three occupations. The more times an individual appeared, the greater the likelihood they had at least one occupational or status term applied to them, and then that they had more than one term applied to them.

Issue 4: Synonyms and compounds

Plaintiffs applied the occupational or status terms they knew and chose to apply. The terms did not come from a list of acceptable terms. Thus, more than 400 distinct terms were used. Sometimes the terms appear to be synonymous, like "shoemaker" and "cordwainer." Others were compounded from other terms. For example, someone could be described as a "merchant and distiller." The same person could, in other circumstances, be defined as either "merchant" or "distiller."

Issue 5: Rank or gradation

Several terms that seem similar appear to have actually had distinct and graduated meanings. Most important here are the differences among merchant, trader, retailer, shopkeeper, and truckman. Some individuals used or had more than one of these terms applied to them, but while merchants were sometimes also called traders, and retailers sometimes called shopkeepers, no one was called both merchant and truckman. Historians of Britain, British North America, and the early United States seem to agree on the broad meanings of at least some of these terms. Thomas Doerflinger, in writing about late-eighteenth-century Philadelphia contends, "Merchants were wholesalers who – in America, at least – were typically active in foreign markets; shopkeepers were general retailers who obtained their goods from merchants."[2] David Hancock, discussing a wide variety of eighteenth-century English writing agrees: "Most contemporaries agreed that a merchant was a wholesale trader who had dealings with foreign countries. Many groups of critical importance to the domestic economy, such as 'artificers' (manufacturers), skilled tradesmen, retailers, and shopkeepers, were not labelled 'merchants.'"[3] This sense is borne out by patterns of litigant behaviour in Halifax. Malachy Salter, a merchant, had significant trade with people outside of Halifax, and more than one-quarter of the people who sued him came from British North America. Compare him to truckman Roger Hill, whose commercial relationships were limited to Halifax. Table A2.1 shows all suits where a Halifax-based plaintiff or defendant was identified as a merchant, trader, retailer, shopkeeper, or truckman. The merchants faced people from outside Halifax in a significantly greater proportion than anyone else; like Salter, more than a quarter of all plaintiffs suing Halifax merchants came from outside of the town. Truckmen sued only within Halifax, and were sued almost exclusively by Haligonians. Traders, retailers, and shopkeepers had some ties outside of Halifax proper, but were more likely than merchants to sue or be sued by Haligonians and Nova Scotians.

To differentiate among traders, retailers, and shopkeepers, it is helpful to differentiate between those who were sued by litigants with these occupations and those who sued them.

- **Merchants** were sued most frequently by merchants (37), mariners and shopkeepers suing them the next-largest number of times (5 and 3 respectively). They sued other merchants (37 times), traders (31), and mariners (30) most often, although they also sued retailers (15), shopkeepers (9), tavern keepers (9), and tailors (9) several times.
- **Traders** were frequently sued by merchants (31) and other traders (17); they were rarely sued by retailers (2) or truckmen (1). Traders sued retailers 9 and truckmen 5 times.

Table A2.1 Halifax commercial litigants' opponents' residences

Litigant	Role	Home of Opponent							
		Halifax		Nova Scotia		BNA		Elsewhere	
		N	%[a]	N	%	N	%	N	%
Merchants	Plt	307	88	32	9	5	1	4	1
	Def	71	80	1	1	5	6	11	13
Traders	Plt	149	95	4	3	3	2	0	n/a
	Def	119	92	6	5	4	3	1	1
Retailers	Plt	42	85	7	14	0	n/a	0	n/a
	Def	86	94	2	2	2	2	1	1
Shopkeepers	Plt	20	83	3	13	0	n/a	1	4
	Def	21	88	0	n/a	0	n/a	3	13
Truckmen	Plt	21	100	0	n/a	0	n/a	0	n/a
	Def	36	97	1	3	0	n/a	0	n/a

[a] Percentage of opponents with a known place of residence.

- **Shopkeepers** were sued most frequently by merchants (9) but sued mariners (4) most frequently.
- Likewise, **retailers** were sued most frequently by merchants (15) and traders (9) but sued carpenters (5), other retailers (4), or yeomen and labourers (3) most often.
- **Truckmen** were sued by yeomen, traders, labourers (5 times each), and merchants (4) most frequently, but while they sued labourers 5 times and yeomen 3 times, they only sued 1 trader and never sued a merchant.

The litigation pattern here suggests that merchants were at the top of commercial occupations extending credit to all of the others, followed in status level by traders, retailers, shopkeepers, and truckmen, with each level lower indebted to those above it and extending credit to others at the same level or below. As other historians have suggested, merchants in Halifax appear to have been wholesalers involved in intercolonial trade. Traders, apparently, were also a variety of wholesaler, but with fewer direct links outside of the colony. Shopkeepers and retailers sold more directly to the public, and relied on wholesalers for their goods. Truckmen were similar to the shopkeepers and retailers, yet operated on an even more local scale than retailers and shopkeepers.

This sort of gradation is most difficult with commercial occupations like merchants and retailers. Among craftspeople and sailors, there were also gradations. Craftspeople could be apprentices learning their craft from others, journeymen who worked for others and on their own, or masters who employed journeymen on a regular or irregular basis. Those who made their life on the sea also had graduated occupation terms, ranging from seamen to masters. With both, however, some terms could be applied regardless of status. For example the term "mariner" was used and applied to any person who made his livelihood at sea and "mason" was applied without distinction to journeymen and masters alike.

Issue 6: Occupation data and class
Thus, it is difficult to simply ascribe social rank, wealth, or even class to individuals based on their occupation terms. Even graduated terms like "merchant" and "retailer" do not necessarily reveal social class. Doerflinger, in describing the merchants of late-eighteenth-century Philadelphia notes, "[T]he merchant community ... was not a tight commercial elite of merchant princes, but a large occupational group

embracing wealthy traders and many petty capitalists who lived no more sumptuously than a successful cooper or grocer."[4] Differentiation is possible, insofar as merchants and traders, as well as retailers, shop-keepers, truckmen, tavern keepers, and innholders made their living buying and selling goods, while craftsmen, labourers, mariners (except those who owned their own vessels perhaps), and yeomen made their living through their labour and from what they produced themselves.

Pre-existing models

Historians have used several models that could be applied to the data available. In *The People of Hamilton, Canada West*, Michael Katz suggests that there are two distinct ways to classify people by occupation. One can rank "occupations in a vertical or hierarchical fashion according to criteria of wealth, status, power, or some combination of these attributes." Or, one can arrange "occupations according to functional groups, that is, on the basis of similarity of their role within the economy or the sort of industry of which they are a part."[5] Essentially, the former is a social class model, the latter an industrial group model. While there may be some relationship to wealth or power in the industrial group model, this is not inherently so.

Both industrial and class models are employed widely by social historians of the law. Deborah Rosen, in describing litigants and jurors at civil courts in eighteenth-century New York, and Peter King, in describing prosecutors, the accused, and jurors in eighteenth-century Essex criminal courts both use industrial group–type models.[6] Both historians group occupations into categories such as "merchant," "craftsmen," or "labourer," although their specific terms and categories differ. The problem with these models is that they offer no consistent breakdown of industry that can be used for comparison from one study to the next. Rosen and King agree that carpenters should not be classified with merchants, but King places tavern keepers with skilled craftspeople, while Rosen places them with merchants. This sort of inconsistency is endemic and makes comparative analysis difficult.

Jim Phillips has attempted a social class model in his study of grand and petty juries in eighteenth-century Nova Scotia. Phillips used a four-class model: elite, upper middling, middling, and lower middling and upper working class. The elite were made up of the "leading merchants, major landowners, and principal office-holders." Malachy Salter fell into this category. The upper middle class comprised "substantial, but not pre-eminent, merchants, former commissioned officers, principal community leaders including some who became members of the assembly after it was founded in 1758, and the like." The middling included "farmers, shopkeepers, small-time merchants, retailers, and publicans." The lower middle or upper working class "were principally successful and independent artisans, smiths, bakers, carpenters, etc., although this category also includes modest fishermen and a variety of other occupations." Placing people within the model proved rather difficult, as no consistent source demonstrating wealth or income is available for the eras (1749–66 and 1787–1800). Significant numbers of jurors were left out of his model. In addition, the differentiation of people between the bottom two categories was difficult. Phillips allows "that some individuals may not be where they should be."[7] Phillips's model holds out the most promise for developing a class model of Halifax, but for the vast majority of litigants at the civil courts, the available information about wealth is so limited that no attempt at recreating his breakdown has been made.

The method applied here

Writing about the urge to model or classify from occupation data, Heinrich Berger has suggested in opposition,

Within the process of classification of occupations there are different possibilities: we can impose a social hierarchy or we can remain very close to the source. When we do the first, considerable interpretation of the source material would be necessary. I think it is much better to interpret as little as possible within the classification and to define the classes with the use of information from the source itself only. Interpretation should be left for the analysis of the data to be a result of research and not the basis.[8]

Following Berger's advice, I decided to analyse litigants first by the occupations ascribed to them on an appearance-by-appearance basis. Thus, Roger Hill was described as a truckman in twenty-five actions, a carter in one, and was not described in thirty actions. In most cases in the analysis, only the twenty-five appearances where he was actually identified as a truckman will be counted when the litigation practices of truckmen are discussed. In some instances, this is not practical (for example, in discussing juries), and litigants will be described as "having been so described one or more times." When this is done, some individuals may be counted more than once: Hill, for example, will be counted in these circumstances as a truckman and as a carter. Unfortunately, while occupation type broadly suggests an individual's relationship to the means of production, it offers relatively little information about either the individual's wealth or his or her access to capital. By holding back from categorizing the different occupations, however, the analysis revealed which occupations seemed to have similar or divergent interests and the points where those similarities and differences appeared.

I then began to break the occupations up into categories based on their main method of working or earning an income. Of the twenty-five most common occupations ascribed to litigants, six were occupations involved in commerce at some level. The individuals who were classified at least once in these occupations litigated often. On average, individuals described at least once as truckmen made 11 litigant appearances, retailers 12, tavern keepers 15, traders 15, merchants 17, and shopkeepers 18. The next largest group were craftspeople; nine of the twenty-five most common occupations were craftspeople: bakers, blacksmiths, butchers, carpenters, coopers, housewrights, masons, shoemakers, and tailors. Others could be classified as seafarers (mariners, master mariners, fishers, and sailors), labourers, professionals (schoolmasters, scriveners, surgeons, and attorneys), soldiers, or agricultural workers (husbandmen and yeomen).

The two largest were commercial and crafts-based occupations. As the discussion of litigants in chapter 2 and of jurors and arbitrators in chapter 5 showed, there were significant differences in the patterns of court use between the people in these groups. On the whole, the amount of litigation engaged in by truckmen was closer to that of traders and merchants than to that of carpenters and coopers. There were outliers for every occupation, but overall it became apparent that these distinctions mattered.

This breakdown suffered from the concern I had with Rosen and King, and so, as much as possible, I refrained from relying on it for the bulk of my analysis and the discussion of it in the body of the book.

Notes

1 Introduction

1 Anne Webb's first appearance is in an action at the September 1757 session, *Tritton v. Webb*, where the writ was issued on 26 August 1757 (NSARM RG 37 (hx) vol. 4 #106). John Webb's last appearance in court before his death was in an ejectment action begun in December 1756 and finally determined on 7 June 1757 (see *Webb v. Prescott*, NSARM RG 37 vol. 3 #44). John likely died between these two moments. For evidence of Anne Webb as a trader on her own, see, for example, *Webb v. Nuttidge*, where all of the trading occurred several years after John Webb's death (NSARM RG 37 (hx) vol. 11 #20). In 1751, John Webb owned the two-masted sailing vessel *Elizabeth* and sailed between the colony and England. In the 1752 census of greater Halifax, he was living alone next door to Robert Ewer. At the end of 1752, John Webb was one of fourteen prominent men in Halifax to sign a memorial accusing several of the colony's justices of bad behaviour.

   For John Webb as master of a vessel, see *Still and Chapman v. Webb*, NSARM RG 1 vol. 491, pp. 13–14. For John Webb in the census, see Thomas B. Akins, *History of Halifax City*, facs. ed. (1895; repr., Belleville, ON: Mika Publishing, 1973), 256. For John Webb and the *Elizabeth*, see John Salusbury, *Expeditions of Honour: The Journal of John Salusbury in Halifax, Nova Scotia, 1749–1753*, 2nd ed., ed. Ronald Rompkey (Montreal: McGill-Queen's University Press, 2011; first published 1982 by University of Delaware Press), 111 and 198n6.

2 Although "truckman" sounds to a modern ear like "trucker," in the eighteenth century, the word referred to "truck" in the sense of commodities or sundries (see *Oxford English Dictionary*, "truck n^1"). For the wedding of Roger Hill and Laetitia Gray, see George T. Bates, "The Great Exodus of 1749: or, The Cornwallis Settlers who Didn't," *Collections of the Nova Scotia Historical Society* 38 (1973): 53. For actions involving Hill in 1750, see *Cummerford v. Hill* and *Dam v. Hill*, NSARM RG 37 A2, pp. 40–9, *Hill v. Shippey*, NSARM RG 37 A2, pp. 50–5. For Hill as a truckman, see, for example, *Salter v. Hill*, NSARM RG 39 "c" (hx) vol. 1 #103 and as a carter, see, for example, *Dwight v. Hill*, NSARM RG 37 (hx) vol. 2 #79.

On the founding of Cow Bay, see "Cow Bay," in Public Archives of Nova Scotia, *Place-Names and Places of Nova Scotia* (Halifax: Provincial Archive of Nova Scotia, 1967), 147. For Hill's death, see Allan E. Marble, *Deaths, Burials, and Probate of Nova Scotians, 1749–1799* (Halifax: Genealogical Association of Nova Scotia, 1990), 119. The closest Hill apparently came to making a mark on the history of Halifax was when he signed a memorial in December 1752 that lambasted the Justices of the Peace, but he was not one of the instigators, and in his discussions of the "Merchants' Affair," John Salusbury makes no reference to him (unlike many of the others involved); even his term for it excludes Hill who was very much not a merchant. (See James Muir, "The Fight for Bourgeois Law in Halifax, Nova Scotia, 1749–1753," *Histoire Sociale/Social History* (2016) 49 no. 98: 15–16, and Salusbury, *Expeditions of Honour*, 129–34.)

3 Litigation rates are difficult to measure, and different historians have offered different methods of measuring it. Christopher Brooks has perhaps done the most sustained study of litigation rates in the common law world and the problems related to measuring litigation rates historically. For a general introduction to the problem, see Brooks, "The Longitudinal Study of Civil Litigation in England, 1200–1996," in *Litigation: Past and Present*, ed. Wilfrid Prest and Sharyn Roach Anleu (Sydney, NSW: UNSW Press, 2004), 24–43.

It is possible to compare the rates in Halifax with those determined for other common law jurisdictions in England or the American colonies in the eighteenth century. For Plymouth County, Massachusetts, in the eighteenth century, William Nelson found family participation rates as high as 24 per cent in the town of Plymouth, but the next-highest rates were 16.3, 15.7, 15.1, and 13.9 per cent. Of the 639 families named in the 1752 Halifax census, the family participation rate was 27 per cent (170). Nelson also notes that intratown litigation rates peaked at 2.57 per 1,000, while the non-commercial litigation rate peaked at 3.21 per 1,000; the

Halifax equivalent measures for 1751–3 were 44 per 1,000 and 14 per 1,000, respectively. See William E. Nelson, *Dispute and Conflict Resolution in Plymouth County, Massachusetts, 1725–1825* (Chapel Hill: University of North Carolina Press, 1981), 52, 64–5, and 67. Craig Muldrew, studying English courts in the 1700s, found rates that ranged from 20 to 73 per 1,000 people in 1750 and actions per household of between 0.08 and 0.3. The equivalent measures for the 1751–3 period in Halifax were 94 actions per 1,000 people or 0.4 actions per household (rates based on the 1752 population, the number of households, and an average household size of 4.7 in the 1752 census) (*The Economy of Obligation: The Culture of Credit and Social Relations in Early Modern England* [Hampshire, UK: Palgrave, 1998], 231–2, 236–7, and 392n105).

John Dickinson has found very high litigation rates for the civilian-law Prévôté de Québec between 1667 and 1675, followed by a generally declining rate through to the 1750s. The procedures do not directly correspond with common law counts, but in the 1670s, the rate of *procès-verbaux* was roughly 200 per 1,000 people per year, while the number of *causes* was only somewhat lower. By the 1750s, just prior to the Seven Years War, the rate was 33.6 *procès-verbaux* per 1,000 people and 23 *causes* per 1,000 people. Later in the same book, however, he provides significantly lower rates for *litiges civils* of 37.9 actions per 1,000 people in the years 1685–9, down to 13.3 per 1,000 people in the years 1750–3. See *Justice et Justiciables: La Procédure Civile à la Prévôté de Québec, 1667–1759* (Québec: Les Presses de l'Université Laval, 1982), 108–11 and 123.

4 This number is based on Statistics Canada's Civil Court Survey (CCS) of general civil cases, which is based on data collected "on civil court events and cases at both the superior and provincial and territorial court levels." The rate of initiated cases per 1,000 people in Canada as a whole between 2010–11 and 2014–15 was approximately 9. The category "general civil cases" includes a variety of disputes not heard in Nova Scotia's civil courts in the 1750s and 1760s: bankruptcy, motor vehicle accidents, malpractice, and negligence. The contemporary numbers do not include family law–related litigation, such as divorce, child custody and access, or support. The numbers quoted above thus overstate contemporary litigation rates that can be directly compared to Nova Scotia in the eighteenth century but also understate total civil litigation rates in Canada today, where family disputes make up a significant proportion of all litigation. See Statistics Canada, *Table 259-0013. Civil court survey, general civil cases by level of court and type of action, annual (number)*, CANSIM (database).

5 The lack of controversy in litigation contrasts with present-day debates

in many parts of the common law world. In Canada, recent debate has focused on access to civil justice and the failure by many to use the courts when they could; see, for example, Trevor Farrow, "Dispute Resolution, Access to Civil Justice and Legal Education," *Alberta Law Review* 42, no. 3 (2005): 741–801, and Beverley McLachlin, "The Challenges We Face: Remarks of the Right Honourable Beverley McLachlin, P.C., Chief Justice of Canada to the Empire Club of Canada," remarks delivered to the Empire Club of Canada, Toronto, ON, 8 March 2007, accessed 31 March 2016. www.cfcj-fcjc.org/sites/default/files/docs/2007/mclachlin-empireclub-en.pdf.

In the United States particularly, but elsewhere as well, it is apparently high litigation rates that are the problem. See from Prest and Anleu, eds., *Litigation: Past and Present*: Prest and Anleu, "Introduction," 6–15; Ted Wright and Angela Melville, "Hey, But Who's Counting? The Metrics and Politics of Trends in Civil Litigation," 96–121; and David Bamford, "Litigation Reform 1980–2000: A Radical Challenge," 147–8 and 155–61. The twin issues of consumer debt and litigation explosion came together nicely in a 13 July 2010 *New York Times* article by Andrew Martin, "Automated Debt-Collection Lawsuits Engulf Courts," accessed 31 March 2016. http://nyti.ms/23HOEyG.

6 A detailed discussion of the sources and my methods of analysis are found in appendix 1.

7 "Merchantocracy" is the term used by Graham D. Taylor and Peter Baskerville in *A Concise History of Business in Canada* (Toronto: Oxford University Press, 1994), 109–14. See the various works at note 3, above, for the history of this development.

8 John Bartlett Brebner, *The Neutral Yankees of Nova Scotia: A Marginal Colony during the Revolutionary Years* (Toronto: McClelland and Stewart, 1969), 15–16.

9 Franco Moretti's *The Bourgeois: Between History and Literature* (New York: Verso Books, 2013) nicely draws together much of this scholarship in an analysis that links great spaces over several centuries.

10 Jürgen Kocka, "The Middle Classes in Europe," *Journal of Modern History* 67, no. 4 (1995): 784. See also his *Civil Society and Dictatorship in Modern German History* (Lebanon, NH: University Press of New England, 2010), 9–15.

11 Moretti, *Bourgeois*, 22.

12 See, for example, Joseph Schumpeter, *Capitalism, Socialism and Democracy* (New York: Harper and Row, 1975; first published 1942 by Harper and Brothers), 156–60; Anthony Giddens, *The Class Structure of the Advanced*

Societies (London: Hutchinson University Library, 1973), 77–80. There are critics of this interpretation, of course. See, for example, the many comments by Ellen Meiksins Wood on the bourgeois, most recently in *Liberty & Property: A Social History of Western Political Thought from Renaissance to Enlightenment* (New York: Verso, 2012), 290–300. Raymond Williams's history of the term remains important in sorting out its general and Marxist connotations in English-language discourse: see "bourgeois," in *Keywords: A Vocabulary of Culture and Society* (London: Fontana Press, 1976), 45–8.

13 Donald Creighton, *The Commercial Empire of the Saint Lawrence, 1760–1850* (New York: Carnegie Endowment for Peace, 1937; repr. as *The Empire of the Saint Lawrence*, Toronto: Macmillan, 1956). See Donald Wright's review of a reissue of the book for a contemporary analysis of Creighton's handling of the "merchant class" in *Canadian Historical Review* 85, no. 3 (2004): 555–8.

14 Brian Young, *George-Etienne Cartier: Montreal Bourgeois* (Montreal: McGill-Queen's University Press, 1981), xii; Don Nerbas, *Dominion of Capital: The Politics of Big Business and the Crisis of the Canadian Bourgeoisie, 1914–1947* (Toronto: University of Toronto Press, 2013), 10–14.

15 See Muir, "The Fight for Bourgeois Law."

16 Margot Finn, *The Character of Credit: Personal Debt in English Culture, 1740–1914* (Cambridge: Cambridge University Press, 2003); Muldrew, *Economy of Obligation.* See also such works as Rowena Olegario, *A Culture of Credit: Embedding Trust and Transparency in American Business* (Cambridge, MA: Harvard University Press, 2006); Roger Fechner, "'The Sacredness of Public Credit': The American Revolution, Paper Currency, and John Witherspoon's *Essay on Money* (1786)," and Seán Moore, "'Vested' Interests and Debt Bondage: Credit as Confessional Coercion in Colonial Ireland," both in *The Empire of Credit: The Financial Revolution in the British Atlantic World, 1688–1815*, ed. Daniel Carey and Christopher J. Finlay (Dublin: Irish Academic Press, 2011).

17 Philip Girard, *Lawyers and Legal Culture in British North America: Beamish Murdoch of Halifax* (Toronto: University of Toronto Press for the Osgoode Society, 2011). For a good recent discussion about what "legal culture" means, see Sally Engle Merry, "What is Legal Culture? An Anthropological Perspective," *Journal of Comparative Law* 5, no. 2 (2010), 43–4 and *passim*. David M. Engel's reply to Merry also merits close reading: "The Uses of Legal Culture in Contemporary Socio-Legal Studies: A Response to Sally Engle Merry," *Journal of Comparative Law* 5, no. 2 (2010), 59–65.

18 Franz von Benda-Beckmann and Keebet von Benda-Beckmann, "Why Not Legal Culture?" *Journal of Comparative Law* 5, no. 2 (2010), 115–16.

19 Wilfrid Prest, "The Experience of Litigation in Eighteenth-Century England," in David Lemmings, ed., *The British and Their Laws in the Eighteenth Century* (Woodridge: The Boydell Press, 2005) 136–7.

20 The most important of these is J.M. Beattie, *Crime and the Courts in England 1660–1800* (Princeton: Princeton University Press, 1986). It and its follow-up, *Policing and Punishment in London 1660–1750: Urban Crime and the Limits of Terror* (Oxford: Oxford University Press, 2001), have deeply influenced the methodology and structure of this work.

21 See the notes in chapters 3 through 6 generally, but the most important studies for this work are three on law in the colonial United States: Bruce Mann, *Neighbors and Strangers: Law and Community in Early Connecticut* (Chapel Hill: University of North Carolina Press, 1987), William E. Nelson, *Dispute and Conflict Resolution*, and Deborah Rosen, *Courts and Commerce: Gender, Law, and the Market Economy in Colonial New York* (Columbus: Ohio State University Press, 1997).

22 The major works on the history of common law civil justice in Canada have remained, for the most part, unpublished. In print, see William Wylie, "Instruments of Commerce and Authority: The Civil Courts in Upper Canada 1789–1812," in *Essays in the History of Canadian Law*, vol. 2 , ed. David Flaherty (Toronto: University of Toronto Press for the Osgoode Society, 1983), 3–48, and Tina Loo, *Making Law, Order, and Authority in Colonial British Columbia, 1821–1871* (Toronto: University of Toronto Press, 1994), 73–92. Paul Craven discusses in some detail the civil jurisdiction of nineteenth-century New Brunswick magistrates in *Petty Justice: Low Law and the Sessions System in Charlotte County, New Brunswick, 1785–1867* (Toronto: University of Toronto Press for the Osgoode Society, 2014).

See also Wylie's unpublished dissertation, "Arbiters of Commerce, Instruments of Power: A Study of the Civil Courts in the Midland District, Upper Canada, 1789–1812" (PhD diss., Queen's University, 1980) and Howard Baker's unpublished master's thesis, "Small Claims, Communal Justice and the Rule of Law in Kingston, Upper Canada, c. 1785–1819" (master's thesis, York University, 1993).

On Quebec, see John Dickinson, *Justice et Justiciables*. Although there is more on the criminal law, it is also under-researched for the eighteenth century. For the work done, see especially the various pieces by Jim Phillips cited throughout this work and Douglas Hay, "The Meanings of the Criminal Law in Quebec, 1764 to 1774," in *Crime and Justice in Europe and Canada*, ed. Louis Knafla (Waterloo: Wilfrid Laurier University Press, 1981), 77–110. The most sustained quantitative study of criminal law history in Canada is Donald Fyson, *Magistrates, Police, and People: Everyday*

Criminal Justice in Quebec and Lower Canada, 1764–1837 (Toronto: University of Toronto Press for the Osgoode Society, 2006). For the rest of the Atlantic world, see the notes earlier in this chapter.

2 Halifax, a Community of Litigants

1 Quoted in William C. Wicken, *Mi'kmaq Treaties on Trial: History, Land and Donald Marshall Junior* (Toronto: University of Toronto Press, 2001), 173. See also Thomas B. Akins, *History of Halifax City* (1895; facs. ed. Belleville, ON: Mika Publishing, 1973), 5, and Nicholas Rogers, *Mayhem: Post-war Crime and Violence in Britain, 1748–53* (New Haven: Yale University Press, 2012), 194–7.
2 Akins, *History*, 4–5; Judith Fingard, Janet Guildford, and David Sutherland, *Halifax: the First 250 Years* (Halifax: Formac Publishing Company, 1999), 9–11; Jeffers Lennox, "An Empire on Paper: The Founding of Halifax and Conceptions of Imperial Space, 1744–55," *Canadian Historical Review* 88, no. 3 (2007): 387–91, and *passim*; Rogers, *Mayhem*, 188–92; Wicken, *Mi'kmaq Treaties*, 182.
3 Lennox, "An Empire on Paper"; Julian Gwyn, *Excessive Expectations: Maritime Commerce and the Economic Development of Nova Scotia, 1740–1870* (Montreal: McGill-Queen's University Press, 1998), 25–9.
4 Wicken, *Mi'kmaq Treaties on Trial*, 178–9. See also Geoffrey Plank, *An Unsettled Conquest: The British Campaigns against the Peoples of Acadia* (Philadelphia: University of Pennsylvania Press, 2001), 127 and 130; Fingard, Guildford, and Sutherland, *Halifax*, 14; John Salusbury, *Expeditions of Honour: Journal of John Salusbury in Halifax, Nova Scotia, 1749–53*, 2nd ed., ed. Ronald Rumpkey (1982; repr. Montreal: McGill-Queen's University Press, 2011), 67. Plank and Wicken disagree as to the particulars of one of the confrontations, including whether a massacre of twenty Mi'kmaq women and children occurred at Canso or in Newfoundland.
5 Wicken, *Mi'kmaq Treaties*, 181; Plank, *An Unsettled Conquest*, 129.
6 See Wicken, *Mi'kmaq Treaties*, chaps. 8 and 9 for an excellent history of Mi'kmaq–British relations in the mid-eighteenth century.
7 Jean Daigle, "Acadian Marshland Settlement," in *The Historical Atlas of Canada*, vol. 1, ed. R. Cole Harris (Toronto: University of Toronto Press, 1987), plate 29.
8 Akins, *History*, 12.
9 See N.E.S. Griffiths, *From Migrant to Acadian: A North American Border People* (Montreal: McGill-Queen's University Press, 2004), 431–64.
10 Rogers, *Mayhem*, 199.

11 Population numbers come from several sources. See Fingard, Guildford, and Sutherland, *Halifax*, 6 and 18; Akins, *History*, 48, 69, and 246–61, Alan Marble, *Surgeons, Smallpox and the Poor* (Montreal: McGill-Queen's University Press, 1993), 27, 33, 52, and 70.

12 Akins, *History*, 248–9.

13 Salusbury, *Expeditions of Honour*, 68. On the Foreign Protestants see Winthrop Bell, *The "Foreign Protestants" and the Settlement of Nova Scotia* (Sackville, NB: Centre for Canadian Studies, Mount Allison University, 1990. First published 1961 by University of Toronto Press) and Barry Cahill, "The 'Hoffman Rebellion' (1753) and Hoffman's Trial (1754): Constructive High Treason and Seditious Conspiracy in Nova Scotia under the Stratocracy," in *Canadian State Trials, Volume 1: Law, Politics, and Security Measures, 1608–1837*, ed. Frank Murray Greenwood and Barry Wright (Toronto: University of Toronto Press for the Osgoode Society, 1996), 72–97.

14 Akins, *History*, 5.

15 To cite, for example, from the men who appear elsewhere in this book: William Hunstable had 6 men over 16, 1 woman over 16, and 1 boy in his house; Joseph Gerrish had 27 men, no women, and 1 boy in his house; Joshua Mauger had 14 men, 3 women, 2 boys, and 1 girl in his; Thomas Saul had 10 men and 1 woman; William Piggott had 7 men, 1 woman, 3 boys, and 4 girls. By way of contrast, John Webb (the husband of Anne Webb, who figures prominently below) was alone in his household at the time of the census. On distinguishing between domestic and other servants in the eighteenth century, see Carolyn Steedman, *Labours Lost : Domestic Service and the Making of Modern England* (Cambridge: Cambridge University Press, 2009), 10–43.

16 Julian Gwyn, *Excessive Expectations*, 16–21 and 28–31.

17 NSARM RG 1 vol. 186, p. 5.

18 NSARM RG 1 vol. 186, p. 15. See also Jim Phillips, "The Criminal Trial in Nova Scotia, 1749–1815," in *Essays in the History of Canadian Law, Volume VIII: In Honour of R.C.B. Risk*, ed. Jim Phillips and G. Blaine Baker, 471–2 (Toronto: University of Toronto Press for the Osgoode Society, 1999).

19 NSARM RG 1 vol. 163, pp. 14, 15, 21, 26–7, and 29. See also James Muir, "The Fight for Bourgeois Law in Halifax, Nova Scotia, 1749–1753," *Histoire Sociale/Social History* (forthcoming).

20 See Susie M. Ames, ed., *County Court Records of Accomack and Northhampton Virginia, 1632–1640*, vol. 7 of *American Legal Records* (Washington, DC: American Historical Association, 1954) and A.G. Roeber, *Faithful Magis-*

trates and Republican Lawyers: Creators of Virginian Legal Culture, 1680–1810 (Chapel Hill: University of North Carolina Press, 1981).

21 For a good discussion of borrowing around the empire focused on master and servant law statutes, see Douglas Hay and Paul Craven, "Introduction," in *Masters, Servants, and Magistrates in Britain and the Empire, 1562–1955*, ed. Douglas Hay and Paul Craven, 14–21 (Chapel Hill: University of North Carolina Press, 2004).

22 NSARM RG 1 vol. 186, pp. 30–40; NSARM RG 37 HX vol. A.

23 Documents produced by the court show it changed names in 1751, but the change was formalized by an order of the governor in council only in May 1752. Charles J. Townsend, *History of the Court of Chancery of Nova Scotia* (Toronto: Carswell, 1900), 34–5.

24 Minutes of the Executive Council, NSARM RG 1 vol. 186, 1749 December 13, pp. 31–40. See also Barry Cahill and Jim Phillips, "The Supreme Court of Nova Scotia: Origins to Confederation," in *From Imperial Bastion to Provincial Oracle: The Supreme Court of Nova Scotia, 1754–2004*, ed. Philip Girard, Jim Phillips, and Barry Cahill, 53–9 (Toronto: University of Toronto Press for the Osgoode Society, 2004).

25 Townsend, *History of the Court of Chancery*, 48–50.

26 The first Marriage and Divorce case was heard 15 May 1750 (*Williams v. Williams*) and is discussed in chapter 7 of this book.

27 Townsend, *History of the Court of Chancery*, 61–7.

28 See chapter 7 of this book.

29 Kimberly Smith Maynard, "Divorce in Nova Scotia, 1750–1890," in *Essays in the History of Canadian Law, Volume III: Nova Scotia*, ed. Philip Girard and Jim Phillips (Toronto: University of Toronto Press for the Osgoode Society, 1990).

30 A great deal of work has now been done on Justices of the Peace and stipendiary justices in other parts of British North America/Canada in the late eighteenth and nineteenth centuries. See, especially, Paul Craven's work, including *Petty Justice: Low Law and the Sessions System in Charlotte County, New Brunswick, 1785–1867* (Toronto: University of Toronto Press for the Osgoode Society, 2014); "Canada, 1670–1935," in *Masters, Servants and Magistrates in Britain and the Empire, 1562–1955*, ed. Douglas Hay and Paul Craven, 175–218 (Chapel Hill: University of North Carolina Press, 2004); "Law and Ideology: The Toronto Police Court, 1850–80," in *Essays in the History of Canadian Law*, vol. 2, ed. David Flaherty, 248–307 (Toronto: Osgoode Society for Canadian Legal History, 1983); and "The Law of Master and Servant in Mid-Nineteenth-Century Ontario," in *Essays in the History of Canadian Law*, vol. 1, ed. David Flaherty, 175–211 (Toronto: Osgoode

Society for Canadian Legal History, 1981). Other work on New Brunswick magistrates and justices has been done by Jacques Paul Couturier; see "Courts and Business Activity in Late 19th Century New Brunswick: A View from the Case Files," *Acadiensis* 26, no. 2 (1997): 77–95. For work on the JP's criminal jurisdiction, see also Donald Fyson, *Magistrates, Police, and People: Everyday Criminal Justice in Quebec and Lower Canada, 1764–1837* (Toronto: University of Toronto Press for the Osgoode Society, 2006); Shelley A.M. Gavigan, *Hunger, Horses, and Government Men: Criminal Law on the Aboriginal Plains, 1870–1905* (Vancouver: UBC Press for the Osgoode Society, 2012); and Susan Lewthwaite's work, including "Law and Authority in Upper Canada: The Justices of the Peace in the Newcastle District, 1803–1840" (PhD diss., University of Toronto, 2001); "The Pre-trial Examination in Upper Canada," in *Criminal Justice in the Old World and the New: Essays in Honour of J.M. Beattie*, ed. Greg T. Smith, Allyson N. May, and Simon Devereaux, 85–103 (Toronto: University of Toronto Centre of Criminology, 1998); and "Violence, Law and Community in Rural Upper Canada," in *Essays in the History of Canadian Law, Volume V: Crime and Criminal Justice*, ed. Jim Phillips, Tina Loo, and Susan Lewthwaite, 353–86 (Toronto: University of Toronto Press for the Osgoode Society, 1994).

31 *The Diary of Simeon Perkins*, in five volumes, ed. Harold A. Innis (vol. 1), D.C. Harvey (vol. 2), and Charles Bruce Fergusson (vols. 3–5) (Toronto: Champlain Society, 1948, 1958, 1961, 1967, 1978).

32 Paul Craven, *Petty Justice*.

33 Carolyn Steedman, *An Everyday Life of the English Working Class: Work, Self and Sociability in the Early Nineteenth Century* (Cambridge: Cambridge University Press, 2013).

34 It is impossible to know what sorts of legal activity occurred solely summarily in this period. Historians of justices in other times and places, especially Paul Craven, Douglas Hay, and their collaborators, have shown that master and servant laws were often enforced by justices of the peace. Craven notes that Nova Scotia's first master and servant act dates from 1765, but it is possible that the justices dealt with and enforced rules like the *Master & Servant Act* before then. See "Canada 1670–1935," 181–3.

35 NS Stats 1758, c. 36, "An Act in Addition to and Explanation of An Act Passed this Session Entitled, An Act for Confirming the Past Proceedings of the Courts of Judicature, and for Regulating the Further Proceedings of the Same."

36 The first detailed exposition of this thesis was made in Beamish Murdoch, "On the Origin and Sources of the Law of Nova Scotia" (Halifax: Law Students' Society, 1863), 3, 4, and 8. See also Beamish Murdoch, *Epitome of*

the Laws of Nova Scotia, vol. 1 (Halifax: Joseph Howe, 1832), 30–41. Girard discusses this briefly in *Lawyers and Legal Culture in British North America: Beamish Murdoch of Halifax* (Toronto: University of Toronto Press for the Osgoode Society, 2011), 184, but see also his discussion of Murdoch on reception, 164–6. See also "'As Near as May be Agreeable to the Laws of this Kingdom': Legal Birthright and Legal Baggage at Chebucto, 1749," in *Law in a Colonial Society: The Nova Scotia Experience*, ed. Peter Waite, Sandra Oxner, and Thomas Barnes (Toronto: Carswell, 1984) 1–23, and Barry Cahill, "'How Far English Laws are in Force Here': Nova Scotia's First Century of Reception Law Jurisprudence," *University of New Brunswick Law Journal* 42 (1993): 113–53.

37 For a detailed discussion of the Justices' Affair and its antecedents, see Muir, "The Fight for Bourgeois Law." The mid-twentieth-century interpretation of the affair is best encapsulated in W.S. MacNutt, *The Atlantic Provinces: The Emergence of a Colonial Society* (Toronto: McClelland and Stewart, 1965), 55.

38 NSARM RG 1 vol. 209, p. 264.

39 NSARM RG 1 vol. 209, p. 264.

40 NSARM RG 1 vol. 209, p. 277.

41 The council's determinations are found in NSARM RG 1 vol. 209, no page number, 1753-02-19, 1753-02-20, 1753-02-23, 1753-03-01 (between pages 308 and 390).

42 NSARM RG 1 vol. 209, pp. 392–3.

43 E.A. Crawley, "An Early Halifax Naval Family," NSARM MG 100, vol. 127, no. 24.

44 Phyllis R. Blakely, "Morris, Charles," in *The Dictionary of Canadian Biography*, vol. 4, ed. Francess G. Halpenny (Toronto: University of Toronto Press, 1979), 559–63. See also Lennox, "An Empire on Paper," 381–5.

45 Phyllis R. Blakeley, "Monk, James," in *The Dictionary of Canadian Biography*, vol. 3, ed. Francess G. Halpenny (Toronto: University of Toronto Press, 1974), 457.

46 See, for example, Douglas Hay, "Legislation, Magistrates, and Judges: High Law and Low Law in England and Empire," in *The British and Their Laws in the Eighteenth Century*, ed. David Lemmings, 59–79 (Woodbridge, UK: Boydell Press, 2005) or many of the essays in Hay and Craven, *Masters, Servants, and Magistrates in Britain and the Empire, 1562–1955* (Chapel Hill: University of North Carolina Press, 2004). In several recent works, Carolyn Steedman has offered a differently nuanced interpretation of the work of Justices of the Peace than that of Hay (and many others). See, especially, Steedman, "At Every Bloody Level: a Magistrate, a Frame-Work

Knitter and the Law," *Law and History Review*, 30, no. 2 (2012): 387–422 and *An Everyday Life of the English Working Class*.

47 For British North America, see Jim Phillips, "A Low Law Counter Treatise? 'Absentees' to 'Wreck' in British North America's First Justice of the Peace Manual," in *Law Books in Action: Essays on the Anglo-American Legal Treatise*, ed. A. Fernandez and M. Dubber, 202–19 (Oxford: Hart Publishing, 2012).

48 J.M. Bumsted, *Land, Settlement, and Politics on Eighteenth-Century Prince Edward Island* (Montreal: McGill-Queen's University Press, 1987), 33–4 and 41.

49 Women's participation in the Supreme Court of Nova Scotia has been studied by Julian Gwyn over a much larger time period than that considered here. There is much of value in Gwyn's study about how women actively took part in litigation in the Supreme Court. My concerns with his study turn on two issues. First, because of the narrow jurisdiction of the Supreme Court, I am wary as to whether Gwyn fully or accurately captures women's participation in either law or commerce (see chapter 7 of this book). Second, because there is no comparison to male participation or use of the court, it is difficult to determine what (if anything) was special about women's use of the courts. Julian Gwyn, "Women as Litigants before the Supreme Court of Nova Scotia, 1754–1830," in *From Imperial Bastion to Provincial Oracle: The Supreme Court of Nova Scotia, 1754–2004*, ed. Philip Girard, Jim Phillips, and Barry Cahill, 298–9.

50 Lee Holcombe, *Wives and Property: Reform of the Married Women's Property Law in Nineteenth-Century England* (Toronto: University of Toronto Press, 1983), 26–7.

51 *King v. Lush*, NSARM RG 37 (hx) vol. 1 #43. On the King and Lush families' make-up, see Akins, *History*, 247 and 250.

52 *Rock v. Maguire* NSARM RG 37 (hx) vol. 7 #6.

53 For wives as litigants, see, for examples, *Nagle & Nagle v. Murray*, NSARM RG 37 (hx) vol. 6 #64 or *Bray v. Simpson & Simpson*, NSARM RG 37 (hx) vol. 9 #2. For an example where the wife was not named as a litigant, see *Gilford v. Fairbanks*, NSARM RG 37 (hx) vol. 4 #42.

54 Rosen, *Courts and Commerce*, 96–100; Cornelia Hughes Dayton, *Women before the Bar* (Chapel Hill: University of North Carolina Press, 1995), 72. See also Peter Charles Hoffer, *Law and People in Colonial America*, rev. ed. (Baltimore: Johns Hopkins University Press, 1998), 82.

55 Rosen found women's participation rates generally decreased over the eighteenth century. She found participation ranged as high as 10 per cent of plaintiffs in the New York City Mayor's Court in the 1700s and 1740s, to

as low as 0.5 per cent of defendants in Dutchess, Orange, and Westchester Counties between 1721 and 1760 (Rosen, ibid.). Halifax's 3 per cent is thus on the low end, but not as low as some of the participation rates Rosen found.

56 See, for example, *Compt v. Whitehand*, NSARM RG 37 (hx) vol. 14 #73, vol. 17 #52, vol. 19 #12; *Giffin v. Whitehand*, NSARM RG 37 (hx) vol. 14 #100, *Whitehand v. Monro*, NSARM RG 37 (hx) vol. 14 #128. As a co-defendant see *Campbell v. Whitehand & Whitehand*, NSARM RG 37 (hx) vol. 14 #74. As a widow, see *Hamman v. Whitehand*, NSARM RG 37 (hx) vol. 17 #140.

57 J.H. Baker, *An Introduction to English Legal History*, 4th ed. (London: Butterworths LexisNexis, 2002), 484. Marylynn Salmon, *Women and the Law of Property in Early America* (Chapel Hill: University of North Carolina Press, 1986), 45–6.

58 Jim Phillips discusses the Halifax case *Sullivan v. Storey* (1789) when the court found for the plaintiff by finding the married female defendant to be acting as a femme sole. Phillips, "The Impeachment of the Judges of the Nova Scotia Supreme Court, 1787–1793: Colonial Judges, Loyalist Lawyers, and the Colonial Assembly," *Dalhousie Law Journal* 34, no. 2 (2011): 313–15.

59 See, for example, *Nathans & Hart v. Hart & Hart*, NSARM RG 37 (hx) vol. 10 #96. In this case, the partnership of Nathan Nathans and Nephtali Hart Jr. were sued by Nephtali Hart Sr. and Isaac Hart.

60 On the intricate legal relationships domestic servants had with their masters, see Carolyn Steedman, *Master and Servant: Love and Labour in the English Industrial Age* (Cambridge: Cambridge University Press, 2007), 66–86 and *Labours Lost*, 105–28 and 172–98.

61 The *Oxford English Dictionary* notes that "widow" could be "prefixed as a title to the name" but has no equivalent meaning to "widower," speaking to the way a woman's identity could be determined by that of her husband in a way that was not common or even generally possible for men and their wives (royal consorts being an obvious but also unusual exception).

62 *Oxford English Dictionary*, 2nd ed., s.v. "yeoman."

63 Allyson May and Jim Phillips, "Homicide in Nova Scotia, 1749–1815," *Canadian Historical Review* 82, no. 4 (2001): 638.

64 The homes of 1,549 (62 per cent) individual litigants, accounting for 8,481 (83 per cent) of litigant appearances, are known. Not all records included the place of residence. Where an individual's place of residence is listed in one set of documents, that residence has been applied to all of the individual's appearances, except where it is clear from the evidence that the individual moved between appearances. Some claims as to place of residence were altered, however. Some plaintiffs would often describe themselves as

being of different places, reflecting the place of Halifax in a trading world. William Maggee, for example, frequently claimed Calcutta to be his home, yet he appeared personally in fifty-two different actions over eleven years in Halifax. In his case, Calcutta was where he came from, not where he lived. In cases like this, where enough evidence shows that the person *actually resided* in Halifax (or somewhere else), their actual place of residence has been applied rather than the residence they claimed. While Maggee's self-characterization is interesting as a marker of place and identity, in this study using Calcutta as the place of residence for someone who lived in Halifax year-round and many years longer than others in the 1750s and 1760s would imply a larger litigation network than actually existed.

65 Of all individuals whose place of residence is known, 1,227, or 79 per cent, were reported as from Halifax. They made 7,683 appearances, or 91 per cent of all litigation appearances by people with known residences.

66 Of all individuals whose place of residence is known, 147, or 9 per cent, were recorded as living elsewhere in Nova Scotia, making a total of 412 appearances (5 per cent). Another 127 (8 per cent) came from other parts of British North America, making 264 appearances (3 per cent). A further 48 (3 per cent) of individuals came from farther away, making 112 (1 per cent) of appearances.

67 Nova Scotians: 134 appearances as plaintiffs, 278 as defendants. British North Americans: 200 appearances as plaintiffs, 64 as defendants. The rest of the world: 81 appearances as plaintiffs, 31 as defendants.

68 This was a measure adopted by the council, following the lead of other earlier colonies, to encourage immigration. See NSARM RG 1, vol. 209, 14 January 1750 (p. 100).

69 Local agents often came to court as "attorneys" (even if they hired a lawyer as well). In these cases, the creditor from outside of Halifax was listed in the papers and considered in this analysis to be the litigant. In some cases, agents may have been hired to carry on all manner of business and sue or be sued in their own names. In such cases, because the local agent was the named litigant, he or she was counted as the litigant, even if the source of the credit or capital was overseas.

70 Susan Buggey, "Salter, Malachy," in *The Dictionary of Canadian Biography*, vol. 4, ed. Francess Halpenny (Toronto: University of Toronto Press, 1979), 695–7. On Salter's career, see also John Bartlett Brebner, *New England's Outpost: Acadia before the Conquest of Canada* (New York: Columbia University Press, 1927), 255–7.

71 Buggey, "Salter, Malachy."

72 John Bartlett Brebner, *The Neutral Yankees of Nova Scotia: A Marginal Colony*

during the Revolutionary Years (Toronto: McClelland and Stewart, 1969), 15–16; Buggey, "Salter, Malachy"; Julian Gwyn, *Excessive Expectations*, 19; Barry Cahill, "The Treason of the Merchants: Dissent and Repression in Halifax in the Era of the American Revolution," *Acadiensis* 26, no. 1 (1996): 52–70.

73 *Mackey v. Innis*, NSARM RG 37 (hx) vol. 6 #31.

74 In addition to ibid., see *Callaghan v. Newton and Mackey* (NSARM RG 37 (hx) vol. 4 #76, #77) and *Rundle & Crawley v. Mackey* (NSARM RG 37 (hx) vol. 8 #86 and vol. 9 #128).

3 Initiating Actions

1 The sort of detailed study of process here has not been done for Nova Scotia, or for civil law in the common law world in the eighteenth century more generally. The historian John Beattie's book *Crime and the Courts in England 1660–1800* (Princeton, NJ: Princeton University Press, 1986) did this for criminal law in England in the eighteenth century. Some elements of civil law process have been described and analysed for several other North American colonies, but none with the detail provided here. See Bruce Mann on Connecticut in *Neighbors and Strangers: Law and Community in Early Connecticut* (Chapel Hill: University of North Carolina Press, 1987) and William Offutt on Delaware in *Of "Good Laws" and "Good Men": Law and Society in the Delaware Valley, 1680–1710* (Urbana and Chicago: University of Illinois Press, 1995). For Massachusetts see David Konig, *Law and Society in Puritan Massachusetts: Essex County, 1626–1693* (Chapel Hill: University of North Carolina Press, 1979) and William E. Nelson, *Dispute and Conflict Resolution in Plymouth County, Massachusetts, 1725–1825* (Chapel Hill: University of North Carolina Press, 1981).

Also see Jerry Bannister on Newfoundland in *The Rule of the Admirals: Law, Custom, and Naval Government in Newfoundland, 1699–1822* (Toronto: University of Toronto Press for the Osgoode Society, 2003), Deborah Rosen on New York in *Courts and Commerce: Gender, Law, and the Market Economy in Colonial New York* (Columbus: Ohio State University Press, 1997), William Wylie on Upper Canada in "Arbiters of Commerce, Instruments of Power: A Study of the Civil Courts in the Midland District, Upper Canada, 1789–1812" (PhD diss., Queen's University, 1980) and "Instruments of Commerce and Authority: The Civil Courts in Upper Canada 1789–1812" in *Essays in the History of Canadian Law*, ed. David Flaherty, vol. 2 (Toronto: University of Toronto Press for the Osgoode Society, 1983), 3–48, and A.G. Roeber on Virginia in *Faithful Magistrates and Republican Lawyers: Creators of Virginia Legal Culture, 1680–1810* (Chapel Hill: University of North Carolina Press, 1981). See also Tina Loo, *Making Law, Order, and Authority in Colonial British Columbia, 1821–1871* (Toronto: University of Toronto Press, 1994), which does something similar for mid-nineteenth-century British Columbia.

2 There is an extensive history that addresses elements of debt, credit, and the importance of merchants in that network for Nova Scotia, Canada and the broader Atlantic world. See, for example, the discussions on Nova Scotia on pages 4–6, 134–5, and 203–24 in Julian Gwyn's *Excessive Expectations: Maritime Commerce and the Economic Development of Nova Scotia, 1740–1870* (Montreal: McGill-Queen's University Press, 1998) and his articles on specific merchants: "Capitalists, Merchants and Manufacturers in Early Nova Scotia, 1769–1791: The Tangled Affairs of John Avery, James Creighton, John Albro, and Joseph Fairbanks," in *Intimate Relations: Family and Community in Planter Nova Scotia, 1759–1800*, ed. Margaret Conrad (Fredericton, NB: Acadiensis Press, 1995), 190–212 and "'A Slave to Business All My Life.' Joshua Mauger, ca. 1712–1788: The Man and the Myth," *Journal of the Royal Nova Scotia Historical Society* 7 (2004): 38–62.

See also Patricia Rogers, "'Unprincipled Men Who Are One Day British Subjects and the Next Citizens of the United States': The Nova Scotian Merchant Community and Colonial Identity Formation, c. 1780–1820" (PhD diss., Michigan State University, 2001); Daniel Samson, *The Spirit of Industry and Improvement* (Montreal: McGill-Queen's University Press, 2008), 29–36 and 225–49; David Sutherland, "The Merchants of Halifax, 1815–1850: A Commercial Class in Pursuit of Metropolitan Status," (PhD diss., University of Toronto, 1975) and "Halifax Merchants and the Pursuit of Development, 1783–1850," *Canadian Historical Review* 59, no. 1 (1978): 1–17.

For Canada more generally, see also, among others, T.W. Acheson, "The Great Merchant and Economic Development in Saint John, 1820–50," *Acadiensis* 8, no. 2 (1979): 3–27; Béatrice Craig, *Backwoods Consumers & Homespun Capitalists: The Rise of a Market Culture in Eastern Canada* (Toronto: University of Toronto Press, 2009), 113–36; Dale Miquelon, "Havy and Lefebvre of Quebec: A Case Study of Metropolitan Participation in Canadian Trade, 1730–60," *Canadian Historical Review* 56, no. 1 (1975): 1–24; Rosemary Ommer, ed., *Merchant Credit & Labour Strategies in Historical Perspective* (Fredericton, NB: Acadiensis Press, 1990); and Eric W. Sager with Gerald E. Panting, *Maritime Capital: The Shipping Industry in Atlantic Canada, 1820–1914* (Montreal: McGill-Queen's University Press, 1990), 16–22 and *passim*.

3 See, for example, "Yearly Supply of Specie in Pence Necessary" and "No Circulating Money amongst German Settlers" in *Documents Relating to Currency, Exchange and Finance in Nova Scotia, with Prefatory Documents, 1675–1758*, ed. Adam Shortt (Ottawa: The King's Printer, 1933), 386 and 411.

4 Anthropologist David Graeber has argued that such economies are essentially mythical creations of economic theorists. See David Graeber, *Debt: The First 5,000 Years* (New York: Melville House, 2011), 34–41. Graeber's work is thought-provoking, and there are many points where his arguments and findings parallel those made here. See also Robin Blackburn, "Finance for Anarchists," *New Left Review* 79 (2013): 141–50 and Benjamin Kunkel, *Utopia or Bust: A Guide to the Present Crisis* (New York: Verso Books, 2014), 118–34.

5 See, for example, Jacob Price, *Capital and Credit in British Overseas Trade: The View from the Chesapeake, 1700–1776* (Cambridge, MA: Harvard University Press, 1980) and "Transaction Costs: A Note on Merchant Credit and the Organization of Private Trade," in *The Political Economy of Merchant Empires: State Power and World Trade, 1350–1750*, ed. James D. Tracey (Cambridge: Cambridge University Press, 1991), 276–97. See also Joseph E. Inkori, *Africans and the Industrial Revolution in England: A Study in International Trade and Economic Development* (Cambridge: Cambridge University Press, 2002), 330–6. Jan de Vries and Ad van der Woude discuss similar developments within the Netherlands and in the Dutch trade in *The First Modern Economy: Success, Failure, and Perseverance of the Dutch Economy, 1500–1815* (Cambridge: Cambridge University Press, 1997), 81–146. Graeber, *Debt*, 333–55 offers a general account of debt in the expansion of European empires.

6 Several of the works discussed throughout this book as comparisons to Halifax deal with local credit. See, for example, Margot Finn, *The Character of Credit: Personal Debt in English Culture, 1740–1914* (Oxford: Oxford University Press, 2003); Bruce Mann, *Neighbors and Strangers: Law and Community in Early Connecticut* (Chapel Hill: University of North Carolina Press, 1987); Craig Muldrew, "Credit and the Courts: Debt Litigation in a Seventeenth-Century Urban Community," *Economic History Review* 46, no. 1 (1993): 23–38; Muldrew, *The Economy of Obligation: The Culture of Credit and Social Relations in Early Modern England* (Hampshire, UK: Palgrave, 1998); Muldrew, "'A Mutual Assent of Her Mind'? Women, Debt, Litigation and Contract in Early Modern England," *History Workshop Journal* 55 (2003): 47–71; Rosen, *Courts and Commerce*; and Serena R. Zabin, *Dangerous Economies: Status and Commerce in Imperial New York* (Philadelphia: Univer-

sity of Pennsylvania Press, 2009). A good description of northern North American colonial credit can be found in Peter E. Pope, *Fish into Wine: The Newfoundland Plantations in the Seventeenth Century* (Chapel Hill: University of North Carolina Press for the Omohundro Institute of Early American History, 2004), 282–4 and 360–5.

7 The definition of "legal system" presented here is drawn from Lawrence Friedman, "Legal Culture and Social Development," *Law & Society Review* 4, no. 2 (1969): 34.

8 The literature is vast on these topics. Histories of empire and the Atlantic world of particular influence in this project are Lauren Benton, *Law and Colonial Cultures: Legal Regimes in World History, 1400–1900* (Cambridge: Cambridge University Press, 2002); David Hancock, *Citizens of the World: London Merchants and the Integration of the British Atlantic Community, 1735–1785* (Cambridge: Cambridge University Press, 1997); Douglas Hay and Paul Craven, *Masters, Servants and Magistrates in Britain and Empire, 1562–1955* (Chapel Hill: University of North Carolina Press, 2004); Allan Kulikoff, *From British Peasants to Colonial American Farmers* (Chapel Hill: University of North Carolina Press, 2000); and Peter Linebaugh and Marcus Rediker, *The Many Headed Hydra: Sailors, Slaves, Commoners and the Hidden History of the Revolutionary Atlantic* (Boston: Beacon Press, 2000).

9 As such, it is in some ways a companion to William E. Nelson's recent and continuing series *The Common Law in Colonial America* (New York: Oxford University Press, vol. 1, 2008; vol. 2, 2013) and Jerry Bannister's *The Rule of the Admirals: Law, Custom, and Naval Government in Newfoundland, 1699–1832* (Toronto: University of Toronto Press for the Osgoode Society, 2003) as well as Bruce Mann's *Neighbors and Strangers*, Christopher Tomlins's *Freedom Bound: Law, Labor, and Civic Identity in Colonizing English America, 1580–1865* (New York: Cambridge University Press, 2010), Tomlins and Mann's co-edited *The Many Legalities of Early America* (Chapel Hill: University of North Carolina Press, 2001), Hay and Craven cited above, and many others whose work dots the notes throughout this book.

10 Descriptions of the type of action are available for 1554 trespasses on the case, 84 per cent of the total for the period 1749 to 1767 in Halifax. Of these 1554 actions, 853 (55 per cent) were for some variety of debts on account and 421 (27 per cent) were for debts by note.

11 Mann, *Neighbors and Strangers*, 36–7.

12 Ibid., 67.

13 Ibid.

14 Ibid.

15 *Power v. Picket*, NSARM RG 37 (hx) vol. 4 #79. See also *Piggot v. Cobb*,

NSARM RG 37 (hx) vol. 4 #78 and *Power v. Brenan*, NSARM RG 39 "c" (hx) vol. 2 #4.

16 *Belcher v. Shepard*, NSARM RG 37 (hx) vol. 5 #7 and RG 39 "c" (hx) vol. 2 #64a; *Butler v. Firth*, NSARM RG 37 (hx) vol. 4 #14; *Butler v. Piggot*, NSARM RG 37 (hx) vol. 4 #15.

17 *Bleigh v. Sutherland*, NSARM RG 37 vol. 9 #3, RG 37 (hx) vol. 9 #177.

18 *Binney v. Lowell*, NSARM RG 39 "c" (hx) vol. 2 #8a–f. See also *Fayerweather v. Jones* for an example of long-held accounts for large volumes of goods and credit set off against each other (NSARM RG 37 (hx) vol. 2 #92, RG 39 (hx) "c" vol. 2 #6a–b).

19 The volume of work on merchants, credit, and community is by now quite large. One of the best works on this continues to be David Hancock's *Citizens of the World*. See also Jacob Price, *Capital and Credit*, and Patricia Rogers, "'Unprincipled Men Who Are One Day British Subjects and the Next Citizens of the United States.'"

20 *Blackburn v. Terlaven*, NSARM RG 39 "c" (hx) vol. 4 #39a, RG 37 (hx) vol. 15 #69, RG 37 (hx) vol. 16 #20.

21 The fishers and mariners could often sue in Vice Admiralty instead of the Inferior Court of Common Pleas.

22 Tomlins, *Freedom Bound*, 313.

23 *Gerrish v. Hunstable*, NSARM RG 39 "c" (hx) vol. 1 #102c.

24 For an example of attaching a house and lot, see *Grant v. Piggot*, NSARM RG 37 (hx) vol. 2 #92 and RG 39 "c" (hx) vol. 2 #12a. For bail, see *Shaw v. Jones*, NSARM RG 39 "c" (hx) vol. 3 #93.

25 *Butler v. Amies*, NSARM RG 37 (hx) vol. 12 #25. See also *Mauger v. Wright*, NSARM RG 37 (hx) vol. 10 #74, 125 and *Wenman v. Moncreif*, NSARM RG 37 (hx) vol. 11 #35, 145.

26 On England see Joanna Innes, "The King's Bench Prison in the Later Eighteenth Century: Law, Authority and Order in London's Debtor's Prison," in *An Ungovernable People: The English and Their Law in the Seventeenth and Eighteenth Centuries*, ed. John Brewer and John Styles (New Brunswick, NJ: Rutgers University Press, 1980), 253. Attachments were similar to the English mesne process, but no one in Halifax appears to have referred to the attachment by its English law Latin term, *capias ad respondendum*. Under the English process, unlike in Halifax, proof of the debt did not have to be presented to the court prior to getting the order. Deborah Rosen found that imprisonment before trial for debts was a regular occurrence in eighteenth-century New York (*Courts and Commerce*, 52).

27 See *Buckley v. Prescott*, NSARM RG 37 (hx) vol. 7 #41, *Quin v. Sullivan*, RG 37 (hx) vol. 4 #83, and *Webb v. Ewer*, RG 37 vol. 3 #12. James Oldham

has shown that trover was used for an even wider range of commercial and private disputes in late-eighteenth-century England than in Halifax (Oldham, *The Mansfield Manuscripts and the Growth of English Law in the Eighteenth Century* [Chapel Hill: University of North Carolina Press, 1992], 1175–81). For a more general discussion of legal fictions see J.M. Baker, *The Law's Two Bodies: Some Evidential Problems in English Legal History* (Oxford: University of Oxford Press, 2001).

28 Of 2,104 actions in which the plea is known, 1,782 were for case. There were 87 ejectment actions.

29 J.H. Baker, *An Introduction to English Legal History*, 4th ed. (London: Butterworths LexisNexis, 2002), 53–61.

30 C.H.S. Fifoot, *History and Sources of the Common Law* (London: Stevens & Sons, 1949), 66. See also Oldham, *The Mansfield Manuscripts*, 214.

31 See Baker, *An Introduction to English Legal History*, 321–6, 333–45.

32 Fifoot, *History and Sources of the Common Law*, 75, 77–8; Baker, *An Introduction to English Legal History*, 84–5. See also A.K. Kiralfy, *The Action on the Case: An Historical Survey of the Development of the Action up to the Year 1700 …* (London: Sweet & Maxwell, 1951), 19–54.

33 *Every Man His Own Lawyer: Or, a Summary of the Laws now in Force in Ireland* (Dublin: Oli. Nelson & Peter Wilson, 1755), 8–9.

34 Bruce Mann has suggested that in seventeenth-century Connecticut, "most civil actions ... were labelled on the case" (*Neighbors and Strangers*, 86). Craig Muldrew found it was used in four-fifths of actions in King's Lynn, Norfolk, England in the 1680s (Muldrew, "Credit and the Courts," 25–6). William E. Nelson found that between 1725 and 1775 case accounted for 51 per cent of actions in Plymouth County, Massachusetts (*Dispute and Conflict Resolution*, 23–4) and Christopher W. Brooks found it accounted for 37 per cent of Common Pleas action in England in 1750, and 42 per cent in King's Bench (Brooks, *Lawyers, Litigation and English Society since 1450* [London: Hambledon Press, 1998], 52–4). Contrary to the above and Muldrew's findings for the county court at King's Lynn, Brooks argues in the passage cited that the use of case in the two central courts increased between the late 1600s and 1750 as the courts became more willing to enforce merchants' customs.

35 Besides the passage from Mann quoted above, see Richard B. Morris, *Studies in the History of American Law, with Special Reference to the Seventeenth and Eighteenth Centuries*, 2nd ed. (Philadelphia: Joseph M. Mitchell Co., 1959), 49–51.

36 The action of debt was available in Halifax, but rarely used except coupled with trespass on the case. There are only sixty-four instances of it in the

Inferior Court between 1750 and 1767, 3 per cent of all cases for which the form of action is known. The action of debt required very specific evidence and applied to only a narrow range of ways credit could be extended. On the action of debt historically, see for example Baker, *An Introduction to English Legal History*, 321–6.

37 Douglas Hay, "Property, Authority and the Criminal Law," in *Albion's Fatal Tree: Crime and Society in Eighteenth-Century England*, ed. Douglas Hay, Peter Linebaugh, John Rule, E.P. Thompson, and Cal Winslow (London: Allen Lane, 1975), 27–8.

38 See *Rundle & Crewly v. Janson*, RG 37 (hx) vol. 4 #25 for an example of a lawyer confessing a debt on his client's behalf.

39 Morris, *Studies in the History of American Law*, 51–9.

40 Many of the court records contain long detailed accounts. See, for examples, *Webb & Ewer v. Franks*, NSARM RG 39 "c" (hx) vol. 1 #97b, c, d, e; *Franklin v. Sterling*, NSARM RG 37 (hx) vol. 21 #25; #5; *Cawthorne v. Hardwell* NSARM RG 37 (hx) vol. 19 #5. See Graeber, *Debt*, 21–41 for a discussion of barter, exchange, and money.

41 "Accompt" was a form of the word "account" in common use well into the eighteenth century.

42 *Halifax Gazette*, 6 April 1752.

43 *Halifax Gazette*, 16 September 1752.

44 See, for example, *Webb & Ewer v. Franks* NSARM RG 39 "c" (hx) vol. 1 #97b, c, d, e; *Webb & Ewer v. King* NSARM RG 37 (hx) vol. 2a #13; and *Webb v. Lukey* NSARM RG 37 vol. 3 #37.

4 Avoiding Trial

1 The Chief Justice of the Supreme Court of Canada, Beverley McLachlin, has discussed this at many points. See, for example, "The Challenges We Face: Remarks of the Right Honourable Beverley McLachlin, P.C., Chief Justice of Canada to the Empire Club of Canada," remarks delivered to the Empire Club of Canada, Toronto, Ontario on 8 March 2007, accessed 31 March 2016, www.cfcj-fcjc.org/sites/default/files/docs/2007/mclachlin-empireclub-en.pdf. For recent research on access issues that speak to the costs of services, see the articles in the Canadian Forum on Civil Justice's *News & Views on Civil Justice Reform* 12 (Spring 2009).

2 If one totals all of the actions at the Inferior Court listed in table 4.1 that must have relied on the defendant deciding to do something or nothing at all (default, confessions, abatement, jury trial, special jury, inquiry, judge trial, arbitration) and divide it by the total number of processes, it appears

that in 82 per cent of the actions *at least*, the defendant played a decisive role in the process adopted to resolve the action.

3 In addition to defaulting and arbitrating, Hill went to trial 10 (21 per cent) times while a defendant had 6 (13 per cent) actions against him withdrawn, and 1 (2 per cent) dismissed.

4 *Leigh v. Jones*, RG 37 (hx) vol. 9 #88.

5 This is narrower than what nonsuits were in England in the mid-eighteenth century. Giles Jacob's *The New Law Dictionary: Containing the Definition of Words and Terms, and also the Whole Law and Practice thereof &c. Carefully Abridged* ... (London: Henry Lintot, 1743) notes under "default" that when plaintiffs failed to attend trial, they were nonsuited. In the entry on "nonsuit," however, they are described as "the Dropping of a Suit or Action; or the Renouncing thereof by the Plaintiff ... which happens most commonly upon the Discovery of some Error in the Plaintiff's proceedings, when the Cause is so far proceeded in, that the Jury is read at the Bar to deliver in their Verdict." In Halifax this would have resulted in a dismissal or a withdrawal, not a nonsuit. See Jacob, *Law Dictionary* (London: Henry Lintot, 1743).

6 The September action is *Binney v. Lowell*, RG 37 vol. 3 #44; the December action is *Binney v. Lowell*, RG 37 vol. 3 #44. These are different than the *Binney v. Lowell* suit described in chapter 3. It was not uncommon for plaintiffs to sue a defendant more than once at the same court in the same session for a different debt or injury.

7 A logistic regression analysis of debt on account actions at the Inferior Court of Common Pleas (n = 669), where the dependent variable is a binary of default (0) and any other trial process (1) produces a probability of not defaulting of 31 per cent (e^b 2.987, sig < 0.001). When the independent variable of the size of claim (0 < £20, 1 ≥ £20) is considered, the probability of a debt on account action not being defaulted when the claim is equal to or exceeds £20 is 75 per cent (e^b 2.987, sig < 0.001).

8 When the claim was equal to or over £20, the defendant had experience as a litigant, the plaintiff had no experience as a litigant, and the plaintiff was not a merchant or trader, the probability was 84 per cent (e^b 5.392, sig < 0.001).

9 A model of experience alone produced the following results: when the defendant was experienced and the plaintiff was not, the probability of not defaulting was 61 per cent; when both litigants had experience the probability of not defaulting was 41 per cent; and when the plaintiff had experience and the defendant did not, the probability was 23 per cent (e^b 1.554, 0.684, 0.315 respectively, sig 0.136). The statistical significance of this

model is not at the 0.05 level, suggesting it is a weak model in explaining the decisions made to default or not.

The table below shows the result of testing the probability of a defendant not defaulting when the plaintiff had never before been a litigant, the defendant was a merchant or trader and had litigation experience, and the claim was equal or greater than £20 was only 79 per cent (e^b 3.695, sig < 0.001); not very different from the probability for account debt actions with a claim of less or more than £20. That is to say, other variables than claim correlated with defendant choices for process, but the correlation between the value of the claim and the decision to contest an action was strongest. The table also shows the basic formula structure for all of my logistic regression analysis.

Logistic regression results, debt on account

Logistic coefficients: plaintiff 0.877, occupation 0.151
defendant 0.555, claim 1.321, constant −1.597
Case values: plaintiff 1, occupation 1, defendant 1, claim 1
Log odds $(Y = 1) = -1.597 + 0.877 + 0.151 + 0.555 + 1.321 = 1.307$

$$\text{Prob}(Y = 1) = \frac{1}{1 + e^{-(1.307)}} = \frac{1}{.270} = 0.787$$

Y process type: 0 default, 1 all other action processes
X_1 plaintiff: 0 prior litigation experience, 1 first action
X_2 occupation: 0 defendant not merchant or trader, 1 defendant merchant or trader
X_3 defendant: 0 first action, 1 prior litigation experience
X_4 claim: 0 claim < £20, 1 claim ≥ £20

10 Nova Scotia Civil Procedure Rules, 2008, amended 2012, rule 8.
11 See, for instance, Alberta Rules of Court, Alberta Regulation 124/2010 rule 3.36 or (Ontario) Rules of Civil Procedure R.R.O. 1990, Regulation 194, rule 19.
12 See Jacob Price, *Capital and Credit in British Overseas Trade: The View from the Chesapeake, 1700–1776* (Cambridge, MA: Harvard University Press, 1980), 44–62.
13 On Halifax currency versus pounds sterling, see John J. McCusker, *Money & Exchange in Europe & America 1600–1775, A Handbook* (Chapel Hill: University of North Carolina Press for the Institute of Early American History and Culture, 1978), 231. Almost all litigation in Halifax was in its local currency.

14 It is likely that *Bourne & Freeman v. Webber* (NSARM RG 37 A2, pp. 99–105), in which the defendant successfully confessed to £12 14s on a bond of £70, was similar. The Halifax courts did not enforce penal bonds like this to their full value. In *Cowie v. Creighton & Hurd*, the plaintiff Robert Cowie sued James Creighton and Benjamin Hurd as guarantors on a bail bond for John Windall, who disappeared before standing trial. The jury awarded Cowie £21 3s 4d in damages, the value of the debt for which he had sued Wendell and not the higher penal sum in the bail bond. Creighton and Hurd's lawyer moved to have judgment against them arrested because the jury had not applied the bond's full value. There is no evidence extant that this was successful (see *Cowie v. Windall*, RG 37 (hx) vol. 17 #81 and *Cowie v. Creighton & Hurd* NSARM RG 37 (hx) vol. 18 #27 and vol. 19 #21).

15 *Ingolls v. Fury*, RG 37 (hx) vol. 13 #22.

16 See, for another example, *Fillis v. Quin*, RG 39 "c" (hx) vol. 4 #14.

17 *Harris v. Shippey*, *Hill v. Shippey*, and *White v. Shippey*, NSARM RG 37 A2, 50–5, 56–87, 87–96; RG 37 (hx) vol. 1 #44. For similar examples of delaying repayment as a condition of the confession, see *Wood v. Cummings* NSARM RG 37 A2, 289–90, RG 37 (hx) vol. 2a #11; *Fillis v. Reynard*, NSARM RG 37 A2, 56–87.

18 *Sharpe v. Shaw*, *Trubee v. Shaw*, *Shipton v. Shaw*, NSARM RG 37 (hx) A2, 19–28.

19 *Jones v. Allen*, RG 37 A2, 15–18.

20 *Chapman v. Erskine*, NSARM RG 37 (hx) A2, 19–28.

21 See Clinton W. Francis, "Practice, Strategy, and Institution: Debt Collection in the English Common-Law Courts, 1740–1840," *Northwestern University Law Review* 80, no. 4 (1985–6): 826–9 and A.G. Roeber, *Faithful Magistrates and Republican Lawyers: Creators of Virginian Legal Culture, 1680–1810* (Chapel Hill: University of North Carolina Press, 1981), 84. Francis argued that in England in the last half of the eighteenth and first half of the nineteenth centuries, confessions were used when defendants could not make payment immediately and needed a delay or a schedule to make payments. The plaintiffs would then hold onto the confession and, if the defendants failed to make payment, seek execution against the defendants without having to return to court. This would be done either through the device of a *cognovit* or a warrant of attorney. In eighteenth-century Virginia, A.G. Roeber reports that some debtors signed over power of attorney to their creditors when they first went into debt so that the creditor could sue and then confess the debt if the debtor failed to make payment. In both cases the process appears to have had more steps than in Halifax and neither of these practices appears to have been in practice in Halifax.

22 Change in procedure might not be the only explanation for the apparent decline in confessions in the mid-1750s. The case files under-reported confessions because of the ways the clerks made notes as to the resolution of actions. For instance, defaults were listed on the writs, but most other resolutions were not. Unlike arbitrations and trials, confessions did not generate additional paper unless the confession was done in writing, and so no written record may have been kept outside of the minute books for most confessions. Minute books exist only for the first five years, so their disappearance from the extant record clearly explains some of the decline. Nevertheless, the change in procedure's importance is demonstrated in two ways. First, the use of confessions is concentrated in 1751 and 1752, when 17 per cent of actions end in confession. This declined precipitously in the following years: to 11 per cent in 1753, 8 per cent in 1754, and 4 per cent in 1755. Second, the uptick in recorded confessions beginning in 1764 coincident with juries of inquiry suggests decisions to confess were driven in part by available processes and by the relative costs of defaulting.

23 *Fillis v. Quin*, NSARM RG 37 (hx) vol. 14 #13; NSARM RG 39 "c" (hx) vol. 4 #14; *Quin v. Fillis*, NSARM RG 39 "c" (hx) vol. 4 #15; NSARM RG 37 (hx) vol. 15 #60.

24 Jacob, *Law Dictionary* (1743), s.v. "abatement."

25 Jacob's *Law Dictionary* (1743) defines demurrer as "an Issue joined upon Matter of Law, which is only determinable by the Judges; and an abiding in and referring to the Judgment of the Court, whether the Declaration or Plea of the adverse Party is sufficient in Law to be maintained." The distinction between them is one of simple error and legal error. In Halifax, as will be seen, this distinction was rarely made. There were examples of pleas of demurrer, such as *Breynton et al. v. Jones* (NSARM RG 37 A2, pp. 334–9), which successfully ended the action for the defendant and *Stewart v. Triton* (NSARM RG 37 No. B, pp. 73–81), which led to a trial by judges without jury.

   Bruce Mann discusses demurrer in his *Neighbors and Strangers: Law and Community in Early Connecticut* (Chapel Hill: University of North Carolina Press, 1987), and on page 82 argues that it was frequently used by defendants to try to stop actions before trial. Pleading demurrer carried a danger, however, because if the defendant failed, the action ended in the plaintiff's favour and there could be no trial on the evidence. In Halifax, even when the defendant explicitly described a plea as demurrer, the court would treat it like abatement, and if the judges rejected the plea, the defendant could go on to try the action on its merits before a jury, although use of the term demurrer to describe a defendant's plea was rare (see *Grant v. Piggot*, NSARM RG 37 (hx) vol. 2 #92; RG 39 "c" (hx) vol. 2 #12a).

26 *Fillis v. Quin*, NSARM RG 39 "c" (hx) vol. 4 #14.

27 *Ferguson & Hammon v. Heffernan & Quin*, NSARM RG 37 (hx) vol. 13 #21, 39.

28 *Bryant v. Sexton*, NSARM RG 37 (hx) vol. 4 #10.

29 *Blackburn v. Terlaven*, NSARM RG 39 "c" (hx) vol. 4 #39a, RG 37 (hx) vol. 15 #69, RG 37 (hx) vol. 16 #20.

30 This is an early run at the petitioners' complaint in the Justices' Affair, discussed in chapter 2. It is worth noting that Ker's complaint is about a writ devised on behalf of Morris, the chief justice on the bench attacked a few months later.

31 Jacobs, *Law Dictionary* (1729), s.vv. "writ, writ of inquiry and damages."

32 Jacobs, *Law Dictionary* (1743), s.v. "writ."

33 William Style, *Style's Practical Register, begin in the Reign of King Charles I …* 3rd ed. (London: Tho, Dring and the Executors of S. Leigh, 1694), 18.

34 *Morris v. Hoare I*, NSARM RG 39 "c" (hx) vol. 1 #133a–h.

35 The bench clearly could act venally, as some of the incidents leading up to the Justices' Affair show, even if it did not have to in this case.

36 For examples of this strategy or the importance of monitoring magistrates for their errors in other circumstances, see for example, Christopher Frank, "'Let But One of Them Come before Me, and I'll Commit Him': Trade Unions, Magistrates, and the Law in Mid-Nineteenth-Century Staffordshire," *Journal of British Studies* 44 (2005): 64–91 and Douglas Hay, "Dread of the Crown Office: The English Magistracy and King's Bench, 1740–1800," in *Law, Crime and English Society 1660–1840*, ed. Norma Landau, 19–45 (Cambridge: Cambridge University Press, 2002).

37 Council minutes, 1752 03 10, NSARM RG 1 vol. 209, 149–50.

38 *Rogers v. Tritton*, NSARM RG 37 A2, pp. 363–5.

39 *Rogers v. Tritton*, NSARM RG 37 B, pp. 1–7.

40 Council minutes, 1752 12 05, NSARM RG 1 vol. 209, 235–7.

41 For the judges, abatements may have offered additional problems: they required the bench, or some portion of it, to meet prior to session to consider the plea and, more generally, they could undermine the court in general by implying that it was poorly organized.

42 NSARM RG 37 A2, pp. 8–9 and 10–12.

43 For examples of lack of service see *Levit v. Hudson* and *Crook v. Main* (both September 1750), NSARM RG 37 A2, pp. 19–28; of missing paperwork, see *Allen v. Willis* and *Stevens v. Davis* (December 1750), NSARM RG 37 A2, pp. 40–9; and of failure to swear see *Allen v. Wallace* or *Smith v. Hunstable* (March 1751), NSARM RG 37 A2, pp. 56–87.

44 *Nagal & wife v. Hoffman*, NSARM RG 37 A2, pp. 118–21.

45 *Willis v. Davidson*, NSARM RG 37 A2, pp. 50–5, *Clerk v. Miller*, NSARM RG 37 A2, pp. 50–5.

46 *Allen v. Wallace*, NSARM RG 37 A2, pp. 56–87, *Hays v. Hunstable*, NSARM RG 37 A2, pp. 56–87.

47 *Jeffrey v. McLean*, NSARM RG 37 A2, pp. 127–36, *Gardner v. Stockley*, NSARM RG 37 A2, pp. 171–9.

48 *Keatin v. Patterson*, NSARM RG 37 A2, pp. 56–87.

49 *Box & Austen v. Sampson*, NSARM RG 37 A2, pp. 127–36.

50 *Mason v. Dawes*, NSARM RG 37 A2, pp. 56–87, *Grant v. Pike*, NSARM RG 37 A2, pp. 87–96, *Armstrong v. Hays*, NSARM RG 37 A2, pp. 267–76.

51 For the forty-four other dismissals there is no plaintiff lawyer listed, but there were few lawyers identified at all in the minute books for these sessions, and so it is possible they were represented but their lawyer was not identified.

5 Going to Trial

1 Deborah Rosen found that only 5 per cent of actions at the New York City mayor's court in 1750 ended in jury trials, down from a high of 25 per cent in 1710. In New York's Dutchess County, the high of 15 per cent in the 1730s had declined to only 1 or 2 per cent in the 1750s. *Courts and Commerce: Gender, Law, and the Market Economy in Colonial New York* (Columbus: Ohio State University Press, 1997), 62–6. Bruce Mann excluded defaults and withdrawn actions in his study of Connecticut. He found that between 5 and 20 per cent of contested actions went to trial by jury in 1745. In Halifax, 41 per cent of contested actions went to jury trials between 1750 and 1766. *Neighbors and Strangers: Law and Community in Early Connecticut* (Chapel Hill: University of North Carolina Press, 1987), 75 and 84.

2 Rosen, *Courts and Commerce*, 65–9, quotations from 68. Mann, *Neighbors and Strangers*, 75–6.

3 *Hill v. Webb*, NSARM RG 39 "c" vol. 3 #105.

4 *Priebst v. Hoffman*, NSARM RG 39 "c" (hx) vol. 1 #96b.

5 J.M. Beattie, *Crime and the Courts in England 1660–1800* (Princeton: Princeton University Press, 1986), 396.

6 *Leigh v. Jones*, NSARM RG 39 "c" (hx) vol. 3 #73b, RG 37 (hx) vol. 9 #88.

7 "An Act to Establish two Rules of the General Court as Laws," NSARM RG 37 B1, 1753-09-61. The Halifax civil practice appears to have conformed with English criminal trial practice, as John Beattie notes that by the mid-

eighteenth century, "depositions were being allowed as evidence [in English criminal trials] only when the accused had had an opportunity to cross-examine the deponent." *Crime and the Courts in England 1660–1800* (Princeton: Princeton University Press, 1986), 273.

8   *Welch v. Campbell*, NSARM RG 37 (hx) vol. 17 #106, vol. 18 #75, NSARM RG 39 "c" (hx) vol. 4 #20.

9   *Nagle & Nagle v. Murray*, NSARM RG 37 (hx) vol. 6 #64.

10 See "Special Court for Collection of Debts," in *Documents Relating to Currency, Exchange and Finance in Nova Scotia, with prefatory documents, 1675–1758,* ed. Adam Shortt (Ottawa: The King's Printer, 1933), 412.

11 James C. Oldham, "The Origins of the Special Jury," *University of Chicago Law Review* 50, no. 1 (1983): 139. Oldham discusses the relationship between trials at bar (that is, before a judge alone) and special juries (190–6). Only one Halifax civil case was recorded as a trial at bar – the assault action *Murphy v. Murphy* (NSARM RG 39 "c" (hx) vol. 3 #100 a, b). Clearly, this was not a viable option in Halifax.

12 *Franks v. Ball*, NSARM RG 37 (hx) vol. 9 #11.

13 *Ball v. Franks*, NSARM RG 37 (hx) vol. 8 #20.

14 In an action involving Anne Webb and her husband's former business partner, they were sued to provide a reasonable account at the Inferior Court in 1759. Of the eight jurors whose occupations can be identified, six were artisans and only two were clearly identified as being involved at some point in commerce: there were two housewrights, two tailors, one joiner, one blockmaker and retailer, one innkeeper and retailer, and one mariner (*Martin v. Webb & Ewer*, NSARM RG 39 (hx) "c" vol. 3 #76d).

15 NSARM RG 1 vol. 209, 14 January 1750/1 ("1750/1" denotes that this order dates before the change in English calendars to recognizing 1 January as the start of the new year).

16 *Hogan v. Jeffrey*, NSARM RG 37 (hx) vol. 19 #36. It is unclear if either Hogan or Monk was present when this was done. In another case referred to a jury of inquiry, the defendant's attorney attended the court but pled nothing in bar or prevention of the plaintiff's case, essentially defaulting despite his presence (*Campbell v. de les Dernier*, NSARM RG 37 (hx) vol. 18 #11).

17 *Webb v. Hill*, NSARM RG 37 (hx) vol. 12 #29.

18 In this period, only men were appointed as arbitrators, although this appears to simply have been the practice rather than a rule.

19 On England, see Henry Horwitz and James Oldham, "John Locke, Lord Mansfield, and Arbitration during the Eighteenth Century," *The Historical Journal* 36, no. 1 (1993), 140–7. The act in question is "An Act for determin-

ing Differences by Arbitration," 9 & 10 William and Mary (1697) c. 15. On Virginia, see Susie M. Ames, *County Court Records of Accomack and North-ampton Virginia, 1632–1640* (Washington, DC: American Historical Asso-ciation, 1954), lvi–lix.

20 Mann, *Neighbors and Strangers*, 128–9.

21 For Ingolls, see, for example, *Gerrish v. Ingolls*, NSARM RG 37 (hx) vol. 16 #27 and *Ingolls v. Charlton*, NSARM RG 39 "c" (hx) vol. 3 #88a, b and RG 37 (hx) vol. 10 #141. For Marshall, see, for example, *Gosbee v. Nuttage*, NSARM RG 37 (hx) vol. 11 #174. For Wakefield, see, for example, *Cunnable v. Fury*, NSARM RG 37 (hx) vol. 10 #11, 23 and *Tufts v. Wakefield*, NSARM RG 37 (hx) vol. 14 #119.

22 *Falkner v. Tritton*, NSARM RG 37 (hx) vol. 4 #30.

23 E.P. Thompson, "In Defence of the Jury," in *Persons and Polemics: Historical Essays* (London: Merlin Press, 1994), 151.

24 Other histories of juries in the eighteenth century include, for juries in civil and criminal courts in colonial Delaware, William M. Offut, Jr., *Of "Good Laws" and "Good Men"* (Urbana: University of Illinois Press, 1995), 57–60. For English juries, the large literature is mostly concerned with criminal trials. These works have, nonetheless, influenced the analysis here: Beattie, *Crime and the Courts*, 327 and 385–7; J.M. Beattie, "London Juries in the 1690s," in *Twelve Good Men and True: The Criminal Trial Jury in England, 1200–1800*, ed. J.S. Cockburn and Thomas A. Green (Princeton: Princeton University Press, 1988), 234–7; P.J.R. King, "'Illiterate Plebeians, Easily Misled': Jury Composition, Experience, and Behaviour in Essex, 1735–1815," in *Twelve Good Men and True*, 285–9; Douglas Hay, "The Class Composition of the Palladium of Liberty: Trial Jurors in the Eighteenth Century," *Twelve Good Men and True*, 346–8. Donald Fyson has described the criminal jury for Quebec after the conquest in *Magistrates, Police, and People: Everyday Criminal Justice in Quebec and Lower Canada, 1764–1837* (Toronto: University of Toronto Press for the Osgoode Society, 2006), esp. 243–5 and (for grand juries, which were quite distinct from the trial juries discussed here) "Jurys, participation civique et representation au Québec et au Bas-Canada: les grands jurys du district de Montréal (1764–1832)," *Revue d'histoire de l'Amerique française* 55, no. 1 (2001): 85–120.

25 English law, in force in both England and the other North American col-onies, limited jury participation to men. This restriction was followed in Nova Scotia as well.

26 *Statutes of Nova Scotia 1758–1759, c. 5, An Act for Regulating Petit Juries, and Declaring the Qualifications of Jurors*, NSARM RG 5, series S, vol. 1. (1758) and RG 5, series S, vol. 1, 1759, c. 5 (1759); Jim Phillips, "Halifax Juries in

the Eighteenth Century," in *Criminal Justice in the Old World and New*, ed. Greg T. Smith, Allyson N. May, and Simon Devereaux, 139–40 (Toronto: Centre of Criminology, University of Toronto, 1998).

27 *Statutes of Nova Scotia 1758–1759, c. 5, An Act for Regulating Petit Juries, and Declaring the Qualifications of Jurors*, NSARM RG 5, series S, vol. 1.

28 NSARM RG 37 (hx) vol. 2 #90, RG 37 (hx) vol. 2 #91, RG 37 (hx) vol. 4 #125, RG 37 (hx) vol. 19 #18, RG 37 (hx) vol. 20 #29.

29 *R v. Ryan* etc., NSARM RG 37 (hx) vol. 12 #75, 76; RG 37 (hx) vol. 13 #17, 96; RG 37 (hx) vol. 14, #76. Juror absenteeism remained a problem into the nineteenth century and has been discussed by two Canadian historians in particular: R. Blake Brown, *A Trying Question: The Jury in Nineteenth-Century Canada* (Toronto: University of Toronto Press for the Osgoode Society, 2009), 29–30 and 49–51, and David Murray, "Just Excuses: Jury Culture in Barrington Township, Nova Scotia, 1795–1837," in *Planter Links: Community and Culture in Colonial Nova Scotia*, ed. Margaret Conrad and Barry Moody, 46 (Fredericton: Acadiensis Press, 2001).

30 Compare this to John Beattie's study of juries in criminal trials in Surrey in the eighteenth century: he found an average of between 1 and 3.5 repeat jurors per jury. See Beattie, *Crime and the Courts*, 386–7. Note that Beattie talks of both sessions and juries, so the comparison is not completely of equal units. Nevertheless, it seems clear that on the whole Halifax civil juries had more experienced members on average than did Surrey criminal juries.

31 *Mackey v. Innis*, NSARM RG 37 (hx) vol. 6 #31. His jury appearances that session were on *Martin v. Webb and Ewer* (involving Anne Webb) (this and the five that follow from NSARM RG 37 (hx) vol. 6) #27, 28, *Parsons v. Brenock*, #35, *Strauch v. Beyer*, #43, *Faulkner v. Baxter*, #83, *Chapman v. King*, #85, *Ainslie v. Gifford*, #89, *Porter v. Shipton* NSARM RG 37 (hx) vol. 7 #50.

32 Mackey claimed £33 16s 7d damages: £13 16s 7d in rent and sundries as debt on account and £20 for damages to the rental house. The jury found for him on both parts, but awarded him £13 8s 1d for the debt and only £4 for the house. As will be seen in the next chapter, this does not appear out of the norm for jury verdicts.

33 Beattie, *Crime and the Courts in England*, 397–8.

34 See Mann, *Neighbors and Strangers*, 36, for an argument that the need for consistency led to practices that kept disputes *away* from juries.

35 These findings bear out those made by Jim Phillips in his study of the Halifax Grand and Petty juries in the eighteenth century, "Halifax Juries in the Eighteenth Century," 140–56; James Muir and Jim Phillips, "Michaelmas Term 1754: The Supreme Court's First Session," in *The Supreme Court*

of Nova Scotia, 1754–2004: From Imperial Bastion to Provincial Oracle, ed. Philip Girard, Jim Phillips, and Barry Cahill (Toronto: University of Toronto Press for the Osgoode Society, 2004), 266–7.

36 Contrast this with Beattie's argument about eighteenth-century Assize juries: many frequent jurors in Surrey were artisans, but they were also frequently important players in local governance. See *Crime and the Courts*, 387–8.

37 By comparison, between 1750 and 1755, 44 per cent of juror appearances were made by first-time jurors, while between 1756 and 1766, 14 per cent of juror appearances were made by first-time jurors.

38 Of all 226 individual arbitrators, 166 (73 per cent) of them were defendants in at least one action while 180 (80 per cent) were plaintiffs at least once.

39 For example, the predominance of merchants among arbitrators was not so disproportionally represented among litigants: of the 105 arbitrations where litigants' occupations were listed, in only 9 actions were the defendants merchants, while in 15 the plaintiffs were merchants. There were 41 actions where the defendants were from some commercial occupation – including not only merchants and traders but the much lower status truckmen, retailers, and shop, inn, and tavern keepers – and 38 where the plaintiffs were from a commercial occupation. By contrast, 28 defendants and 33 plaintiffs turning to arbitration were artisans.

40 None of the 8 most frequent arbitrators were among the 49 most frequent jurors, but 3 were among the frequent litigants. Only 5 of the frequent litigants were among the frequent jurors.

6 Ending the Action

1 The costs taxed for the Supreme Court hearing and arbitration are not recorded. In most cases, these too would be taxed against Webb, on top of the costs Webb was already taxed at the Inferior Court.

2 *Watson v. Rockett*, NSARM RG 37 (hx) vol. 20 #36 and vol. 21 #6.

3 The *Oxford English Dictionary* cites a source from 1792 that defines shoremen as "the people who are employed on shore, to head, split, and salt the codfish." In this case, Stirling was likely more of a foreman for a crew of on-shore workers.

4 Note that in this case the default order was issued not because the defendant was not present, but because the defendant who was present offered no defence. Nesbitt's role in this case is not unique: in other cases where damages were determined by juries of inquiry, lawyers appeared for defaulting defendants to say nothing in bar of the action.

246 Notes to pages 130–40

5 *Franklin v. Stirling*, NSARM RG 37 (hx) vol. 20 #50, 62; vol. 21 #5, 25.

6 See, for example, *Barkeley & Ross v. Clark & Eardly*, NSARG RG 37 (hx) vol. 18 #4, vol. 20 #57.

7 In six cases, defendants confessed for more than was claimed against them. It is not clear why this was the case. In one action, *Jackson v. Hoar*, the remaining account is for the debt confessed to (£22 12s 8d) but the claim was only for £18 17s 8d. It is possible that the evidence presented with the declaration, and thus the claimed debt, was for the smaller sum, but the evidence available at the sitting of the court was for the higher value (NSARM RG 37 (hx) vol. 19 #39).

8 See, for instance, J.M. Beattie, *Crime and the Courts in England, 1660–1800*, pp. 419–30 and *Policing and Punishment in London, 1660–1750*, pp. 304–6, 339–44.

9 The demands in assault actions ranged from £20 to £500, while awards ranged from 5 shillings to £100.

10 *Gibbons v. Quin*, NSARM RG 37 (hx) vol. 18 #49 and RG 39 "c" (hx) vol. 4 #30.

11 *Jones v. Mauger*, NSARM RG 37 (hx) vol. 14 #144.

12 The Franks and Ball actions described in chapter 5 ended in a similar fashion: the special jury found for Franks as plaintiff in his claim on debt, and found for Franks again as defendant against Ball's action demanding a reasonable account (*Franks v. Ball*, NSARM RG 37 (hx) vol. 9 #11; *Ball v. Franks*, NSARM RG 37 (hx) vol. 8 #20). A series of suits in 1764 over a covenant held in escrow that was to be exchanged for real property similarly found the special jury splitting its decisions, finding for the same party (in this case John Anderson and Robert Campbell) whether they were defendant or plaintiff in the several actions the jury heard at once (see *Chorley v. Anderson and Campbell*, NSARM RG 37 (hx) vol. 17 #80, 136 and NSARM RG 39 "c" (hx) vol. 4 #25; *Blackburn v. Anderson*, NSARM RG 37 (hx) vol. 17 #33; *Anderson v. Blackburn*, NSARM RG 37 (hx) vol. 17 #6 and NSARM RG 39 "c" (hx) vol. 4 #20a).

13 *Kennedy v. Easton*, NSARM RG 37 (hx) vol. 10 #137, vol. 11 #61; *Easton v. Kennedy*, NSARM RG37 (hx) vol. 10 #150 and NSARM RG 39 "c" (hx) vol. 3 #90; *McGee v. Kennedy*, NSARM RG 39 "c" (hx) vol. 3 #97.

14 *Webb & Ewer v. Franks*, NSARM RG 39 "c" (hx) vol. 1 #97b, c, d, e.

15 *Heffernan v. Murray*, NSARM RG 37 (hx) vol. 9 #23, vol. 10 #38, vol. 13 #79. The sharing of costs by both litigants was rare in arbitration awards: in most cases, arbitrators followed the loser-pays-all-costs rule.

16 Clinton Francis found English litigants agreeing to prorate costs in proportion to damages when the defendant was successful in reducing the

plaintiff's claim. There is no evidence of this in Halifax. Francis, "Practice, Strategy, and Institution: Debt Collection in the English Common-Law Courts, 1740–1840," *Northwestern University Law Review* 80, no. 4 (1985–6): 822.

17 Plaintiffs were responsible for more of the fees of court going through the process of litigation, and so more would be charged to defendants than would be charged to plaintiffs in cases where defendants received their cost.

18 Excluding those defaults referred to a jury of inquiry.

19 *Wood v. Heffernan*, NSARM RG 37 vol. 13 #71. Most appearances at trial were charged at 6 shillings 8 pence when at the Interior Court and the Quarter Sessions (the criminal jurisdiction court that sat at the same time and with the same judges). At the Supreme Court, arguing an action cost 1 pound. In addition, Wood appears to have done a variety of other tasks as lawyer for Heffernan. For example, in February of 1762 he accompanied Heffernan "by particular desire to demand Money due from Thomas Bleigh on a note and after," for which he charged 3 shillings 4 pence, half of his lower-court appearance fee.

20 John A. Dickinson, "Court Costs in France and New France in the Eighteenth Century," *Historical Papers / Communications Historiques* 12, no. 1 (1977): 53.

21 The writ of *scire facias* had to be issued by the court which issued the original judgment. If a judgment from the Inferior Court of Common Pleas was unsuccessfully appealed to the Supreme Court, and then no satisfaction made, the writ of *scire facias* would have to be issued by the Supreme Court. The Supreme Court issued three writs of *scire facias* between 1750 and 1766.

22 *Purcel v. Landres & Healy*, NSARM RG 37 (hx) vol. 8 #91. For the full litigation history of this case, see also *Purcel v. Fitzpatrick*, NSARM RG 37 (hx) vol. 7 #22, vol. 8 #92, vol. 9 #149; *Galland v. Fitzpatrick*, NSARM RG 37 (hx) vol. 10 #60.

23 NSARM CO 217 vol. 9 F. 156 and F. 163. It is possible that this is the same Stephen Theodore Janssen who acted as MP for and Sheriff of London in late 1749. On Janssen's sheriff work, see Peter Linebaugh, "The Tyburn Riot against the Surgeons," in *Albion's Fatal Tree: Crime and Society in Eighteenth-Century England*, ed. Douglas Hay et al. (London: Allen Lane, 1975), 99–102.

24 *Janssen v. Cook*, NSARM RG 37 vol. 2 #85, vol. 3 #24, RG 37 No. B, pp. 133–6.

25 *McMar & Reynolds v. Cook*, NSARM RG 37 (hx) vol. 2 #92; *Townsend v.*

Cook, NSARM RG 37 (hx) vol. 2 #92; *Baxter v. Cook,* NSARM RG 37 No. B, pp. 126–32; *Grahame v. Cook,* NSARM RG 37 No. B, pp. 126–32. A fifth action was launched against Cook at the same session by William Nesbitt, but Cook fought this one with a countersuit. Both Nesbitt and Cook were victorious at the June court. Nesbitt did not get a clear victory over Cook until the September session – too late to be included in the execution of the June actions. *Nesbitt v. Cook I* and *Nesbitt v. Cook II,* NSARM RG 37 (hx) vol. 2 #88; *Cook v. Nesbitt,* NSARM RG 37 (hx) vol. 2 #87.

26 George Chumbley, *Colonial Justice in Virginia: The Development of a Judicial System, Typical Laws and Cases of the Period* (Richmond: The Dietz Press, 1938), 101.

27 *Piggot v. Cobb,* NSARM RG 39 "c" (hx) vol. 2 #10a.

28 *Hunstable v. Gleason,* NSARM RG 39 "c" (hx) vol. 1 #81a, b, d. Although Hunstable was a frequent litigant prior to his disappearance, he does not reappear in Halifax legal documents before at least 1767, if at all. See also *Porter v. Hoare,* NSARM RG 39 "c" (hx) vol. 1 #133g, h, *Seaflower,* NSARM RG 39 "c" (hx) vol. 4 #23a.

29 *Recovery of Debts in American Plantations Act,* 5 Geo II, c. 7 (1732).

30 Bruce H. Mann, *Republic of Debtors: Bankruptcy in the Age of American Independence* (Cambridge, MA: Harvard University Press, 2002), 30.

31 Adam Shortt and Arthur G. Doughty, *Documents Relating to the Constitutional History of Canada 1759–1791,* 2nd rev. ed. (Ottawa: J de L. Tache, 1918), part 1, 399.

32 *An Act for Making Lands and Tenements Liable to the Payment of Debts, Statutes of Nova Scotia,* 1758, c. 15.

33 Margot Finn, *The Character of Credit: Personal Debt in English Culture, 1740–1914* (Cambridge: Cambridge University Press, 2003), 111–12. See also Ian P.H. Duffy, "English Bankrupts, 1571–1861," *American Journal of Legal History* 24, no. 4 (1980): 285.

34 Bruce Kercher, *Debt, Seduction and Other Disasters: The Birth of the Civil Law in Convict New South Wales* (Leichhardt, NSW: The Federation Press, 1996), 198–200.

35 *Ewer v. Webb* and *Ewer, Ewer v. Webb, Ewer v. Webb,* NSARM RG 37 (hx) vol. 5 #33 & 34.

36 David Sugarman and Ronnie Warrington, "Land Law, Citizenship, and the Invention of 'Englishness': The Strange World of the Equity of Redemption," in *Early Modern Conceptions of Property,* ed. John Brewer and Susan Staves (London and New York: Routledge, 1995), 113–17.

37 William S. Holdsworth, *An Historical Introduction to the Land Law* (Oxford: The Clarendon Press, 1927), 257.

38 Neither Holdsworth nor the historian of the equity of redemption, Richard
    Turner, addresses the question of improvements directly. They are clear
    that the mortgagor could be held to only the principle and interest. Even
    in cases where mortgagors were foreclosed, they could have the Chancery
    reopen the mortgage and award redemption if they paid off the debt with
    interest. See Holdsworth, *An Historical Introduction to the Land Law*, 259
    and 262, and Richard W. Turner, *The Equity of Redemption: Its Nature, His-
    tory and Connection with Equitable Estates Generally* (Cambridge: Cambridge
    University Press, 1931), 52–64 and 175–9.

39 NSARM RG 1 vol. 209, 1750/1-01-14, p. 100.

40 *Gordon v. Nesbitt*, NSARM RG 37 A2, pp. 167–70; *Gordon v. Nesbitt II*, RG
    37 (hx) vol. 4 #43, vol. 5 #26. See Turner, *The Equity of Redemption*, 88–97,
    on mortgagor's possession of land in English law in the seventeenth and
    eighteenth centuries.

41 J.H. Baker, *An Introduction to English Legal History*, 4th ed. (London: Butter-
    worths LexisNexis, 2002), 66.

42 By contrast, for the older colonies to the south, see Alan Kulikoff, *From
    British Peasants to Colonial American Farmers* (Chapel Hill: University of
    North Carolina Press, 2000), 225.

43 In four instances it is unclear if the imprisonment occurred prior to or after
    trial.

44 *Nathans v. Reed*, NSARM RG 37 (hx) vol. 7 #23 and vol. 9 #162.

45 *Power v. Ryan*, NSARM RG 37 (hx) vol. 11 #7; *Salter v. Hopkins*, NSARM RG
    37 (hx) vol. 7 #69; *Binning v. Pierce*, NSARM RG 37 (hx) vol. 9 #160; *Jeffery v.
    Abrahams*, NSARM RG 37 (hx) vol. 2a #17; *Nathans v. Reed*, NSARM RG 37
    (hx) vol. 7 #23 and vol. 9 #162. Jail returns: NSARM RG 39 "c" (hx) vol. 4
    #27c, RG 37 (hx) vol. 19 #48, and RG 37 (hx) vol. 9 #182.

46 Thomas B. Akins, *History of Halifax City*, facs. ed. (1895; repr., Belleville,
    ON: Mika Publishing, 1973) (Halifax, 1895), 258.

47 On the English rules, see Paul H. Haagen, "Eighteenth-century English So-
    ciety and the Debt Law," in *Social Control and the State*, ed. Stanley Cohen
    and Andrew Scull (Oxford: Basil Blackwell Press, 1985), 226–31. For Mas-
    sachusetts, see Robert A. Feer, "Imprisonment for Debt in Massachusetts
    before 1800," *The Mississippi Valley Historical Review* 48, no. 2 (1961): 255–7.
        Haagen has found that in mid-century London no fewer than 1,000 and
    up to 2,000 debtors were imprisoned a year, while in England and Wales
    up to 4,000 a year were imprisoned. He estimates that over the century, be-
    tween 1 in 375 and 1 in 1,000 adult men were imprisoned in England and
    Wales each year, but in some towns it could be as high as 1 in 125 (New-
    castle, 1720) or 1 in 55 (Norwich, 1720). By mid-century, the length of in-

carceration for debt was usually less than a year, but at the Fleet Prison in London in 1734, 25 per cent of prisoners had been incarcerated for three or more years (Haagan, 58–9, 62, 66–7, and 80). Robert Feer found 1,902 debtors imprisoned in Massachusetts from 1695–1800, fewer than 20 a year. Of these, only 35 were incarcerated for more than a year (Feer, 258–60 and 264–5).

7 Appeals and Other Courts

1 The history of the General Court is covered briefly in Barry Cahill and Jim Phillips's, "The Supreme Court of Nova Scotia: Origins to Confederation," in *The Supreme Court of Nova Scotia, 1754–2004: From Imperial Bastion to Provincial Oracle*, ed. Philip Girard, Jim Phillips, and Barry Cahill (Toronto: University of Toronto Press for the Osgoode Society, 2004), 54–5. See their note 2 on page 112 for other historians who have touched on the court. The General Court case for £7 10s, *Taylor v. Hudson & Thompson*, NSARM RG 39 "c" (hx) vol. 1 #98, was heard at the winter session in 1752.

2 Susan Buggey, "Belcher, Jonathan," in *The Dictionary of Canadian Biography*, vol. 4, ed. Francess G. Halpenny (Toronto: University of Toronto Press, 1979), 50–4; James Muir and Jim Phillips, "Michaelmas Term 1754: The Supreme Court's First Session," in *The Supreme Court of Nova Scotia, 1754–2004*, 263; Paul Craven, "Master & Servant Legislation of Atlantic Canada in Imperial Context" (paper presented at the Atlantic Law & History Workshop II, Dalhousie Law School, Halifax, NS, 3–4 March 1995).

3 For a good introduction to the building of Westminster Hall and the placement of the courts inside, see Leonard W. Cowie, "Justice at Westminster Hall," *History Today* 21, no. 3 (1971): 178–86.

4 J.H. Baker, *An Introduction to English Legal History*, 4th ed. (London: Butterworths LexisNexis, 2002), 84–5, 136–7, and 148–9 and Douglas Hay, "Origins: The Courts of Westminster Hall in the Eighteenth Century," in *The Supreme Court of Nova Scotia, 1754–2004*, 13–29. The writ of error could be issued by the Exchequer Chambers for actions in King's Bench as well as the Exchequer of Pleas.

5 Mary Sarah Bilder, "The Origin of the Appeal in America," *Hastings Law Journal* 48 (1996–7): 924–47.

6 Thomas Garden Barnes, "'The Dayly Cry for Justice': The Juridical Failure of the Annapolis Royal Regime, 1713–1749," in *Essays in the History of Canadian Law, Volume III: Nova Scotia*, ed. Philip Girard and Jim Phillips (Toronto: University of Toronto Press for the Osgoode Society, 1990), 14–17.

7 NSARM RG 1 vol. 29, document #2, 1749–02–18.

8 *Monk v. Quin*, NSARM RG 37 (hx) vol. 18 #55.

9 NSARM RG 37 (hx) vol. A, 13 December 1749, 4 December 1752 (p. 234). A later statute of the assembly repeated the rules; see "An Act in addition to an Act entitled an Act for regulating the Proceedings of the Courts of Judicature," 1763 8th Assembly Cap. 6, NSARM RG 5 "s" v. 2.

10 Bilder, "Origin of Appeal," 934–6.

11 *Piggot v. Grant*, NSARM RG 39 "c" (hx) vol. 2 #11b; RG 36 Series A bx. 2 #10, doc. 26.

12 See, for example, Bruce Mann, *Neighbors and Strangers: Law and Community in Early Connecticut* (Chapel Hill: University of North Carolina Press, 1987), 138–9.

13 Jim Cruikshank, "The Chancery Court of Nova Scotia: Jurisdiction and Procedure 1751–1855," *Dalhousie Journal of Legal Studies* 1, no. 1 (1992): 33–4.

14 See Ernest Clark and Jim Phillips, "'The Course of Law Cannot Be Stopped': The Aftermath of the Cumberland Rebellion in the Civil Courts of Nova Scotia," *Dalhousie Law Journal* 21, no. 2 (1998): 470–2 and Philip Girard, "Taking Litigation Seriously: The Market Wharf Controversy at Halifax, 1785–1820," in *Essays in the History of Canadian Law, Volume VIII: In Honour of R.C.B. Risk*, ed. Jim Phillips and G. Blaine Baker (Toronto: University of Toronto Press for the Osgoode Society, 1999), 217–18.

15 Cruikshank, "The Chancery Court of Nova Scotia," 36–43.

16 *Grant v. Piggot*, NSARM RG 37 (hx) vol. 2 #92, NSARM RG 39 "c" (hx) vol. 2 #12a.

17 See Mann, *Neighbors and Strangers*, 82. The Nova Scotian practice of tentatively allowing demurrers and going forward with a trial if they failed seems similar to medieval English practice (see Baker, *An Introduction to English Legal History*, 79).

18 *Piggot v. Grant I*, NSARM RG 39 "c" (hx) vol. 2 #11c.

19 *Piggot v. Grant II*, NSARM RG 39 "c" (hx) vol. 2 #11b, RG 36 Series A bx. 2 #10, RG 36 vol. 75a.

20 *Piggot v. Grant III*, NSARM RG 39 "c" (hx) vol. 2 #11b, RG 36 #8 17b.

21 *Piggot v. Grant IV*, RG 36 #10 22.

22 David Sugarman and Ronnie Warrington, "Land Law, Citizenship, and the Invention of 'Englishness': The Strange World of the Equity of Redemption," in *Early Modern Conceptions of Property*, ed. John Brew and Susan Staves (London: Routledge, 1995), 126.

23 In *Porter v. Shipton*, a 1759 Inferior Court trial, John Porter sued Samuel Shipton demanding Shipton present a reasonable account of all of the money Porter had paid Shipton since 1752, when Porter had transferred title of a plot of land to Shipton for a debt of £19 1s 8d. Porter intended

to exercise his equity of redemption. The judge told the jury, "Your issue is to try whether the Plt is Entitled to the Possession of the House & if he be upon the Adjustment of the Account what is due either to the Plt or Defendant and return your Verdict According to Evidence." The jury returned, "The Jurors finde for ye Plantife ye Position of his house & Lott he paying ye Defendent ye Sum of Nineteen pounds one shilling & 8d & Costs of Corte [*sic*][.]" Porter's right to the equity was maintained, but the jury did not count the rents Porter paid for six and a half years towards the original debt. See NSARM RG 37 (hx) vol. 7 #50.

24 Of 106 actions, 31 (29 per cent) were for prize, 25 (24 per cent) for wages owed, 15 (14 per cent) for illegal trading, 10 (10 per cent) for salvage, 4 (4 per cent) for insurance, and 2 (2 per cent) for negligence.

25 Arthur J. Stone, "The Admiralty Court in Colonial Nova Scotia," *Dalhousie Law Journal* 17 (1994): 363–79.

26 Donald Chard, "Green, Benjamin," in *The Dictionary of Canadian Biography*, vol. 4, 312–13; William Hamilton, "Collier, John," in *The Dictionary of Canadian Biography*, vol. 3, ed. Francess G. Halpenny, 130–1 (Toronto: University of Toronto Press, 1974).

27 *Handly v. Cook*, NSARM RG 1 vol. 491, pp. 1–4. Cook faced other sailors' wages actions from mariners on the *Baltimore* in 1750; see *Dixon v. Cook* and *Palmer v. Cook*, NSARM RG 1 vol. 491, pp. 145–7. On the appeal of Vice Admiralty to seamen seeking wages in the North American colonies, see David Owen and Michael Tolley, *Courts of Admiralty in Colonial America: The Maryland Experience, 1634–1776* (Durham, NC: Carolina Academic Press, 1995), 2–3 and Richard B. Morris, *Government and Labor in Early America* (New York: Octagon Books, 1965), 232–3.

28 The act in question is *The Act for the Better Regulation and Government of the Merchant Service, 1729*, which formalized sailors' employment contracts and required that the route of the voyage be specified in the contract. For a discussion of the act and its general effect on sailors, see Marcus Rediker, *Between the Devil and the Deep Blue Sea* (Cambridge: Cambridge University Press, 1987), 140–1.

29 See Morris, *Government and Labor in Early America*, 242–3.

30 The value of the decrees ranged from only a halfpenny less than the sailors claim to one where the awarded wages of 15s 5d was only 6 per cent of the claimed loss. The median value of a wage decree was 41.6 per cent of the sailors' demand.

31 See, for example, *Mundi v. Dunn*, NSARM RG 1 vol. 492, pp. 1–15 and *St. Francis*, NSARM RG 1 vol. 491, pp. 113–44. See also Rediker, *Between the Devil and the Deep Blue Sea*, 119–21.

32 See, for example, *St. Peters*, NSARM RG 1 vol. 491, pp. 195–203.
33 E.P. Thompson, *Customs in Common* (New York: New Press, 1991), 404–66.
34 Nancy F. Cott, "Divorce and the Changing Status of Women in Eighteenth-Century Massachusetts," *William and Mary Quarterly* 33, no. 4 (1976): 587–90, Henry S. Cohn, "Connecticut's Divorce Mechanism: 1636–1969," *American Journal of Legal History* 14, no. 1 (1970): 37–9, Roderick Phillips, *Putting Asunder: A History of Divorce in Western Society* (Cambridge: Cambridge University Press, 1988), 134–40, 227–8, 239–42. On the sale of wives, see Thompson, *Customs in Common*, 404–66.
35 *Williams v. Williams*, NSARM RG 1 vol. 209, 1750-05-15. See the description in Charles J. Townsend, *History of the Court of Chancery of Nova Scotia* (Toronto: Carswell, 1990), 16–17.
36 Thomas B. Akins, *History of Halifax City* (Halifax: Nova Scotia Historical Society, 1895), 256.
37 Judicial divorce was available in Scotland. The method there was very different than that of the New England colonies or Nova Scotia. It is unlikely, despite its nominal "Scottishness," that eighteenth-century Nova Scotian rules for divorce owed anything directly to the Scottish rules. On Scotland see Leah Leneman, *Alienated Affections: The Scottish Experience of Divorce and Separation 1684–1830* (Edinburgh: Edinburgh University Press, 1998).
38 Kimberley Smith Maynard, "Divorce in Nova Scotia, 1750–1890," in *Essays in the History of Canadian Law, Volume III: Nova Scotia*, ed. Philip Girard and Jim Phillips (Toronto: University of Toronto Press for the Osgoode Society, 1990), 234–5.
39 *The King in Proh. v. Ryan*, Edward Belcher Family Papers, University of British Columbia Special Collections, file 1–45. Unfortunately, the available records do not record the date of this action.
40 Rediker, *Between the Devil and the Deep Blue Sea*, 119–20.
41 Holt KB 595 (90 E.R. 1229 [B]); 1 Salk. 33 (91 E.R. 34 [B]); 1 ld. Raym. 576 (91 E.R. 1285); Carth. 518 (90 E.R. 896 [A]).
42 Richard Morris states that in other British North American Vice Admiralty courts in the eighteenth century, all officers except the master could sue for wages. Morris writes, "The courts justified this distinction on the ground that the mariners contracted on the credit of the ship, but the master contracted on the credit of the owner … It must be borne in mind that in colonial times many masters owned their ships or were part owners." See Morris, *Government and Labor*, 244.
43 In *Hickey v. the King's Advocate*, from September 1761, Belcher again ruled

against an attempt to remove a case from Vice Admiralty (NSARM RG 36 vol. 75, pp. 95–8, RG 36 vol. 74 [a] p. 1).

44 On the response to the courts in the rest of British North America, see Lawrence M. Friedman, *A History of American Law* (New York: Simon and Schuster, 1973), 45–6.

45 *R. v. Power*, NSARM RG 1 vol. 491, pp. 158–64.

46 See, on the enforcement of *Navigation Acts* in Maryland and other parts of British North America, Owen and Tolley, *Courts of Admiralty*, 102–3, 133–6, and 101–36 generally.

47 At the same time as the Vice Admiralty suit, Power was being sued in the Inferior Court of Common Pleas by John Owen and other members of the *Francis*'s crew for their shares of the summer's catch. *Owen v. Power, Hagarty v. Power, Chellis v. Power, Oakes v. Power, Power v. Owen*, NSARM RG 37 (hx) vol. 1 #85, 86, 87, 88.

48 *R. v. Power*, NSARM RG 1 vol. 491, pp. 158–64.

49 An anchor of wine contained "10 old wine gallons or 8 1/3 imperial gallons." See "anker," *Oxford English Dictionary* (Oxford: Oxford University Press, 1933).

50 I have been unable to find a reply to Green's memo to the Board of Trade. The High Court of Admiralty had no jurisdiction over the *Navigation Acts*. Instead, all cases in England were to be tried at a court of record in Westminster, which, in practice, was the Court of Exchequer. As a reference, this case would probably first have gone to the Board of Trade who may have referred it elsewhere as they saw necessary. See Owen and Tolley, *Courts of Admiralty*, 106.

51 See, for example, Cal Winslow, "Sussex Smugglers," in *Albion's Fatal Tree: Crime and Society in Eighteenth-Century England*, ed. Douglas Hay, Peter Linebaugh, John Rule, E.P. Thompson, and Cal Winslow (London: Allen Lane, 1975), 140–7. Barry Moody notes the existence of a great deal of illegal trade between Louisburg, English Nova Scotia, and New England in the 1730s. See Barry Moody, "Making a British North America," in *The "Conquest" of Acadia, 1710: Imperial, Colonial, and Aboriginal Constructions*, ed. John G. Reid, Maurice Basque, Elizabeth Mancke, Barry Moody, Geoffrey Plank, and William Wicken (Toronto: University of Toronto Press, 2003), 153.

52 Donald F. Chard, "Mauger, Joshua," in *The Dictionary of Canadian Biography*, vol. 4, 526; see also A.A. Mackenzie, "Zouberbuhler, Sebastian," in *The Dictionary of Canadian Biography*, vol. 4, 780.

53 W.A.B. Douglas, "Halifax as an Element of Sea Power 1749–1766" (master's thesis, Dalhousie University, 1966), 48.

8 Conclusion

1 William Nelson, *Dispute and Conflict Resolution in Plymouth County, Massachusetts, 1725–1825* (Chapel Hill: University of North Carolina Press, 1981), 68.

2 Craig Muldrew, *The Economy of Obligation: The Culture of Credit and Social Relations in Early Modern England* (Hampshire, UK: Palgrave, 1998), 239.

3 Julian Gwyn, *Excessive Expectations: Maritime Commerce and the Economic Development of Nova Scotia, 1740–1870* (Montreal: McGill-Queen's University Press, 1998), 30.

4 John Bartlett Brebner, *The Neutral Yankees of Nova Scotia: A Marginal Colony during the Revolutionary Years* (1937; repr., Toronto: McClelland and Stewart, 1969), 1–104.

5 John A. Dickinson, *Justice et Justiciables: La Procédure Civile à la Prévôté de Québec, 1667–1759* (Québec: Les Presses de l'Université Laval, 1982), 110–11.

6 Tina Loo, *Making Law, Order, and Authority in British Columbia, 1821–1871* (Toronto: University of Toronto Press, 1994), 74–5, 90.

7 Christopher W. Brooks, "The Longitudinal Study of Civil Litigation in England 1200–1996," in *Litigation: Past and Present*, ed. Wilfrid Prest and Sharyn Roach Anleu (Sydney, Australia: UNSW Press, 2004), 28.

8 Allan Kulikoff, *From British Peasants to Colonial American Farmers* (Chapel Hill: University of North Carolina Press, 2000), 220, but 216–26 *passim*.

9 Gwyn, *Excessive Expectations*, 5, 6.

10 The debate can be followed through T.W. Acheson, "The Great Merchant and Economic Development in Saint John, 1820–50," *Acadiensis* 8, no. 2 (1979): 3–27; Ian McKay, "The Crisis of Dependent Development: Class Conflict in the Nova Scotia Coalfields, 1872–1876," in *Class, Gender, and Region: Essays in Canadian Historical Sociology*, ed. Gregory S. Kealey (St. John's, NL: Committee on Canadian Labour History, 1988), 13–30; Eric W. Sager with Gerald E. Panting, *Maritime Capital: The Shipping Industry in Atlantic Canada, 1820–1914* (Montreal: McGill-Queen's University Press, 1990), 16–22; Graham D. Taylor and Peter A. Baskerville, *A Concise History of Business in Canada* (Toronto: Oxford University Press, 1994), 109–16; Gwyn, *Excessive Expectations*, 4–6, 134–5, and 203–24; Daniel Samson, *The Spirit of Industry and Improvement: Liberal Government and Rural-Industrial Society, Nova Scotia, 1790–1862* (Montreal: McGill-Queen's University Press, 2008), 29–36, 225–49.

11 Alternative modes of capitalist development in colonial North America are discussed in several works. Robert Sweeney compared seventeenth-

century modes of development in "What Difference Does a Mode Make? A Comparison of Two Seventeenth-Century Colonies: Canada and Newfoundland," *William and Mary Quarterly* 63, no. 2 (2006): 281–304. Robert B. Kristofferson's *Craft Capitalism: Craftworkers and Early Industrialization in Hamilton, Ontario, 1840–1872* (Toronto: University of Toronto Press, 2007) describes how craft-based industrialization occurred in nineteenth-century Canada.

Agrarian capitalism has also been at the centre of a long debate in colonial and antebellum American history. See, for example, Alan Kulikoff, "The Transition to Capitalism in Rural America," *William and Mary Quarterly* 46, no. 1 (1989): 120–44; Gary Kornblith and John Murrin, "The Making and Unmaking of an American Ruling Class," in *Beyond the American Revolution: Explorations in the History of American Radicalism*, ed. Alfred Young, 27–79 (Decal: Northern Illinois University Press, 1993); Michael Merrill, "Putting 'Capitalism' in Its Place: A Review of Recent Literature," *William and Mary Quarterly* 52, no. 2 (1995): 315–26; Naomi R. Lamoreaux, "Rethinking the Transition to Capitalism in the Early American Northeast," *Journal of American History* 90, no. 2 (2003): 437–61. This debate is discussed in the Canadian context in Béatrice Craig's *Backwoods Consumers & Homespun Capitalists: The Rise of a Market Culture in Eastern Canada* (Toronto: University of Toronto Press, 2009), 3–22.

Appendix 1

1 On the importance of generalizations for social science research and the necessity of being self-aware of the generalizations one makes, see Howard S. Becker, *Tricks of the Trade: How to Think about Your Research While You're Doing It* (Chicago: University of Chicago Press, 1998).

Appendix 2

1 W.A. Armstrong, "The Use of Information about Occupation," in *Nineteenth-Century Society: Essays in the Use of Quantitative Methods for the Study of Social Data*, ed. E.A. Wrigley (Cambridge: Cambridge University Press, 1972), 191–2. All emphases in the original.
2 Thomas Doerflinger, *A Vigorous Spirit of Enterprise: Merchants and Economic Development in Revolutionary Philadelphia* (Chapel Hill: University of North Carolina Press, 1986), 17.
3 David Hancock, *Citizens of the World: London Merchants and the Integration of the British Atlantic Community, 1735–1785* (Cambridge: Cambridge University Press, 1995), 10.

4 Doerflinger, *A Vigorous Spirit of Enterprise*, 15.
5 Michael B. Katz, *The People of Hamilton, Canada West* (Cambridge, MA: Harvard University Press, 1975), 51.
6 Deborah Rosen, *Courts and Commerce: Gender, Law, and the Market Economy in Colonial New York* (Columbus: Ohio State University Press, 1997), 88–91, 146–7, and 183. Peter King, *Crime, Justice, and Discretion in England, 1740–1820* (Oxford: Oxford University Press, 2000), 35–9 and 52. The categories he uses are based on Arthur F.J. Brown, *Essex at Work 1700–1815* (Chelmsford, UK: Essex County Council, 1969), 108. A similar model is offered in William M. Offut, Jr., *Of "Good Laws" and "Good Men": Law and Society in the Delaware Valley, 1680–1710* (Urbana: University of Illinois Press, 1995), 32–3 and 278.
7 Jim Phillips, "Halifax Juries in the Eighteenth Century," in *Criminal Justice in the Old World and New*, ed. Greg T. Smith, Allyson N. May, and Simon Devereaux (Toronto: Centre of Criminology, University of Toronto, 1998), 141–4. Michael Katz, offered a five-class model based on occupation and wealth in *The People of Hamilton*, 69, but see 69–71 and 343–8.
8 Heinrich Berger, "Occupational Titles of the 'Vienna Database on European Family History,'" in *Occupational Titles and Their Classification: The Case of the Textile Trade in Past Times*, ed. Herman Diedrecks and Marjan Balkestein (St. Katharinen, Germany: Max-Planck-Institut für Geschichte, in Kommission bei Scripta Mercaturae Verlag, 1995), 64.

Bibliography

Acheson, T.W. "The Great Merchant and Economic Development in Saint John, 1820–50." *Acadiensis* 8, no. 2 (1979): 3–27.

Akins, Thomas B. *History of Halifax City*. Halifax: Nova Scotia Historical Society, 1895. Facsimile of the first edition 1973 by Mika Publishing.

Ames, Susie M., ed. *County Court Records of Accomack and Northhampton Virginia, 1632–1640*. Vol. 7 of *American Legal Records*. Washington, DC: American Historical Association, 1954.

Armstrong, W.A. "The Use of Information about Occupation." In *Nineteenth-Century Society: Essays in the Use of Quantitative Methods for the Study of Social Data*, edited by E.A. Wrigley, 191–223. Cambridge: Cambridge University Press, 1972.

Baker, Howard. "Small Claims, Communal Justice and the Rule of Law in Kingston, Upper Canada, c. 1785–1819." Master's thesis, York University, 1993.

Baker, J.H. *The Law's Two Bodies: Some Evidential Problems in English Legal History*. Oxford: Oxford University Press, 2001.

– *An Introduction to English Legal History*. 4th ed. London: Butterworths LexisNexis, 2002.

Bamford, David. "Litigation Reform 1980–2000: A Radical Challenge." In *Litigation: Past and Present*, edited by Wilfrid Prest and Sharyn L. Roach Anleu, 146–70. Sydney, Australia: UNSW Press, 2004.

Bannister, Jerry. *The Rule of the Admirals: Law, Custom, and Naval Government in Newfoundland, 1699–1832*. Toronto: University of Toronto Press for the Osgoode Society, 2003.

Barnes, Thomas Garden. "'As Near as May be Agreeable to the Laws of this Kingdom': Legal Birthright and Legal Baggage at Chebucto, 1749." In *Law in a Colonial Society: The Nova Scotia Experience*, edited by Peter Waite, Sandra Oxner, and Thomas Barnes, 1–23. Toronto: Carswell, 1984.

– "'The Dayly Cry for Justice': The Judicial Failure of the Annapolis Royal Regime, 1713–1749." In *Essays in the History of Canadian Law, Volume III: Nova Scotia*, edited by Philip Girard and Jim Phillips, 10–41. Toronto: University of Toronto Press for the Osgoode Society, 1990.

Bates, George T. "The Great Exodus of 1749: Or, The Cornwallis Settlers who Didn't." *Collections of the Nova Scotia Historical Society* 38 (1973): 27–62.

Beattie, J.M. *Crime and the Courts in England 1660–1800*. Princeton: Princeton University Press, 1986.

– "London Juries in the 1690s." In *Twelve Good Men and True: The Criminal Trial Jury in England, 1200–1800*, edited by J.S. Cockburn and Thomas A. Green, 214–53. Princeton: Princeton University Press, 1988.

– *Policing and Punishment in London, 1660–1750: Urban Crime and the Limits of Terror*. Oxford: Oxford University Press, 2001.

Becker, Howard S. *Tricks of the Trade: How to Think about Your Research While You're Doing It*. Chicago: University of Chicago Press, 1998.

Bell, Winthrop. *The "Foreign Protestants" and the Settlement of Nova Scotia*. Sackville, NB: Centre for Canadian Studies, Mount Allison University, 1990. First published 1961 by University of Toronto Press.

Benton, Lauren. *Law and Colonial Cultures: Legal Regimes in World History, 1400–1900*. Cambridge: Cambridge University Press, 2002.

Berger, Heinrich. "Occupational Titles of the 'Vienna Database on European Family History.'" In *Occupational Titles and Their Classification: The Case of the Textile Trade in Past Times*, edited by Herman Diedrecks and Marjan Balkestein, 61–74. St. Katharinen, Germany: Max-Planck-Institut für Geschichte, in Kommission bei Scripta Mercaturae Verlag, 1995.

Bilder, Mary Sarah. "The Origin of Appeal in America." *Hastings Law Journal* 48 (1996–7): 913–68.

Blackburn, Robin. "Finance for Anarchists." *New Left Review* 79 (2013): 141–50.

Blakeley, Phyllis R. "Monk, James." In *The Dictionary of Canadian Biography*. Vol. 3. Edited by Francess G. Halpenny, 457. Toronto: University of Toronto Press, 1974.

– "Morris, Charles." In *The Dictionary of Canadian Biography*. Vol. 4. Edited by Francess G. Halpenny, 559–63. Toronto: University of Toronto Press, 1979.

Brebner, John Bartlett. *New England's Outpost: Acadia before the Conquest of Canada*. New York: Columbia University Press, 1927.

– *The Neutral Yankees of Nova Scotia: A Marginal Colony during the Revolutionary*

Years. Toronto: McClelland and Stewart, 1969. First published 1937 by Columbia University Press.

Brooks, Christopher W. *Lawyers, Litigation and English Society since 1450*. London: Hambledon Press, 1998.

– "The Longitudinal Study of Civil Litigation in England, 1200–1996." In *Litigation: Past and Present*, edited by Wilfrid Prest and Sharyn Roach Anleu, 24–43. Sydney, Australia: UNSW Press, 2004.

Brown, Arthur F.J. *Essex at Work 1700–1815*. Chelmsford, UK: Essex County Council, 1969.

Brown, R. Blake. *A Trying Question: The Jury in Nineteenth-Century Canada*. Toronto: University of Toronto Press for the Osgoode Society, 2009.

Buggey, Susan. "Belcher, Jonathan." In *The Dictionary of Canadian Biography*. Vol. 4. Edited by Francess G. Halpenny, 50–4. Toronto: University of Toronto Press, 1979.

– "Salter, Malachy." In *The Dictionary of Canadian Biography*. Vol. 4. Edited by Francess G. Halpenny, 695–7. Toronto: University of Toronto Press, 1979.

Bumstead, J.M. "Little, Otis." In *The Dictionary of Canadian Biography*. Vol. 3. Edited by Francess G. Halpenny, 403–5. Toronto: University of Toronto Press, 1974.

– *Land, Settlement, and Politics on Eighteenth-Century Prince Edward Island*. Montreal: McGill-Queen's University Press, 1987.

Cahill, Barry. "'How Far English Laws are in Force Here': Nova Scotia's First Century of Reception Law Jurisprudence." *University of New Brunswick Law Journal* 42 (1993): 113–53.

– "The 'Hoffman Rebellion' (1753) and Hoffman's Trial (1754): Constructive High Treason and Seditious Conspiracy in Nova Scotia under the Stratocracy." In *Canadian State Trials, Volume 1: Law, Politics, and Security Measures, 1608–1837*, edited by Frank Murray Greenwood and Barry Wright, 72–97. Toronto: University of Toronto Press for the Osgoode Society, 1996.

– "The Treason of the Merchants: Dissent and Repression in Halifax in the Era of the American Revolution." *Acadiensis* 26, no. 1 (1996): 52–70.

Cahill, Barry, and Jim Phillips. "The Supreme Court of Nova Scotia: Origins to Confederation." In *The Supreme Court of Nova Scotia, 1754–2004: From Imperial Bastion to Provincial Oracle*, edited by Philip Girard, Jim Phillips, and Barry Cahill, 53–139. Toronto: University of Toronto Press for the Osgoode Society, 2004.

Chard, Donald F. "Green, Benjamin." In *The Dictionary of Canadian Biography*. Vol. 4. Edited by Francess G. Halpenny, 312–13. Toronto: University of Toronto Press, 1979.

– "Mauger, Joshua." In *The Dictionary of Canadian Biography*. Vol. 4. Edited by

Francess G. Halpenny, 525–9. Toronto: University of Toronto Press, 1979.

Chumbley, George. *Colonial Justice in Virginia: The Development of a Judicial System, Typical Laws and Cases of the Period.* Richmond: The Dietz Press, 1938.

Clark, Ernest, and Jim Phillips. "'The Course of Law Cannot Be Stopped': The Aftermath of the Cumberland Rebellion in the Civil Courts of Nova Scotia." *Dalhousie Law Journal* 21, no. 2 (1998): 440–74.

Cohn, Henry S. "Connecticut's Divorce Mechanism: 1636-1969." *American Journal of Legal History* 14, no. 1 (1970): 35–54.

Cott, Nancy F. "Divorce and the Changing Status of Women in Eighteenth-Century Massachusetts." *William and Mary Quarterly* 33, no. 4 (1976): 586–614.

Couturier, Jacques Paul. "Courts and Business Activity in Late 19th Century New Brunswick: A View from the Case Files." *Acadiensis* 26, no. 2 (1997): 77–95.

"Cow Bay." In Public Archives of Nova Scotia, *Place-Names and Places of Nova Scotia,* 147. Halifax: Provincial Archive of Nova Scotia, 1967.

Cowie, Leonard W. "Justice at Westminster Hall." *History Today* 21, no. 3 (1971): 178–86.

Craig, Béatrice. *Backwoods Consumers & Homespun Capitalists: The Rise of a Market Culture in Eastern Canada.* Toronto: University of Toronto Press, 2009.

Craven, Paul. "The Law of Master and Servant in Mid-Nineteenth-Century Ontario." In *Essays in the History of Canadian Law.* Vol. 1. Edited by David Flaherty, 175–211. Toronto: University of Toronto Press for the Osgoode Society, 1981.

– "Law and Ideology: The Toronto Police Court, 1850–80." In *Essays in the History of Canadian Law.* Vol. 2. Edited by David Flaherty, 248–307. Toronto: University of Toronto Press for the Osgoode Society, 1983.

– "Master & Servant Legislation of Atlantic Canada in Imperial Context." Paper presented at the Atlantic Law & History Workshop II, Dalhousie Law School, Halifax, NS, 3–4 March 1995.

– "Canada, 1670–1935." In *Masters, Servants and Magistrates in Britain and the Empire, 1562–1955,* edited by Douglas Hay and Paul Craven, 175–218. Chapel Hill: University of North Carolina Press, 2004.

– *Petty Justice: Low Law and the Sessions System in Charlotte County, New Brunswick, 1785–1867.* Toronto: University of Toronto Press for the Osgoode Society, 2014.

Crawley, E.A. "An Early Halifax Naval Family." Unpublished. At Nova Scotia Archives and Records Management, MG 100, vol. 127, no. 24.

Creighton, Donald. *The Commercial Empire of the Saint Lawrence, 1760–1850*. New York: Carnegie Endowment for Peace, 1937. Reprinted in 1956 as *The Empire of the Saint Lawrence* by Macmillan.

Cruikshank, Jim. "The Chancery Court of Nova Scotia: Jurisdiction and Procedure 1751–1855." *Dalhousie Journal of Legal Studies* 1, no. 1 (1992): 27–48.

Daigle, Jean. "Acadian Marshland Settlement." In *The Historical Atlas of Canada*. Vol. 1. Edited by R. Cole Harris, 29. Toronto: University of Toronto Press, 1987.

Dayton, Cornelia Hughes. *Women before the Bar: Gender, Law, & Society in Connecticut, 1639–1789*. Chapel Hill: University of North Carolina Press, 1995.

Dickinson, John A. "Court Costs in France and New France in the Eighteenth Century." *Historical Papers / Communications Historiques* 12, no. 1 (1977): 48–64.

– *Justice et Justiciables: La Procédure Civile à la Prévôté de Québec, 1667–1759*. Québec: Les Presses de l'Université Laval, 1982.

Doerflinger, Thomas. *A Vigorous Spirit of Enterprise: Merchants and Economic Development in Revolutionary Philadelphia*. Chapel Hill: University of North Carolina Press, 1986.

Douglas, W.A.B. "Halifax as an Element of Sea Power 1749–1766." Master's thesis, Dalhousie University, 1966.

Duffy, Ian P.H. "English Bankrupts, 1571–1861." *American Journal of Legal History* 24, no. 4 (1980): 283–305.

Engel, David M. "The Uses of Legal Culture in Contemporary Socio-Legal Studies: A Response to Sally Engle Merry." *Journal of Comparative Law* 5, no. 2 (2010): 59–65.

Every Man His Own Lawyer: Or, a Summary of the Laws Now in Force in Ireland. Dublin: Oli. Nelson & Peter Wilson, 1755.

Farrow, Trevor. "Dispute Resolution, Access to Civil Justice and Legal Education." *Alberta Law Review* 42, no. 3 (2005): 741–801.

Fechner, Roger. "'The Sacredness of Public Credit': The American Revolution, Paper Currency, and John Witherspoon's *Essay on Money* (1786)." In *The Empire of Credit: The Financial Revolution in the British Atlantic World, 1688–1815*, edited by Daniel Carey and Christopher J. Finlay, 141–70. Dublin: Irish Academic Press, 2011.

Feer, Robert A. "Imprisonment for Debt in Massachusetts before 1800." *The Mississippi Valley Historical Review* 48, no. 2 (1961): 252–69.

Fergusson, Charles Bruce, ed. *The Diary of Simeon Perkins*. Vols. 3–5. Toronto: Champlain Society, 1961–78.

Fifoot, C.H.S. *History and Sources of the Common Law*. London: Stevens & Sons, 1949.

Fingard, Judith, Janet Guildford, and David Sutherland. *Halifax: The First 250 Years*. Halifax: Formac Publishing Company, 1999.

Finn, Margot. *The Character of Credit: Personal Debt in English Culture, 1740–1914*. Cambridge: Cambridge University Press, 2003.

Francis, Clinton W. "Practice, Strategy, and Institution: Debt Collection in the English Common-Law Courts, 1740–1840." *Northwestern University Law Review* 80, no. 4 (1985–6): 807–955.

Frank, Christopher. "'Let But One of Them Come before Me, and I'll Commit Him': Trade Unions, Magistrates, and the Law in Mid-Nineteenth-Century Staffordshire." *Journal of British Studies* 44 (2005): 64–91.

Friedman, Lawrence. "Legal Culture and Social Development." *Law & Society Review* 4, no. 2 (1969): 29–44.

– *A History of American Law*. New York: Simon and Schuster, 1973.

Fyson, Donald. "Jurys, Participation Civique et Representation au Québec et au Bas-Canada: Les Grands Jurys du District de Montréal (1764–1832)." *Revue d'histoire de l'Amerique française* 55, no. 1 (2001): 85–120.

– *Magistrates, Police, and People: Everyday Criminal Justice in Quebec and Lower Canada, 1764–1837*. Toronto: University of Toronto Press for the Osgoode Society, 2006.

Gavigan, Shelley A.M. *Hunger, Horses, and Government Men: Criminal Law on the Aboriginal Plains, 1870–1905*. Vancouver: UBC Press for the Osgoode Society, 2012.

Giddens, Anthony. *The Class Structure of the Advanced Societies*. London: Hutchinson University Library, 1973.

Girard, Philip. "Married Women's Property, Chancery Abolition, and Insolvency Law: Law Reform in Nova Scotia, 1820–1867." In *Essays in the History of Canadian Law, Volume III: Nova Scotia*, edited by Philip Girard and Jim Phillips, 80–127. Toronto: University of Toronto Press for the Osgoode Society, 1990.

– "Taking Litigation Seriously: The Market Wharf Controversy at Halifax, 1785–1820." In *Essays in the History of Canadian Law, Volume VIII: In Honour of R.C.B. Risk*, edited by Jim Phillips and G. Blaine Baker, 213–40. Toronto: University of Toronto Press for the Osgoode Society, 1999.

– *Lawyers and Legal Culture in British North America: Beamish Murdoch of Halifax*. Toronto: University of Toronto Press for the Osgoode Society, 2011.

Girard, Philip, and Jim Phillips, eds. *Essays in the History of Canadian Law, Volume III: Nova Scotia*. Toronto: University of Toronto Press for the Osgoode Society, 1990.

Girard, Philip, Jim Phillips, and Barry Cahill, eds. *The Supreme Court of Nova*

Scotia, 1754–2004: From Imperial Bastion to Provincial Oracle. Toronto: University of Toronto Press for the Osgoode Society, 2004.

Graeber, David. *Debt: The First 5,000 Years*. New York: Melville House, 2011.

Griffiths, Naomi E.S. *From Migrant to Acadian: A North American Border People*. Montreal: McGill-Queen's University Press, 2004.

Gwyn, Julian. "Capitalists, Merchants and Manufacturers in Early Nova Scotia, 1769–1791: The Tangled Affairs of John Avery, James Creighton, John Albro, and Joseph Fairbanks." In *Intimate Relations: Family and Community in Planter Nova Scotia, 1759–1800*, edited by Margaret Conrad, 190–212. Fredericton, NB: Acadiensis Press, 1995.

– *Excessive Expectations: Maritime Commerce and the Economic Development of Nova Scotia, 1740–1870*. Montreal: McGill-Queen's University Press, 1998.

– "'A Slave to Business All My Life.' Joshua Mauger, ca. 1712–1788: The Man and the Myth." *Journal of the Royal Nova Scotia Historical Society* 7 (2004): 38–62.

– "Women as Litigants before the Supreme Court of Nova Scotia, 1754–1830." In *The Supreme Court of Nova Scotia, 1754–2004: From Imperial Bastion to Provincial Oracle*, edited by Philip Girard, Jim Phillips, and Barry Cahill, 294–320. Toronto: University of Toronto Press for the Osgoode Society, 2004.

Haagen, Paul H. "Eighteenth-Century English Society and the Debt Law." In *Social Control and the State*, edited by Stanley Cohen and Andrew Scull, 222–47. New York: St. Martin's Press, 1983. Reprinted in 1985 by Basil Blackwell Press.

Hamilton, William. "Collier, John." In *The Dictionary of Canadian Biography*. Vol. 3. Edited by Francess G. Halpenny, 130–1. Toronto: University of Toronto Press, 1974.

Hancock, David. *Citizens of the World: London Merchants and the Integration of the British Atlantic Community, 1735–1785*. Cambridge: Cambridge University Press, 1995.

Harvey, D.C., ed. *The Diary of Simeon Perkins*. Vol. 2. Toronto: Champlain Society, 1958.

Hay, Douglas. "Property, Authority and the Criminal Law." In *Albion's Fatal Tree: Crime and Society in Eighteenth-Century England*, edited by Douglas Hay, Peter Linebaugh, John Rule, E.P. Thompson, and Cal Winslow, 17–63. London: Allen Lane, 1975.

– "The Meanings of the Criminal Law in Quebec, 1764 to 1774." In *Crime and Justice in Europe and Canada*, edited by Louis Knafla, 77–110. Waterloo: Wilfrid Laurier University Press, 1981.

– "The Class Composition of the Palladium of Liberty: Trial Jurors in the Eighteenth Century." In *Twelve Good Men and True: The Criminal Trial Jury in*

England, 1200–1800, edited by J.S. Cockburn and Thomas A. Green, 305–57. Princeton: Princeton University Press, 1988.

– "Dread of the Crown Office: The English Magistracy and King's Bench, 1740–1800." In *Law, Crime and English Society 1660–1840,* edited by Norma Landau, 19–45. Cambridge: Cambridge University Press, 2002.

– "Origins: The Courts of Westminster Hall in the Eighteenth Century." In *The Supreme Court of Nova Scotia, 1754–2004: From Imperial Bastion to Provincial Oracle,* edited by Philip Girard, Jim Phillips, and Barry Cahill, 13–29. Toronto: University of Toronto Press for the Osgoode Society, 2004.

– "Legislation, Magistrates, and Judges: High Law and Low Law in England and Empire." In *The British and Their Laws in the Eighteenth Century,* edited by David Lemmings, 59–79. Woodbridge, UK: Boydell Press, 2005.

Hay, Douglas, and Paul Craven. *Masters, Servants and Magistrates in Britain and Empire, 1562–1955.* Chapel Hill: University of North Carolina Press, 2004.

Hoffer, Peter Charles. *Law and People in Colonial America.* Rev. ed. Baltimore: Johns Hopkins University Press, 1998.

Holcombe, Lee. *Wives and Property: Reform of the Married Women's Property Law in Nineteenth-Century England.* Toronto: University of Toronto Press, 1983.

Holdsworth, William A. *An Historical Introduction to the Land Law.* Oxford: The Clarendon Press, 1927.

Horwitz, Henry, and James Oldham. "John Locke, Lord Mansfield, and Arbitration during the Eighteenth Century." *The Historical Journal* 36, no. 1 (1993): 137–59.

Inkori, Joseph E. *Africans and the Industrial Revolution in England: A Study in International Trade and Economic Development.* Cambridge: Cambridge University Press, 2002.

Innes, Joanna. "The King's Bench Prison in the Later Eighteenth Century: Law, Authority and Order in a London Debtors' Prison." In *An Ungovernable People: The English and Their Law in the Seventeenth and Eighteenth Centuries,* edited by John Brewer and John Styles, 250–98. New Brunswick, NJ: Rutgers University Press, 1980.

Innis, Harold A., ed. *The Diary of Simeon Perkins.* Vol. 1. Toronto: Champlain Society, 1948.

Jacob, Giles. *A New Law-Dictionary: Containing, the Interpretation and Definition of Words and Terms used in the Law* ... London: E. and R. Nutt and R. Gosling, 1729.

– *The New Law Dictionary: Containing the Definition of Words and Terms, and also the Whole Law and Practice thereof &c. Carefully Abridged* ... London: Henry Lintot, assignee of Edward Sayer, 1743.

Katz, Michael B. *The People of Hamilton, Canada West*. Cambridge, MA: Harvard University Press, 1975.

Kercher, Bruce. *Debt, Seduction and Other Disasters: The Birth of the Civil Law in Convict New South Wales*. Leichhardt, NSW: The Federation Press, 1996.

Kernaghan, Lois. "Nesbitt, William." In *The Dictionary of Canadian Biography*. Vol. 4. Edited by Francess G. Halpenny, 581–2. Toronto: University of Toronto Press, 1979.

King, Peter J.R. "'Illiterate Plebeians, Easily Misled': Jury Composition, Experience, and Behaviour in Essex, 1735–1815." In *Twelve Good Men and True: The Criminal Trial Jury in England, 1200–1800*, edited by J.S. Cockburn and Thomas A. Green, 254–304. Princeton: Princeton University Press, 1988.

– *Crime, Justice, and Discretion in England, 1740–1820*. Oxford: Oxford University Press, 2000.

Kiralfy, A.K. *The Action on the Case: An Historical Survey of the Development of the Action up to the Year 1700 …* London: Sweet & Maxwell, 1951.

Kocka, Jürgen. "The Middle Classes in Europe." *Journal of Modern History* 67, no. 4 (1995): 783–806.

– *Civil Society and Dictatorship in Modern German History*. Lebanon, NH: University Press of New England, 2010.

Konig, David. *Law and Society in Puritan Massachusetts: Essex County, 1626–1693*. Chapel Hill: University of North Carolina Press, 1979.

Kornblith, Gary, and John Murrin. "The Making and Unmaking of an American Ruling Class." In *Beyond the American Revolution: Explorations in the History of American Radicalism*, edited by Alfred Young, 27–79. Decal: Northern Illinois University Press, 1993.

Kristofferson, Robert B. *Craft Capitalism: Craftworkers and Early Industrialization in Hamilton, Ontario, 1840–1872*. Toronto: University of Toronto Press, 2007.

Kulikoff, Allan. "The Transition to Capitalism in Rural America." *William and Mary Quarterly* 46, no. 1 (1989): 120–44.

– *From British Peasants to Colonial American Farmers*. Chapel Hill: University of North Carolina Press, 2000.

Kunkel, Benjamin. *Utopia or Bust: A Guide to the Present Crisis*. New York: Verso Books, 2014.

Lamoreaux, Naomi R. "Rethinking the Transition to Capitalism in the Early American Northeast." *Journal of American History* 90, no. 2 (2003): 437–61.

Leneman, Leah. *Alienated Affections: The Scottish Experience of Divorce and Separation, 1684–1830*. Edinburgh: Edinburgh University Press, 1998.

Lennox, Jeffers. "An Empire on Paper: The Founding of Halifax and Conceptions of Imperial Space, 1744–55." *Canadian Historical Review* 88, no. 3 (2007): 373–412.

Lewthwaite, Susan. "Violence, Law and Community in Rural Upper Canada." In *Essays in the History of Canadian Law, Volume V: Crime and Criminal Justice*, edited by Jim Phillips, Tina Loo, and Susan Lewthwaite, 353–86. Toronto: University of Toronto Press for the Osgoode Society, 1994.

– "The Pre-Trial Examination in Upper Canada." In *Criminal Justice in the Old World and the New: Essays in Honour of J.M. Beattie*, edited by Greg T. Smith, Allyson N. May, and Simon Devereaux, 85–103. Toronto: University of Toronto Centre of Criminology, 1998.

– "Law and Authority in Upper Canada: The Justices of the Peace in the Newcastle District, 1803–1840." PhD diss., University of Toronto, 2001.

L'Heureux, Jacques. "Suckling, George." In *The Dictionary of Canadian Biography*. Vol. 4. Edited by Frances G. Halpenny, 724–6. Toronto: University of Toronto Press, 1979.

Linebaugh, Peter. "The Tyburn Riot against the Surgeons." In *Albion's Fatal Tree: Crime and Society in Eighteenth-Century England*, edited by Douglas Hay, Peter Linebaugh, John G. Rule, E.P. Thompson, and Cal Winslow, 65–117. London: Allen Lane, 1975.

Linebaugh, Peter, and Marcus Rediker. *The Many Headed Hydra: Sailors, Slaves, Commoners, and the Hidden History of the Revolutionary Atlantic*. Boston: Beacon Press, 2000.

Loo, Tina. *Making Law, Order, and Authority in Colonial British Columbia, 1821–1871*. Toronto: University of Toronto Press, 1994.

Mackenzie, A.A. "Zouberbuhler, Sebastian." In *The Dictionary of Canadian Biography*. Vol. 4. Edited by Frances G. Halpenny, 780–1. Toronto: University of Toronto Press, 1979.

MacNutt, Wallace Stewart. *The Atlantic Provinces: The Emergence of a Colonial Society*. Toronto: McClelland and Stewart, 1965.

Mancke, Elizabeth. *The Fault Lines of Empire: Political Differentiation in Massachusetts and Nova Scotia, ca. 1760–1830*. New York: Routledge, 2005.

Mann, Bruce. *Neighbors and Strangers: Law and Community in Early Connecticut*. Chapel Hill: University of North Carolina Press, 1987.

– *Republic of Debtors: Bankruptcy in the Age of American Independence*. Cambridge, MA: Harvard University Press, 2002.

Marble, Allan E. *Deaths, Burials, and Probate of Nova Scotians, 1749–1799*. Halifax: Genealogical Association of Nova Scotia, 1990.

– *Surgeons, Smallpox and the Poor: A History of Medicine and Social Conditions in Nova Scotia, 1749–1799*. Montreal: McGill-Queen's University Press, 1993.

Martin, Andrew. "Automated Debt-Collection Lawsuits Engulf Courts." *New York Times*, 13 July 2010. http://nyti.ms/23HOEyG.

May, Allyson, and Jim Phillips. "Homicide in Nova Scotia, 1749–1815." *Canadian Historical Review* 82, no. 4 (2001): 625–61.

– "The Criminality of Women in Eighteenth-Century Halifax." *Acadiensis* 31, no. 2 (2002): 71–97.

Maynard, Kimberley Smith. "Divorce in Nova Scotia, 1750–1890." In *Essays in the History of Canadian Law, Volume III: Nova Scotia*, edited by Philip Girard and Jim Phillips, 232–72. Toronto: University of Toronto Press for the Osgoode Society, 1990.

McCusker, John J. *Money & Exchange in Europe & America, 1600–1775: A Handbook*. Chapel Hill: University of North Carolina Press for the Institute of Early American History and Culture, 1978.

McKay, Ian. "The Crisis of Dependent Development: Class Conflict in the Nova Scotia Coalfields, 1872–1876." In *Class, Gender, and Region: Essays in Canadian Historical Sociology*, edited by Gregory S. Kealey, 9–48. St. John's, NL: Committee on Canadian Labour History, 1988.

McLachlin, Beverley. "The Challenges We Face: Remarks of the Right Honourable Beverley McLachlin, P.C., Chief Justice of Canada to the Empire Club of Canada." Remarks delivered to the Empire Club of Canada, Toronto, Ontario on 8 March 2007. Accessed 31 March 2016. www.cfcj-fcjc.org/sites/default/files/docs/2007/mclachlin-empireclub-en.pdf.

Merrill, Michael. "Putting 'Capitalism' in Its Place: A Review of Recent Literature." *William and Mary Quarterly* 52, no. 2 (1995): 315–26.

Merry, Sally Engle. "What Is Legal Culture? An Anthropological Perspective." *Journal of Comparative Law* 5, no. 2 (2010): 40–58.

Miquelon, Dale. "Havy and Lefebvre of Quebec: A Case Study of Metropolitan Participation in Canadian Trade, 1730–60." *Canadian Historical Review* 56, no. 1 (1975): 1–24.

Moody, Barry. "Making a British North America." In *The "Conquest" of Acadia, 1710: Imperial, Colonial, and Aboriginal Constructions*, edited by John G. Reid, Maurice Basque, Elizabeth Mancke, Barry Moody, Geoffrey Plank, and William Wicken, 127–54 .Toronto: University of Toronto Press, 2003.

Moore, Seán. "'Vested' Interests and Debt Bondage: Credit as Confessional Coercion in Colonial Ireland." In *The Empire of Credit: The Financial Revolution in the British Atlantic World, 1688–1815*, edited by Daniel Carey and Christopher J. Finlay, 209–28. Dublin: Irish Academic Press, 2011.

Moretti, Franco. *The Bourgeois: Between History and Literature*. New York: Verso Books, 2013.

Morgan, R.J. "Gibbons, Richard." In *The Dictionary of Canadian Biography*. Vol. 4. Edited by Francess G. Halpenny, 292–3. Toronto: University of Toronto Press, 1979.

Morris, Richard B. *Studies in the History of American Law, with Special Reference to the Seventeenth and Eighteenth Centuries.* 2nd ed. Philadelphia: Joseph M. Mitchell Co., 1959.

– *Government and Labor in Early America.* New York: Octagon Books, 1965.

Muir, James. "The Fight for Bourgeois Law in Halifax, Nova Scotia, 1749–1753." *Histoire Sociale/Social History* 49, no. 98 (2016): 1–25.

Muir, James, and Jim Phillips. "Michaelmas Term 1754: The Supreme Court's First Session." In *The Supreme Court of Nova Scotia, 1754–2004: From Imperial Bastion to Provincial Oracle,* edited by Philip Girard, Jim Phillips, and Barry Cahill, 259–93. Toronto: University of Toronto Press for the Osgoode Society, 2004.

Muldrew, Craig. "Credit and the Courts: Debt Litigation in a Seventeenth-Century Urban Community." *Economic History Review* 46, no. 1 (1993): 23–38.

– *The Economy of Obligation: The Culture of Credit and Social Relations in Early Modern England.* Hampshire, UK: Palgrave, 1998.

– "'A Mutual Assent of Her Mind'? Women, Debt, Litigation and Contract in Early Modern England." *History Workshop Journal* 55 (2003): 47–71.

Murdoch, Beamish. *Epitome of the Laws of Nova Scotia.* 4 vols. Halifax: Joseph Howe, 1832–3.

– "On the Origin and Sources of the Law of Nova Scotia." Halifax: Law Students' Society, 1863.

Murray, David. "Just Excuses: Jury Culture in Barrington Township, Nova Scotia, 1795–1837." In *Planter Links: Community and Culture in Colonial Nova Scotia,* edited by Margaret Conrad and Barry Moody, 36–57. Fredericton, NB: Acadiensis Press, 2001.

Nelson, William E. *Dispute and Conflict Resolution in Plymouth County, Massachusetts, 1725–1825.* Chapel Hill: University of North Carolina Press, 1981.

– *The Chesapeake and New England, 1607–1660.* Vol. 1 of *The Common Law in Colonial America.* New York: Oxford University Press, 2008.

– *The Middle Colonies and the Carolinas, 1660–1730.* Vol. 2 of *The Common Law in Colonial America.* New York: Oxford University Press, 2013.

Nerbas, Don. *Dominion of Capital: The Politics of Big Business and the Crisis of the Canadian Bourgeoisie, 1914–1947.* Toronto: University of Toronto Press, 2013.

Offutt, William M., Jr. *Of "Good Laws" and "Good Men": Law and Society in the Delaware Valley, 1680–1710.* Urbana: University of Illinois Press, 1995.

Oldham, James C. "The Origins of the Special Jury." *University of Chicago Law Review* 50, no. 1 (1983): 137–221.

– *The Mansfield Manuscripts and the Growth of English Law in the Eighteenth Century.* Chapel Hill: University of North Carolina Press, 1992.

Olegario, Rowena. *A Culture of Credit: Embedding Trust and Transparency in American Business*. Cambridge, MA: Harvard University Press, 2006.

Ommer, Rosemary E., ed. *Merchant Credit & Labour Strategies in Historical Perspective*. Fredericton, NB: Acadiensis Press, 1990.

Owen, David R., and Michael C. Tolley. *Courts of Admiralty in Colonial America: The Maryland Experience, 1634–1776*. Durham, NC: Carolina Academic Press, 1995.

Phillips, Jim. "Halifax Juries in the Eighteenth Century." In *Criminal Justice in the Old World and New*, edited by Greg T. Smith, Allyson N. May, and Simon Devereaux, 135–82. Toronto: Centre of Criminology, University of Toronto, 1998.

– "The Criminal Trial in Nova Scotia, 1749–1815." In *Essays in the History of Canadian Law, Volume VIII: In Honour of R.C.B. Risk*, edited by Jim Phillips and G. Blaine Baker, 469–511. Toronto: University of Toronto Press for the Osgoode Society, 1999.

– "The Impeachment of the Judges of the Nova Scotia Supreme Court, 1787–1793: Colonial Judges, Loyalist Lawyers, and the Colonial Assembly." *Dalhousie Law Journal* 34, no. 2 (2011): 313–15.

– "A Low Law Counter Treatise? 'Absentees' to 'Wreck' in British North America's First Justice of the Peace Manual." In *Law Books in Action: Essays on the Anglo-American Legal Treatise*, edited by A. Fernandez and M. Dubber, 202–19. Oxford: Hart Publishing, 2012.

Phillips, Roderick. *Putting Asunder: A History of Divorce in Western Society*. Cambridge: Cambridge University Press, 1988.

Plank, Geoffery. *An Unsettled Conquest: The British Campaign against the Peoples of Acadia*. Philadelphia: University of Pennsylvania Press, 2001.

Pope, Peter E. *Fish into Wine: The Newfoundland Plantations in the Seventeenth Century*. Chapel Hill: University of North Carolina Press for the Omohundro Institute of Early American History, 2004.

Prest, Wilfrid. "The Experience of Litigation in Eighteenth-Century England." In *The British and Their Laws in the Eighteenth Century*, edited by David Lemmings, 133–54. Woodridge: The Boydell Press, 2005.

Prest, Wilfrid, and Sharyn Roach Anleu, eds. *Litigation: Past and Present*. Sydney, NSW: UNSW Press, 2004.

Price, Jacob M. *Capital and Credit in British Overseas Trade: The View from the Chesapeake, 1700–1776*. Cambridge, MA: Harvard University Press, 1980.

– "Transaction Costs: A Note on Merchant Credit and the Organization of Private Trade." In *The Political Economy of Merchant Empires: State Power and World Trade, 1350–1750*, edited by James D. Tracey, 276–97. Cambridge: Cambridge University Press, 1991.

Rediker, Marcus. *Between the Devil and the Deep Blue Sea*. Cambridge: Cambridge University Press, 1987.

Reid, John G., Maurice Basque, Elizabeth Mancke, Barry Moody, Geoffrey Plank, and William Wicken. *The "Conquest" of Acadia, 1710: Imperial, Colonial, and Aboriginal Constructions*. Toronto: University of Toronto Press, 2003.

Roeber, A.G. *Faithful Magistrates and Republican Lawyers: Creators of Virginian Legal Culture, 1680–1810*. Chapel Hill: University of North Carolina Press, 1981.

Rogers, Nicholas. *Mayhem: Post-War Crime and Violence in Britain, 1748–53*. New Haven, CT: Yale University Press, 2012.

Rogers, Patricia. "'Unprincipled Men Who Are One Day British Subjects and the Next Citizens of the United States': The Nova Scotian Merchant Community and Colonial Identity Formation, c. 1780–1820." PhD diss., Michigan State University, 2001.

Rosen, Deborah A. *Courts and Commerce: Gender, Law, and the Market Economy in Colonial New York*. Columbus: Ohio State University Press, 1997.

Sager, Eric W., with Gerald E. Panting. *Maritime Capital: The Shipping Industry in Atlantic Canada, 1820–1914*. Montreal: McGill-Queen's University Press, 1990.

Salmon, Marylynn. *Women and the Law of Property in Early America*. Chapel Hill: University of North Carolina Press, 1986.

Salusbury, John. *Expeditions of Honour: The Journal of John Salusbury in Halifax, Nova Scotia, 1749–53*. Edited by Ronald Rompkey. Montreal: McGill-Queen's University Press, 2011. First published 1982 by University of Delaware Press.

Samson, Daniel. *The Spirit of Industry and Improvement: Liberal Government and Rural-Industrial Society, Nova Scotia, 1790–1862*. Montreal: McGill-Queen's University Press, 2008.

Schumpeter, Joseph. *Capitalism, Socialism and Democracy*. New York: Harper and Row, 1975. First published 1942 by Harper and Brothers.

Shortt, Adam, ed. *Documents Relating to Currency, Exchange and Finance in Nova Scotia, with Prefatory Documents, 1675–1758*. Ottawa: The King's Printer, 1933.

Shortt, Adam, and Arthur G. Doughty. *Documents Relating to the Constitutional History of Canada 1759–1791*. Rev. ed. Ottawa: J de L. Tache, 1918.

Statistics Canada. *Table 259–0013. Civil court survey, general civil cases by level of court and type of action, annual (number)*, CANSIM (database).

Steedman, Carolyn. *Master and Servant: Love and Labour in the English Industrial Age*. Cambridge: Cambridge University Press, 2007.

- *Labours Lost: Domestic Service and the Making of Modern England*. Cambridge: Cambridge University Press, 2009.
- "At Every Bloody Level: A Magistrate, a Frame-Work Knitter and the Law." *Law and History Review* 30, no. 2 (2012): 387–422.
- *An Everyday Life of the English Working Class: Work, Self and Sociability in the Early Nineteenth Century*. Cambridge: Cambridge University Press, 2013.

Stone, Arthur J. "The Admiralty Court in Colonial Nova Scotia." *Dalhousie Law Journal* 17 (1994): 363–427.

Style, William. *Style's Practical Register, begin in the Reign of King Charles I ...* 3rd ed. London: Tho. Dring and the executors of S. Leigh, 1694.

Sugarman, David, and Ronnie Warrington. "Land Law, Citizenship, and the Invention of 'Englishness': The Strange World of the Equity of Redemption." In *Early Modern Conceptions of Property*, edited by John Brewer and Susan Staves, 111–43. London: Routledge, 1995.

Sutherland, David Alexander. "The Merchants of Halifax, 1815–1850: A Commercial Class in Pursuit of Metropolitan Status." PhD diss., University of Toronto, 1975.

- "Halifax Merchants and the Pursuit of Development, 1783–1850." *Canadian Historical Review* 59, no. 1 (1978): 1–17.

Sweeney, Robert. "What Difference Does a Mode Make? A Comparison of Two Seventeenth-Century Colonies: Canada and Newfoundland." *William and Mary Quarterly* 63, no. 2 (2006): 281–304.

Taylor, Graham D., and Peter A. Baskerville. *A Concise History of Business in Canada*. Toronto: Oxford University Press, 1994.

Thompson, E.P. "In Defence of the Jury." In *Persons and Polemics: Historical Essays*, 143–68. London: Merlin Press, 1984.

- *Customs in Common*. New York: New Press, 1993.

Tomlins, Christopher. *Freedom Bound: Law, Labor, and Civic Identity in Colonizing English America, 1580–1865*. New York: Cambridge University Press, 2010.

Tomlins, Christopher, and Bruce Mann, eds. *The Many Legalities of Early America*. Chapel Hill: University of North Carolina Press, 2001.

Townsend, Charles J. *History of the Court of Chancery of Nova Scotia*. Toronto: Carswell, 1900.

Turner, Richard W. *The Equity of Redemption: Its Nature, History and Connection with Equitable Estates Generally*. Cambridge: Cambridge University Press, 1931.

von Benda-Beckmann, Franz, and Keebet von Benda-Beckmann. "Why Not Legal Culture?" *Journal of Comparative Law* 5, no. 2 (2010): 104–17.

Vries, Jan de, and Ad van der Woude. *The First Modern Economy: Success, Failure, and Perseverance of the Dutch Economy, 1500–1815*. Cambridge: Cambridge University Press, 1997.

Wicken, William C. *Mi'kmaq Treaties on Trial: History, Land and Donald Marshall Junior*. Toronto: University of Toronto Press, 2002.

Williams, Raymond. *Keywords: A Vocabulary of Culture and Society*. London: Fontana Press, 1976.

Winslow, Cal. "Sussex Smugglers." In *Albion's Fatal Tree: Crime and Society in Eighteenth-Century England*, edited by Douglas Hay, Peter Linebaugh, John Rule, E.P. Thompson, and Cal Winslow, 119–68. London: Allen Lane, 1975.

Wood, Ellen Meiksins. *Liberty & Property: A Social History of Western Political Thought from Renaissance to Enlightenment*. New York: Verso, 2012.

Wright, Donald. "The Empire of the St. Lawrence: A Study of Commerce and Politics (review)." *Canadian Historical Review* 85, no. 3 (2004): 555–8.

Wright, Ted, and Angela Melville. "Hey, But Who's Counting? The Metrics and Politics of Trends in Civil Litigation." In *Litigation: Past and Present*, edited by Wilfrid Prest and Sharyn L. Roach Anleu, 24–43. Sydney, NSW: UNSW Press, 2004.

Wylie, William N.T. "Arbiters of Commerce, Instruments of Power: A Study of the Civil Courts in the Midland District, Upper Canada, 1789–1812." PhD diss., Queen's University, 1980.

– "Instruments of Commerce and Authority: The Civil Courts in Upper Canada, 1789–1812." In *Essays in the History of Canadian Law*. Vol. 2. Edited by David Flaherty, 3–48. Toronto: University of Toronto Press for the Osgoode Society, 1983.

Young, Brian. *George-Etienne Cartier: Montreal Bourgeois*. Montreal: McGill-Queen's University Press, 1981.

Zabin, Serena R. *Dangerous Economies: Status and Commerce in Imperial New York*. Philadelphia: University of Pennsylvania Press, 2009.

Index

Philip Girard, *Lawyers and Legal Culture in British North America: Beamish Murdoch of Halifax*

John McLaren, *Dewigged, Bothered, and Bewildered: British Colonial Judges on Trial, 1800–1900*

Lesley Erickson, *Westward Bound: Sex, Violence, the Law, and the Making of a Settler Society*

2010   Judy Fudge and Eric Tucker, eds., *Work on Trial: Canadian Labour Law Struggles*

Christopher Moore, *The British Columbia Court of Appeal: The First Hundred Years*

Frederick Vaughan, *Viscount Haldane: 'The Wicked Step-father of the Canadian Constitution'*

Barrington Walker, *Race on Trial: Black Defendants in Ontario's Criminal Courts, 1858–1958*

2009   William Kaplan, *Canadian Maverick: The Life and Times of Ivan C. Rand*

R. Blake Brown, *A Trying Question: The Jury in Nineteenth-Century Canada*

Barry Wright and Susan Binnie, eds., *Canadian State Trials, Volume III: Political Trials and Security Measures, 1840–1914*

Robert J. Sharpe, *The Last Day, the Last Hour: The Currie Libel Trial* (paperback edition with a new preface)

2008   Constance Backhouse, *Carnal Crimes: Sexual Assault Law in Canada, 1900–1975*

Jim Phillips, R. Roy McMurtry, and John T. Saywell, eds., *Essays in the History of Canadian Law, Volume X: A Tribute to Peter N. Oliver*

Greg Taylor, *The Law of the Land: The Advent of the Torrens System in Canada*

Hamar Foster, Benjamin Berger, and A.R. Buck, eds., *The Grand Experiment: Law and Legal Culture in British Settler Societies*

2007   Robert Sharpe and Patricia McMahon, *The Persons Case: The Origins and Legacy of the Fight for Legal Personhood*

Lori Chambers, *Misconceptions: Unmarried Motherhood and the Ontario Children of Unmarried Parents Act, 1921–1969*

Jonathan Swainger, ed., *A History of the Supreme Court of Alberta*

Martin Friedland, *My Life in Crime and Other Academic Adventures*

2006   Donald Fyson, *Magistrates, Police, and People: Everyday Criminal Justice in Quebec and Lower Canada, 1764–1837*

Dale Brawn, *The Court of Queen's Bench of Manitoba, 1870–1950: A Biographical History*

R.C.B. Risk, *A History of Canadian Legal Thought: Collected Essays*, edited and introduced by G. Blaine Baker and Jim Phillips

2005 Philip Girard, *Bora Laskin: Bringing Law to Life*
Christopher English, ed., *Essays in the History of Canadian Law: Volume IX – Two Islands: Newfoundland and Prince Edward Island*
Fred Kaufman, *Searching for Justice: An Autobiography*

2004 Philip Girard, Jim Phillips, and Barry Cahill, eds., *The Supreme Court of Nova Scotia, 1754–2004: From Imperial Bastion to Provincial Oracle*
Frederick Vaughan, *Aggressive in Pursuit: The Life of Justice Emmett Hall*
John D. Honsberger, *Osgoode Hall: An Illustrated History*
Constance Backhouse and Nancy Backhouse, *The Heiress versus the Establishment: Mrs Campbell's Campaign for Legal Justice*

2003 Robert Sharpe and Kent Roach, *Brian Dickson: A Judge's Journey*
Jerry Bannister, *The Rule of the Admirals: Law, Custom, and Naval Government in Newfoundland, 1699–1832*
George Finlayson, *John J. Robinette, Peerless Mentor: An Appreciation*
Peter Oliver, *The Conventional Man: The Diaries of Ontario Chief Justice Robert A. Harrison, 1856–1878*

2002 John T. Saywell, *The Lawmakers: Judicial Power and the Shaping of Canadian Federalism*
Patrick Brode, *Courted and Abandoned: Seduction in Canadian Law*
David Murray, *Colonial Justice: Justice, Morality, and Crime in the Niagara District, 1791–1849*
F. Murray Greenwood and Barry Wright, eds., *Canadian State Trials, Volume II: Rebellion and Invasion in the Canadas, 1837–1839*

2001 Ellen Anderson, *Judging Bertha Wilson: Law as Large as Life*
Judy Fudge and Eric Tucker, *Labour before the Law: The Regulation of Workers' Collective Action in Canada, 1900–1948*
Laurel Sefton MacDowell, *Renegade Lawyer: The Life of J.L. Cohen*

2000 Barry Cahill, *'The Thousandth Man': A Biography of James McGregor Stewart*
A.B. McKillop, *The Spinster and the Prophet: Florence Deeks, H.G. Wells, and the Mystery of the Purloined Past*
Beverley Boissery and F. Murray Greenwood, *Uncertain Justice: Canadian Women and Capital Punishment*
Bruce Ziff, *Unforeseen Legacies: Reuben Wells Leonard and the Leonard Foundation Trust*

1999 Constance Backhouse, *Colour-Coded: A Legal History of Racism in Canada, 1900–1950*
G. Blaine Baker and Jim Phillips, eds., *Essays in the History of Canadian Law: Volume VIII – In Honour of R.C.B. Risk*
Richard W. Pound, *Chief Justice W.R. Jackett: By the Law of the Land*
David Vanek, *Fulfilment: Memoirs of a Criminal Court Judge*

1998   Sidney Harring, *White Man's Law: Native People in Nineteenth-Century Canadian Jurisprudence*

Peter Oliver, *'Terror to Evil-Doers': Prisons and Punishments in Nineteenth-Century Ontario*

1997   James W.St.G. Walker, *'Race,' Rights and the Law in the Supreme Court of Canada: Historical Case Studies*

Lori Chambers, *Married Women and Property Law in Victorian Ontario*

Patrick Brode, *Casual Slaughters and Accidental Judgments: Canadian War Crimes and Prosecutions, 1944–1948*

Ian Bushnell, *The Federal Court of Canada: A History, 1875–1992*

1996   Carol Wilton, ed., *Essays in the History of Canadian Law: Volume VII – Inside the Law: Canadian Law Firms in Historical Perspective*

William Kaplan, *Bad Judgment: The Case of Mr Justice Leo A. Landreville*

Murray Greenwood and Barry Wright, eds., *Canadian State Trials: Volume I – Law, Politics, and Security Measures, 1608–1837*

1995   David Williams, *Just Lawyers: Seven Portraits*

Hamar Foster and John McLaren, eds., *Essays in the History of Canadian Law: Volume VI – British Columbia and the Yukon*

W.H. Morrow, ed., *Northern Justice: The Memoirs of Mr Justice William G. Morrow*

Beverley Boissery, *A Deep Sense of Wrong: The Treason, Trials, and Transportation to New South Wales of Lower Canadian Rebels after the 1838 Rebellion*

1994   Patrick Boyer, *A Passion for Justice: The Legacy of James Chalmers McRuer*

Charles Pullen, *The Life and Times of Arthur Maloney: The Last of the Tribunes*

Jim Phillips, Tina Loo, and Susan Lewthwaite, eds., *Essays in the History of Canadian Law: Volume V – Crime and Criminal Justice*

Brian Young, *The Politics of Codification: The Lower Canadian Civil Code of 1866*

1993   Greg Marquis, *Policing Canada's Century: A History of the Canadian Association of Chiefs of Police*

Murray Greenwood, *Legacies of Fear: Law and Politics in Quebec in the Era of the French Revolution*

1992   Brendan O'Brien, *Speedy Justice: The Tragic Last Voyage of His Majesty's Vessel Speedy*

Robert Fraser, ed., *Provincial Justice: Upper Canadian Legal Portraits from the Dictionary of Canadian Biography*

1991   Constance Backhouse, *Petticoats and Prejudice: Women and Law in Nineteenth-Century Canada*

1990 Philip Girard and Jim Phillips, eds., *Essays in the History of Canadian Law: Volume III – Nova Scotia*
Carol Wilton, ed., *Essays in the History of Canadian Law: Volume IV – Beyond the Law: Lawyers and Business in Canada, 1830–1930*
1989 Desmond Brown, *The Genesis of the Canadian Criminal Code of 1892*
Patrick Brode, *The Odyssey of John Anderson*
1988 Robert Sharpe, *The Last Day, the Last Hour: The Currie Libel Trial*
John D. Arnup, *Middleton: The Beloved Judge*
1987 C. Ian Kyer and Jerome Bickenbach, *The Fiercest Debate: Cecil A. Wright, the Benchers, and Legal Education in Ontario, 1923–1957*
1986 Paul Romney, *Mr Attorney: The Attorney General for Ontario in Court, Cabinet, and Legislature, 1791–1899*
Martin Friedland, *The Case of Valentine Shortis: A True Story of Crime and Politics in Canada*
1985 James Snell and Frederick Vaughan, *The Supreme Court of Canada: History of the Institution*
1984 Patrick Brode, *Sir John Beverley Robinson: Bone and Sinew of the Compact*
David Williams, *Duff: A Life in the Law*
1983 David H. Flaherty, ed., *Essays in the History of Canadian Law: Volume II*
1982 Marion MacRae and Anthony Adamson, *Cornerstones of Order: Courthouses and Town Halls of Ontario, 1784–1914*
1981 David H. Flaherty, ed., *Essays in the History of Canadian Law: Volume I*